French Cinema:
A Student's Guide

French Cinema:
A Student's Guide

Phil Powrie and Keith Reader

HODDER
EDUCATION
PART OF HACHETTE LIVRE UK

The authors and publishers would like to thank the following for permission to reproduce copyright illustrative material:

bfi Collections 15, 25, 34, 43, 47, 50, 100, 111; bfi Stills, Posters and Designs 52; Ronald Grant Archive 32, 42, 94

Orders: please contact Bookpoint Ltd, 130 Milton Park, Abingdon, Oxon OX14 4SB. Telephone: (44) 01235 827720. Fax: (44) 01235 400454. Lines are open from 9.00 - 5.00, Monday to Saturday, with a 24 hour message answering service.

British Library Cataloguing in Publication Data
A catalogue record for this title is available from the British Library

ISBN 978 0 340 76004 8

First Published 2002
Impression number   10 9 8 7 6 5
Year   2008

Typeset by Phoenix Photosetting
Printed in India for Hodder Education, part of Hachette Livre UK, 338 Euston Road, London NW1 3BH

Contents

Further reading   **196**

Bibliography   **199**

Index of films and proper names   **209**

This book is dedicated to the memory of our colleague and friend Jill Forbes, Professor of French at Queen Mary & Westfield College, London. Jill was one of the finest writers on French cinema; she died at the far too early age of 54 on Friday, 13 July 2001.

INTRODUCTION

Since the early 1980s there has been a gradual increase in the number of people teaching and researching French cinema courses in UK universities. There are now some 45 staff members in universities in the UK alone publishing material on this subject; these and many more also teach French cinema on a regular basis. French cinema forms an integral part of many French/Modern Languages university degrees, as well as being an important component of what is now called World Cinema in Film Studies degrees, in both the UK and the USA. Surprisingly, though, there is no single volume that serves as a reasonably comprehensive background for such study.

Although there have been many histories of the French cinema, French-specific theorising on the cinema has not to our knowledge formed part of any introductory texts; 'film theory' is seen as a global phenomenon that tends to elide French-specific continuities. There are guidebooks on how to study or write on film, but, again, these are not French-specific. There are no books for students outlining the different types of research in French cinema; this is confined to scattered reviews in learned journals or alluded to in a fragmentary way in scholarly tomes. Our volume is an attempt to combine all of these strands – history, theory, practice – with the more usual statistics one might expect to find in a student handbook.

We have decided to focus specifically on French, rather than Francophone, cinema. The reader will therefore not find references to French-speaking African cinema, nor to Swiss cinema (for example, the films of Alain Tanner), nor, finally, to Belgian cinema.

We have included an annotated Bibliography in addition to the usual References, which will act as 'further reading' for those readers wishing to pursue some of the strands outlined in this volume.

Film titles are given in their original French version, without a translation (unless this is necessary in the context).

The volume has been written in collaboration; however, there has usually been a main writer for each section. The credits are as follows.

- History   1930–1939, 1939–1945, 1945–1959, 1959–1968, 1968–1981 and Conclusion (Keith Reader); 1896–1929 and 1981–2001 (Phil Powrie)
- Theory   Introduction, 1945–1960 and 'The spaces of cinema' (Keith Reader); all other sections (Phil Powrie)
- Practice   Phil Powrie
- Writing about French films   Phil Powrie
- Appendices   Phil Powrie

We would like to thank Manchester University Press for allowing us to use part of Phil Powrie's volume, *Jean-Jacques Beineix* (2001b), in one of the sequence analyses, and the *Journal of Romance Studies* for allowing us to rework a review article by Phil Powrie for the section on 'Practice' (Powrie, 2002). Particular thanks too to our students – Abigail Murray, Ellen Parker and John Williams – for allowing us to use their work.

Chapter One

HISTORY

The world's first screening of a motion picture to a paying audience took place at the Grand Café in Paris on 28 December 1895; it was a programme of short films by Louis Lumière, who with his brother Auguste ran a photography firm in Lyon. Ever since that date, cinema has occupied a central place in the culture of France, a place the French state, as we shall see, has always been concerned to protect and promote. The Paris *Cinémathèque*, founded by Henri Langlois and Georges Franju in 1936, has remained since then the world's best-known cinematic archive, and there is no city in which it is possible to see a greater range and variety of films than Paris. The cinematic involvement of leading figures from the worlds of literature and theatre, from Sacha Guitry to Marguerite Duras, is another indication of how important a place in French culture cinema holds. Pride in a national invention, the dominant place of Paris in the national culture (not even London or New York can lay claim to such hegemony), the city's reputation as a byword for intellectual and cultural innovation and, after the Second World War especially, France's long-standing love/hate relationship with the United States, epicentre of world cinema, are among the main reasons for this centrality.

1896–1929: THE SILENT PERIOD

The two best-known names in French silent cinema are those of Lumière and Georges Méliès. This is largely because between them they permit the division of the field into two conveniently complementary halves. Lumière allegedly described the cinema as 'a fairground showman's trade', and the brothers, initially at least, saw their short films as valuable publicity for their photographic business. Their titles, such as *Sortie d'usine/Workers Leaving the Lumière Factory* or *Arrivée des congressistes à Neuville-sur-Saone/Debarcation of Photographic Congress Members at Lyon*, suggest the careful documentary observation of bourgeois life that caused them to be hailed as the first cinematic realists. Renoir, Duvivier and Truffaut are among the leading inheritors of this tradition.

Méliès, on the other hand, was a conjurer and illusionist whose short films now appear as naive precursors of Surrealism. *Le Voyage dans la Lune* (1902) parodies the ambitions of scientists and shows an oddly winsome form of sadism in the scene where a space rocket lands in one of the moon's 'eyes', causing it to weep. *Le Royaume des fées* (1903) features a line-up of 'fairies' more reminiscent of dancing showgirls. The *fantastique* tradition in which Méliès's work is now generally read can be traced through Cocteau and the Surrealists to culminate, in a manner technically at least far more sophisticated, in the extravagant illusionism of a contemporary film-maker such as Léos Carax.

This binary reading is given further credence by the differing fortunes of the film-makers. Lumière retained his fortune thanks to a swift move out of film-making into production and, once the market became saturated, concentrated again on the photography business. Méliès, bankrupted by changing public tastes and the First World War, wound up living on charity in a home for retired artists. Realism/the bourgeoisie/money as against imagination/bohemia/impoverishment – the dichotomy is a seductive one, but open to criticism and modification. For one thing, Méliès also filmed studio reconstructions of real-life events (including the coronation of Edward VII). For another, the Lumière films are not of interest solely as items of documentary record. *L'Arroseur arrosé* of 1896 is probably the first cinematic comedy, with a closely structured symmetrical narrative. For yet a third, the bourgeoisie and money were to make their most serious appearance with the foundation of the Pathé Frères company in 1897, followed by Gaumont.

Charles Pathé and Léon Gaumont were businessmen, who left the film-making to others: for Pathé, the main director was Ferdinand Zecca, whose five-minute shorts included such titles as *Les Victimes de l'alcoolisme* (a compressed retelling of one of Zola's great novels, *L'Assommoir*). For Gaumont, it was his erstwhile secretary, Alice Guy, who was the first professional woman director anywhere in the world. Pathé succeeded where Méliès had failed disastrously and Lumière got out scarcely in time, in becoming the first major French cinematic entrepreneur. By the early 1900s, Pathé had branches all over the world, and was particularly well established in the USA; the studios were turning out something like ten films a week. The role of the multi-media conglomerate – Pathé had started out as a phonograph manufacturer – dates back almost as far as the cinematic medium itself. The interpenetration of realist observation and constructed fantasy, neither readily conceivable without the other, was to prove a guiding principle of that medium and of its major French practitioners. 'Lumière' and 'Méliès' increasingly appear as complements rather than irreconcilable opposites, both in different ways digested by the 'dream factory' (the very expression is redolent of their interdependence) that the cinema industry early became.

That similarity is all the more obvious when one remembers that these early films, irrespective of who made them, were at first a fairground attraction, literally in the case of Lumière, whose films travelled around the country, while Méliès showed his films in his theatre, where they gradually supplanted performing magicians. These early films were very short, and tended to fall into the following types. The first type was what Lumière called *vues*, landscapes, buildings, the roads of Paris, official occasions such as royal visits or parades. Similar to this was the dramatisation of news items, such as, for example, the Russian Revolution of 1905. A more moralising documentary type, of which Zecca's film on alcoholism, mentioned above, is a good example, is the cautionary tale. In what was still a religious country, a fourth type was the religious film. But the more frequent type was the comic film, which has remained the most popular French genre to this day.

A new development occurred in 1908 with the creation of the Société du Film d'Art. The purpose of this organisation was to lift film out of its popular origins in fairground entertainment, and to give it cultural (for which read middle-class) respectability. These films, often historical epics, as was the case with the first one, *L'Assassinat du Duc de Guise*, are the forerunners of the *tradition de qualité* of the 1950s and the heritage film of the 1980s and 1990s. This expansion of the French cinema marks a high point. French films accounted for something like 60 per cent of the world market. Pathé had built his own filmstock factories, so he was no longer dependent on American filmstock; indeed, there were twice as many Pathé films on the US market as all American-produced films put together. A further example to add to the dominance of the French industry in the pre-war years was that the first global star, established around 1910, was the Gaumont comic Max Linder, arguably the first film star, even before the notion of the film director had taken root.

Nevertheless, with hindsight, historians of the French cinema have isolated a number of important directors: Léonce Perret was a realist; Albert Capellani tended to make literary adaptations and historical epics; and, perhaps the most important of these pre-war directors, there was Louis Feuillade, at once a senior executive with Gaumont and an idol of the Surrealists, who found in his bizarrely stylised *Fantômas* series (1913–1914) and *Les Vampires* (1915), the dreamlike amalgam of reality and imagination that was their artistic ideal. *Les Vampires'* black-tighted *femme fatale* and mysterious criminal mastermind are precursors of *film noir* – evidence that the European cinema was to exercise a significant influence over Hollywood as well as the other way round.

French dominance was to change dramatically with the First World War, as a result of which the studios lost staff, and the French industry never fully recovered. The 1920s were, nevertheless, a time when cinema began to interest artists and intellectuals. As the post-war industry expanded, even if never recovering its hege-mony, film magazines were established and a star system took root. If serials seemed to remain extremely popular, with some 60 of them produced in the first five years of the 1920s, there was an extraordinary variety of films, including the most important development for many French film historians, a film avant-garde, linked to writers and intellectuals. Along with Soviet cinema and German Expressionism, French Impressionist cinema, as it is usually called, constitutes the major French contribution to the development of cinema as an art, along with Surrealist film, with which it is sometimes linked.

The Impressionists were Dulac, Epstein, Gance and L'Herbier. Germaine Dulac (along with Alice Guy) is the best-known woman silent film-maker, whose avant-garde psychodrama *La Coquille et le Clergyman* (1927) aroused controversy little inferior to that provoked by Buñuel's Surrealist classics *Un chien andalou* (1929) and *L'Age d'Or* (1930) a few years later. Perhaps more powerful now is the explicitly feminist *La Souriante Madame Beudet* (1923), whose heroine fantasises about killing her oafish bourgeois husband and about love affairs with tennis stars who walk out of the pages of her women's magazine. Jean Epstein made three major films in 1923 alone, but his greatest is perhaps the 1928 adaptation of Edgar Allan Poe's *The Fall of the House of Usher*, a horror film that still manages to disturb.

Abel Gance was, along with Marcel L'Herbier whose *L'Argent* (1929) is a virtuoso updating of Émile Zola's novel, the most epically ambitious of the silent directors. He had made a four-hour epic, *La Roue*, in 1923. But nowhere is his ambition more apparent than in the five-hour *Napoléon* (1927), whose use of split screen (up to three images side by side), superimposition and ultra-rapid montage evince a grandiose ambition often compared to that of the film's subject. Gance provided the film with a soundtrack in 1934, but it was not until Kevin Brownlow restored it to its full length in 1981 that *Napoléon* could be seen by a contemporary audience as its maker had intended. The heroic populism much in evidence in the film was to make of Gance an ardent supporter of Marshal Pétain, and his post-war unpopu-larity was neither aesthetically nor politically surprising.

The advent of sound cinema marks a break for the French industry, but it is impor-tant to recognise that many of the directors who are more familiar from their work in the 1930s, began their careers with sometimes substantial films in the silent period. Jean Renoir's *Nana* (1926) is an adaptation of a Zola novel. Jacques Feyder, a Belgian, who began his career in 1915, made, amongst others, a silent adaptation of the Carmen story (1926), and an adaptation of another Zola novel, *Thérèse Raquin* (1928). René Clair, best known for his musical comedies *Sous les toits de Paris*

(1930) and *Le Million* (1931), began his career with a zany Dada-Surrealist film *Entr'acte* (1924), but also produced two superb comedies, *Un chapeau de paille d'Italie* (1927) and *Les Deux Timides* (1928), a Keatonesque comedy starring the protagonist of Buñuel's *Un chien andalou*, Pierre Batcheff, a matinée idol who was perhaps the only major star of the 1920s to straddle the divide between avant-garde and commercial cinema.

1930–1939: THE 'EARLY CLASSIC ERA' – FROM SOUND TO THE SECOND WORLD WAR

The advent of sound in 1929 inaugurated what is usually called the classic French cinema. Sound was a mixed blessing, at first viewed with suspicion by the industry because of the costly technological investment it required, all the costlier since France's only home-grown sound system was of poor quality and rapidly taken over by the German Tobis Klangfilm company. On the other hand, the language barrier introduced by sound ensured a viable domestic market for French films, while the standardisation of projection speed and running times imposed by higher overheads ensured that 'the cinema finally became a fully rationalised, mass-produced spectacle' (Williams, 1992: 182). The modern cinema industry can be said to have been born with the advent of sound.

Yet it is the 'classic' rather than the 'modern' label that seems on the whole more appropriate to the cinema of the 1930s – partly because so many of the French films now thought of as 'classics' date from this period, partly because it was characterised by the dominance of the classic industrial model of production. This was nowhere near as closely integrated in France as in the United States; Crisp speaks of 'the atomised and relatively artisanal nature of the film "industry" in France . . . and the lack of vertical integration of production, distribution and exhibition sectors' (Crisp, 1993: xvi). Any national cinema in this period, however, was to some extent forced to define itself in relation to Hollywood, and the examples of Gaumont and Pathé – still major names in France – illustrate how important a factor the industrialisation of the medium was. Both companies, however, were to lose out to the USA in the 'trade wars', Pathé selling off its factory to Eastman-Kodak and Gaumont pyrrhically merging with MGM. Without the state and governmental support it was to enjoy in later years, this was a difficult period for French cinema.

Sound had a more conservative effect than we might imagine, for the opportunity to transfer literary and theatrical classics to the screen was liberally used, leading to a large number of uninspired journeyman adaptations. Moreover, despite a 1932 governmental decree that dubbing of foreign films into French had to be done in

France with French personnel, widespread fears were expressed that 'American cultural colonialism of the world could proceed unimpeded and French screens would be flooded with foreign imports' (Crisp, 1993: 25). The justification for such fears is nowadays, of course, all too plain to see; but the French film industry, and the French state, have always shown great tenacity in defending what is often known as France's 'cultural exception', and even without large-scale governmental assistance in the 1930s the industry's artisanal structure and largely successful resistance to the Depression were to ensure the production of many outstanding films.

Given the other constraints mentioned, however, it is possible to see how a film-maker such as René Clair may have been more justified than might now appear in lamenting the loss of the silent cinema's originality and universality. Clair, nevertheless, adapted rapidly enough to become the French cinema's first, and (apart from Jacques Demy) to this day only, leading director of musical comedies. *Sous les toits de Paris* (1930) is, as its title suggests, an evocation of the picturesque 'people's Paris' that was to figure importantly in films of the period, culminating in Renoir's *Le Crime de Monsieur Lange* (1936). *A nous la liberté* (1931) satirises the very mass-production technologies of entertainment that made it possible, with its scenes in a prison and a phonograph factory structurally almost indistinguishable from each other. *Le Million* (1931) choreographs the frantic search for a missing lottery ticket; even from so apparently Arcadian a world as Clair's, the economy of pleasure is rarely absent. Clair's work may now appear slightly fey and insubstantial, but the visual verve of *A nous la liberté* in particular, and its satirisation of the nascent modern entertainment industry of which the film is itself an example, do not deserve the neglect into which they have latterly fallen.

Jean Vigo made only two films of any length before his death at the age of 29 in 1934. *Zéro de conduite* (1933) had to be left partially incomplete because his time in the studio ran out, and *L'Atalante* (1934) was not a script of his choosing. Yet the first film's evocation of a revolt in a boys' boarding school, and the second's tale of life on a canal barge, have nothing of the journeyman about them; cinema as dream – the Surrealists' ideal – here reaches an apotheosis. *Zéro de conduite* was banned by the government virtually on release, perhaps surprisingly considering the innocence of its central characters' uprising (they use no weapons more deadly than tiles torn from the school roof). Yet we should remember that the 1930s was a decade of intense social instability in France, threatened with recession in the aftermath of the Wall Street Crash and for much of the decade at risk from German expansionism. The brief interlude of the left-wing Popular Front government, which introduced paid holidays and the 40-hour working week before its downfall, came to stand out in popular memory as a moment of solidarity and togetherness amid a decade of turmoil. Censorial trigger-happiness, subsequently evidenced in the banning of Renoir's *La Règle du jeu*, doubtless owed much to this precarious position.

L'Atalante owes much of its impact to the extraordinary performance of Michel Simon as the barge-hand Père Jules. Simon – Swiss, but at the very antipodes of the anodine cleanliness normally associated with that country – is the great visceral star of classic French cinema. Even at his most benignly disruptive, as in this film or Renoir's *Boudu sauvé des eaux* (1932), there is something satyr-like and perturbing about him; in Carné's *Le Quai des brumes* (1938), where he plays the monstrous Zabel, driven nearly mad by his quasi-incestuous fascination with his goddaughter, his performance evokes depths of which scarcely any other French actor was capable. *L'Atalante* is among the most visually striking films of its period, thanks to the superb camerawork of Boris Kaufman in the night-time and dream sequences in particular. It was a comparative failure at the box office, though its classic status is now unquestioned.

Much more of a journeyman than either Clair or Vigo was Julien Duvivier, whose *La Belle Équipe* (1936) features one of the definitive performances from the working-class hero of the time, Jean Gabin, and replicates the debates and uncertainties surrounding the Popular Front government in its two alternative endings – one affirmative of solidarity, the other homicidal and elegiac. Duvivier's artisanal competence and lengthy career, much of it in Hollywood, make of him, as it were, the anti-Vigo, and there has perhaps been a consequent tendency to under-rate his work, which does a film like the Algiers-set drama *Pépé le Moko* (1937) little service. *Pépé le Moko*, like *La Belle Équipe*, stars Gabin, who in the later film dies a violent death as he was so often to do on screen, notably for Carné in *Le Quai des brumes* and *Le Jour se lève* (1939). The critic André Bazin memorably described Gabin as 'Oedipus in a cloth cap' – a reference to his archetypal role as a decent man of modest origins driven to madness and despair by the malignity of fate. Celebrated for his on-screen outbursts of anger, he was to undergo a class meta-morphosis after the war, featuring (significantly thicker-set) in more bourgeois roles and thus becoming an icon of social change in France.

The relationship between literature and the cinema became an increasingly complex one during this period. Marcel Pagnol not merely adapted many of his own works for the screen (such as *César*, 1936, later to be 'adapted back' into a stage play), he was also to become one of the most important producers of the classic years, and an early practitioner of location filming. Sacha Guitry's coruscating the-atrical dialogues made his plays natural choices for screen adaptation; the use of off-screen sound in *Le Roman d'un tricheur* (1936) and his free reworking of French history in *Remontons les Champs-Élysées* (1938) illustrate how his early disdain for the medium gave way to an innovative use of it, by turns frolicsome and sardonic. His career, like a great many others, never fully recovered from his collaboration with the Germans under the Occupation.

Jean Cocteau's later interest in cinema was prefigured by *Le Sang d'un poète* (1931), one of the most celebrated cinematic products of the pre-war avant-garde. The literary figure whose trace is most perceptible in the 1930s films still watched today, however, never himself directed a film. Jacques Prévert, Surrealist expulsee and Marxist fellow traveller, made his name as a writer of film scripts before becoming even more widely known as a poet in his own right. His best-known work was for Marcel Carné, the apostle of what André Bazin was to dub 'poetic realism'. This term relates to an aesthetic that has much in common with the Hollywood genre of *film noir*, not least in the jadedness and pessimism of the world it evokes. *Drôle de drame* (1937) is a preposterous fantasy set in a half-Dickensian, half-Surrealist London, with Michel Simon and Louis Jouvet. Jouvet's sardonic, haughty demeanour here perhaps figures his slightly condescending attitude towards the filmic medium, for he had long been renowned as a serious theatre actor, above all in the works of Jean Giraudoux, and came belatedly to the cinema, which he always professed to regard as a commercial rather than an artistic medium. *Le Quai des brumes* and *Le Jour se lève*, both starring Gabin, take place on studio sets designed by Alexandre Trauner in which every detail is at once plausible and charged with poetic significance. The mists that cloak the port of Le Havre in the earlier film, like the wardrobe with which Gabin walls himself up in his attic room in *Le Jour se lève*, suggest a mood of exhaustion and defeat over and above their realistically motivated place in the films. *Le Quai des Brumes* pits Gabin against Simon in their only screen appearance together, and made a star of the young Michèle Morgan to whom Gabin famously says, 'T'as de beaux yeux, tu sais/You've got lovely eyes, you know.' More interesting formally is *Le Jour se lève*, unusually for its time told largely in flashback (which apparently confused many spectators). Gabin's nemesis here is the splendidly yet repulsively oleaginous Jules Berry, star also of *Le Crime de M. Lange* and Carné's *Les Visiteurs du soir* (1943). Carné has become a byword for cinematic fatalism, the doomed love so characteristic of his work being associated by Edward Baron Turk with his homosexuality. The three years that separated *La Belle Équipe*, in its happy ending at least the apotheosis of Gabin triumphant, from the same actor's tragic demise in *Le Jour se lève* were the years during which France slid from the initial optimism of the Popular Front to the verge of war, a congruence of cinema and history that powerfully reinforces the individual fatalism so clearly present in much of Carné's work. Yet viewing his films is a less uniformly dispiriting experience than this may suggest, for their dialogues are studded with the mordant wit so characteristic of Prévert.

This is still more in evidence in Prévert's only script for Jean Renoir, almost universally regarded as the greatest of French directors. *Le Crime de Monsieur Lange*, about a publishing firm whose workers form themselves into a cooperative when their dastardly boss Batala (Jules Berry) absconds owing money, is both one of Renoir's finest works and the film that most clearly embodies the exhilaration of the early Popular Front period. The film is celebrated above all for the so-called 360° pan around the courtyard immediately before Lange, the gentle author of escapist western novels, shoots Batala, who has come back to help himself to the cooperative's proceeds. This shot evokes the sense of community and solidarity that motivates Lange's shooting and, thanks largely to Bazin's masterly analysis of it, has become a classic of political cinema.

Renoir's subsequent work may lack the overt ideological edge of *Le Crime de Monsieur Lange*, but as a cinematic anatomy of a society, and a class, on the brink of collapse it is without rival. *La Grande Illusion* (1937) counterposes the realities of national rivalry (between France and Germany) with those of class conflict. Set in a German prisoner-of-war camp for officers during the First World War, it strikingly prefigures the conflict that was to erupt two years after its making. The aristocrats de Boieldieu/Pierre Fresnay and von Rauffenstein/Erich von Stroheim have in common a civilised, chivalrous lifestyle and ethic clearly doomed by the looming realities of twentieth-century warfare, and one in which their less opulent fellow soldiers, such as Maréchal/Jean Gabin, cannot share. The 'illusion' of the title thus seems to be that national loyalties are more important than those of class, yet the film's setting, and continuing relevance in the Europe of today, suggest that questions of nationhood are not to be so easily discarded. *La Marseillaise* (1938) – designed as the apotheosis of the Popular Front, in fact its artistic swansong – depicts the French Revolution as the achievement of ordinary women and men, in a reaction against the 'great names' school of history that places it at the opposite extreme to *Napoléon*.

Renoir's filming is characterised by a stylistic openness and a collaborative use of actors that enable him to articulate the social contradictions of his time with remarkable subtlety. Martin O'Shaughnessy's observation that *La Marseillaise* can be seen as 'the welding together of two conflicting gendered stories' – a 'male narrative of coming of age' and one in which 'women are seen to play an assertive, powerful and violent role' (O'Shaughnessy, 2000: 137) – foregrounds the otherwise largely neglected importance of gender in Renoir's work. Ethnicity too, notably through the anti-Semitic remarks of which Rosenthal/Marcel Dalio is the target in *La Grande Illusion*, is a prominent issue.

These potential conflicts, in addition to the pervasive theme of class, help us to understand what Renoir meant when he said of France before the Second World War: 'We are dancing on a volcano.' That remark could serve as epigraph to his outstanding work, *La Règle du jeu* (1939). An aristocratic country-house party is the setting in which all manner of repressed conflicts – sexual, social, ethnic, class-based – come to the surface. This happened in the cinema too; riots broke out on the film's first screening in Paris and it was banned successively by the pre-war and by the Vichy and Occupation governments. The savagery with which Renoir anatomises the hypocrisy and bad faith of pre-war French society may take some time for a contemporary audience to appreciate. The film features no truly major star (Gaston Modot, Julien Carette and even Marcel Dalio were all minor ones at best), relying rather on the group dynamic that, from *Le Crime de Monsieur Lange* onwards, is so characteristic of Renoir's work. The world it evokes will seem impossibly stylised and mannered to most contemporary audiences, for whom elaborate amateur theatricals and the etiquette of pheasant shooting are unlikely to be familiar territory. The film's visual verve, however, is apparent at first viewing, notably in the rabbit hunt scene near the beginning and the frantic chase through the corridors of the château towards the end, two scenes that echo and mirror each other. Hunting is a leitmotif of *La Règle du jeu*, all at once visually (as in the two scenes just mentioned), emotionally (to the pursuit of game corresponds the pursuit of love, both likely to lead to bloody consequences) and in the wider social context (the pursuit of territorial ambition was even as Renoir filmed pushing Europe towards war). The film's astonishing unity-in-diversity helps to explain Pierre Billard's judgement that Renoir's 'freedom kills the myth of representation', so that he 'takes his place in the cinema of modernity twenty years ahead of his time' (Billard, 1995: 341). Neither truly 'classic' – though the summit of the French cinema that generally goes by that name – nor yet 'modern(ist)', *La Règle du jeu* marks the transition *par excellence* from one kind of cinema to another.

That judgement, of course, is necessarily influenced by the immense historical rupture brought about by the outbreak of war, which makes *La Règle du jeu*'s transitional status only too apparent. It was one of 51 French films – along with *Le Quai des brumes* and Renoir's 1938 Zola adaptation *La Bête humaine* – to be banned by the censor just before war was declared, while the first Cannes festival, due to take place in September 1939, had to be cancelled. The decade that was ending so ominously had nevertheless been a productive one for the cinema. The *Conseil supérieur du cinéma*, set up in 1931, had shown the beginnings of state and governmental interest in this (comparatively) new art form, and the founding of the *Cinémathèque française* in 1936 went on to reinforce this, providing the institutional context within which generations of young critics and film-makers would get to know not only French, but European and American cinema. Between 94 and 158 films were produced each year during the decade (not counting 1939 which, for obvious reasons, was 'incomplete'), and something of the order of 225 000 000 admissions were annually recorded. It might have been thought that the social and economic disruption caused by wartime and the Occupation would have a calamitous effect on the nascent industry, but as we shall see that was to be only part of the story.

1939–1945: THE WAR YEARS

To speak of the Occupation as having positive effects on the French cinema industry may appear perverse, even seditious, but it is a position increasingly widely accepted by film historians. The unavailability of American films meant that the French industry had the field to itself far more than in normal circumstances; a character in Jean-Pierre Melville's Resistance epic *L'Armée des ombres* (1969) says that France will know she is free when it is possible to watch *Gone With The Wind* on the Champs-Élysées, which poignantly suggests the cultural deprivation of which French film-makers were able to take (often against their will) advantage. The Occupation cinema was brought under central – i.e. German-dominated – control in a way that severely restricted freedom of expression, but also introduced the first system of advances to producers and made the industry much more efficient. If this sounds suspiciously like a variant of 'Mussolini made the trains run on time', it should be borne in mind that many of the structures of post-war state aid to the cinema were modelled on those imposed under the Occupation. The legal requirement to lodge a copy of any new film was introduced in 1943, and the following year saw the foundation of the IDHEC (now FEMIS), France's first national film school.

Against this has to be set, of course, the loss of key personnel to the industry. Many of the leading producers, being Jewish, were not permitted to work. Renoir left for the USA where he was thenceforth to spend most of his time; Clair and Duvivier, more briefly, did likewise. Renoir's American work is by common consent less outstanding than his great films of the 1930s, not least because he was working within the constraints of the Hollywood system and had lost the acute sense of French society that makes *La Grande Illusion* or *La Règle du jeu* so remarkable. Even so, the moody evocation of the Deep South in *Swamp Water* (1941) and the black comedy of *The Diary of a Chambermaid* (1946) remain powerful. His work of the 1950s and 1960s, less mordant than that of the pre-war years, is nevertheless recognisably by the same hand. *Le Carrosse d'or* (1953) and *French Can-Can* (1955), both in what was known at the time as 'glorious Technicolor', feature in more historically remote settings – respectively, colonial Peru and *belle époque* Montmartre – the stress on the interplay, and ultimate indistinguishability, of theatricality and 'real life' so important in the earlier works. Clair enlisted Marlene Dietrich for *The Flame of New Orleans* (1941), while Duvivier's post-war career reached its height with the sour and misanthropic *Voici le temps des assassins* (1956), starring Jean Gabin. The loss or diminished glory of these figures, and of others, was in a sense replicated on a smaller scale at the Liberation, when such figures as Guitry, Arletty and the actor Robert Le Vigan – a prominent collaborator who was never to work in France again – were tried and briefly imprisoned.

The leading pre-war director to remain in France was Carné, who worked in the Victorine Studios in Nice – thus within the Vichy zone. The first of his two wartime films, both scripted by Prévert, *Les Visiteurs du soir*, is a surreal medieval fantasy, featuring Arletty as the duplicitously androgynous emissary of Jules Berry's camp Devil in knee-breeches. This film, for all its visual extravagance, is alas characterised by some rather listless acting – something that is emphatically not true of Carné's best-known and most ambitious work, *Les Enfants du Paradis* (released in 1945 though shot in 1943–1944), set in the Paris theatre world of the 1830s (see Figure 1.1). Superb performances from such as Arletty, Jean-Louis Barrault and Pierre Brasseur have helped to make it probably the best-loved of French film classics, along with the richness of its *mise-en-scène* of the world of popular entertainment, which owes much to the magnificent sets designed by the Hungarian Jew Alexandre Trauner, working for obvious reasons clandestinely. Its at first tenuous-seeming relationship to the society of its time has of course to do with the omnipresence of censorship, but Edward Baron Turk finds liberating possibilities in its sexual politics: 'By calling into question the authority of the family, the repression of sexual deviance, rigid gender roles, and the dependence of women on men, *Les Enfants du Paradis* assailed the foundation of Vichy's social order' (Turk, 1989: 268).

Two of the outstanding film-makers to have made their mark under the Occupation were Jacques Becker (whose *Goupi Mains Rouges* of 1943 is an almost Gothic drama of peasant life) and Jean Grémillon, for whom Prévert scripted *Lumière d'été* (1943). This film, about a *Règle du jeu*-like tangle of love and class relationships in the Midi, was along with Grémillon's aviation drama *Le Ciel est à vous* (1944) among the few major Occupation films to present a critical view of contemporary society. *Le Ciel est à vous*, indeed, has often been seen as a parable of the solidarity of the Resistance. Grémillon's post-war career was a sorry catalogue of aborted or curtailed projects; he was to make only three feature films between 1945 and his death in 1959, and remains an unjustly little-known director.

Figure 1.1   Les Enfants du paradis

15

The Liberation proved barely less disruptive to the cinema than the Occupation. Collaborators, as we have seen, found their careers blighted or destroyed, while the disappearance of the protected domestic market seemed briefly to threaten the very foundations of the French industry. The Blum–Byrnes agreement of May 1946 allowed American films unrestricted access to the French market, but also introduced a quota of French films to be screened – initially 30 per cent, rising to 38 per cent in 1948. The agreement, widely denounced at the time as an act of treachery, appears in retrospect not only highly realistic, but premonitory of subsequent French cultural and cinematic relations with the USA, seeking accommodation of the 'cultural exception' within an American hegemony the French industry could not hope to vanquish. Along with the nationalisation of large exhibition circuits at the end of the war and the continuation of 'outrageously protectionist' (Crisp, 1993: 77) government advances and funding, the agreement protected the industry far more effectively than might have been thought at the time. The *Centre national de la cinématographie* (CNC) was set up in 1946 to oversee film finance – a striking example of the readiness the French state has always shown to intervene in cultural matters – and in 1948 established a fund to assist French film production and distribution, which has been largely responsible for the industry's high international profile ever since.

1945–1959: LE CINÉMA DE PAPA

The period between 1945 and 1959 was for long stigmatised as what Truffaut called the *cinéma de papa* ('daddy's cinema'), a sneering reference to the supposed political and aesthetic paralysis of the Fourth Republic; his vitriolic 1954 article lambasts a cinema locked into tedious literary adaptations (see Truffaut, 1976). Squeezed between the heyday of the classic cinema and the burgeoning of the New Wave, it remains, in both senses of the word, largely invisible. Not a single film by Claude Autant-Lara, Jacques Becker or Christian-Jaque, three of the period's major directors, is available on video in the UK, and only one example of those directors' work – Becker's *Casque d'or* (1952) – has been shown on British television. Such neglect, while comprehensible, is scarcely justifiable.

The period in question also marked the beginning, or culmination, of three of the major post-war directorial careers. Robert Bresson's eschewal of professional actors and refusal of psychological depth in favour of an austerely materialist Catholic spirituality first becomes marked in his Bernanos adaptation *Journal d'un curé de campagne* (1951). This account of a young priest's suffering, clearly an analogy for the holy agony of Christ, derives much of its force from the doubling of its narration; we see the priest writing his diary at the same time as we hear him reading from it, emphasising how he is 'the unwilling (at first) victim of an overwhelming and self-mortifying passion' (Schrader, 1972: 73). Bresson's second feature, *Un condamné à mort s'est échappé* (1956), details the escape (based on real life) of a Resistance detainee from Montluc prison in Lyon, presented as a sustained and suspenseful exercise in the operation of grace.

Jacques Tati once said that he would like to work with Bresson – an odd remark considering the conspicuous lack of humour in the latter's films, but less anomalous than it might appear if we bear in mind the meticulously choreographed style and innovatively dislocatory use of sound that characterise Tati's work. His three features of the period – *Jour de fête* (1949), *Les Vacances de Monsieur Hulot* (1953) and *Mon oncle* (1958) – are among the most acute satires of the galloping modernisation that in some 30 years transformed France from a largely rural into a primarily industrial economy. The cults of speed (explicitly linked with the USA), the seaside holiday and household gadgets are his targets in the three features; to describe M. Hulot as a 'reflection of the increased standardization of daily life in France' (Ross, 1995: 174), however portentous it may sound, says a good deal about his enduring appeal and relevance.

Cocteau's two best-known films are *La Belle et la bête* (1946) and *Orphée* (1950), imbued with the spirit of what, in a doubtless conscious response to Carné and Bazin, he dubbed 'magical realism'. The earlier film's evocation of the world of Dutch painting and *Orphée*'s sumptuous special effects have lasted rather better than the matinee-idol narcissism of Jean Marais in the leading roles. The 'real objects' in these films may appear to be very far removed from the France of the time at which they were made, but this would be to disregard the strong homosexual element in *La Belle et la bête*'s 'love that dare not speak its name', or the allusions to the heavily coded world of the Resistance in *Orphée*'s abundance of seemingly nonsensical passwords. The fantasy/reality antithesis, yet again, turns out to be more illusory than real.

Jean-Pierre Melville in 1950 directed (by all accounts with considerable interference from the author) the cinematic adaptation of Cocteau's best-known text, *Les Enfants terribles*. Melville's place in the history of French cinema, however, rests less on this or his earlier literary adaptation, of Vercors's *Le Silence de la mer* (1949), than on the influence of Hollywood 'action cinema' on his work. The work of directors such as Howard Hawks and Samuel Fuller, with its stress on laconic, often violent action and its narrative terseness, was to have a major effect on the New Wave filmmakers of the succeeding generation – an effect for which Melville was in large part responsible. He was also the first major French director (after Pagnol) to set up his own production company, operating artisanally on the fringes of the industry. This enabled him to reconcile financial autonomy – if he and the New Wave directors so admired the 'action cinema' school it was largely because it had been able to produce memorable films often on very low budgets – and a degree of artistic independence that for his critics verges on the mannered. *Bob le flambeur* (1956) was the first of his gangster movies, a stylised riposte to the production-line *série noire* films, often starring Eddie Constantine, that constituted the French mainstream cinema's first response to the influx of American productions after the war.

The film-makers so far mentioned in this section are all in greater or lesser degree atypical of the dominant Fourth Republic cinema. That cinema's frequent recourse to literary adaptation, its reliance on careful scriptwriting (often by the duo of Jean Aurenche and Pierre Bost), its general air of businesslike professionalism and supposed unadventurousness, were all laughed out of fashion by the New Wave, but have in the past decade or so staged a resurgence through the popularity of the 'heritage film'. The strictures of Truffaut may well have been applicable to the journeyman work of such as Jean Delannoy, who signed forgettable adaptations of Cocteau (*L'Éternel Retour*, 1943) and Sartre (*Les Jeux sont faits*, 1946), but two film-makers of the period at least display subversive and ironic qualities that should not pass unnoticed. Claude Autant-Lara's move from Communist Party activist after the war to Front National MEP in the mid-1980s scarcely did him credit, but the dozen or so films he made under the Fourth Republic often give a mordant portrayal of the suffocating pettiness and hypocrisy of the time. *Le Diable au corps* (1947) and *Le Blé en herbe* (1954), adapted from Radiguet and Colette respectively, both deal with burgeoning adolescent sexuality and caused scandals through their depiction of relationships between a younger man and an older woman. *Le Blé en herbe* was among the first post-war films to fall foul of the power exercised by French mayors to ban from their cities films that had received the national censor's authorisation. *La Traversée de Paris* (1956) teamed Gabin and Bourvil in a tale of black-marketeering in occupied Paris – the forerunner of the determinedly unheroic view of the Occupation years that was to come to the fore in the 1970s.

More bilious and misanthropic still is the work of Henri-Georges Clouzot, who found himself for a while banished from the industry at the Liberation because of the harshly cynical view of provincial life in his poison-pen drama, *Le Corbeau* (1943). *Le Salaire de la peur* (1953) sustains for more than two and a half hours the suspense of its tale of European expatriates driving lorryloads of nitroglycerine over treacherous Central American roads to quench an oil-rig fire. Yves Montand, first drawn to public attention in Carné's *Les Portes de la nuit* (1946), gives one of the defining performances of his career here. Most frightening of all his works perhaps is *Les Diaboliques* (1955), with Simone Signoret in one of her best-known roles. The film's sadistic martyrisation of the character played by Véra Clouzot (the director's wife) becomes even more chilling when we know that she suffered in real life from a weak heart that was not long afterwards to kill her. The film's ending clearly inspired that, more than 30 years later, of Adrian Lyne's *Fatal Attraction*, but in its manipulation of actors and audience alike is surely closer to Hitchcock – a major influence on the New Wave, present here too in what it would be quite unjust to dismiss as *cinéma de papa*.

René Clément is the other directorial name most often associated with the cinema of this period. *Jeux interdits* (1952) tells of the impact of the war on two young children who create an animals' cemetery before being roughly separated from each other. The film's view of childhood, while less barbed than that of Vigo, is nevertheless a determinedly unidealised one, a very long way from the Hollywood of the time. Clément's other major work of the period took the form of literary adaptations, from Zola (*Gervaise* of 1956) or Marguerite Duras (*Barrage contre le pacifique* of 1958).

Carné proved unable to sustain his pre-war popularity after the Liberation. *Les Portes de la nuit* was severely criticised as *déjà vu*, the doom-laden Prévert script and heavy fatalism with which it is imbued not suiting the more upbeat expectations of the post-Liberation era. Thenceforth his career tailed off sadly, the Zola adaptation *Thérèse Raquin* (1953) being his most successful later film, thanks largely to Simone Signoret's vampish performance in the title role. Becker produced at once his most lyrical and his most doom-laden film with *Casque d'or*, a reconstruction of the nine-teenth-century Parisian underworld, as well as such realistically observed dramas as *Rue de l'Estrapade* (1953), a forerunner of the New Wave. Signoret gives what is probably the performance of her life, and Serge Reggiani as her doomed young lover exudes tragic intensity. Becker went on to give Jean Gabin one of his great post-war roles as the portly gangster yearning for retirement in the *série noire Touchez pas au grisbi* (1954). This director's reputation is less by some way than it deserves to be, for he died prematurely in 1960, just before the release of the prison escape drama *Le Trou*, which remains among the finest French films of its period.

Industrially and aesthetically alike, the 'Fourth Republic years' were, it is now beginning to be recognised, richer and more complex than might at first appear. Yet – with the handful of exceptions already mentioned – it lacked the innovative verve of earlier and later periods. It was a time of reconstruction and consolidation for the industry, which for most of the period succeeded in attracting more specta-tors to French than to American films. The seeds of innovation were being sown elsewhere, in the pages of the new cinematic journals that appeared during and after the war. *L'Écran français* began clandestinely in 1943 and lasted ten years, during which it brought to the fore notions of the cinema as a vehicle for ideological engagement and as a language in its own right. Alexandre Astruc's 1948 'Naissance d'une nouvelle avant-garde' ('Birth of a new avant-garde') inaugurated a mode of writing on the cinema which the journals *Positif* and *Cahiers du cinéma* were to continue into the 1950s.

It is in a sense provocative to bracket those names together for, in their earlier days at least, the two journals cordially detested each other. *Positif* was sympathetic to Surrealism and to the French Communist Party, while among the major influences on *Cahiers* was the existentialist Catholicism of André Bazin. Half a century on, both journals still exist and thrive, albeit with much ideological passion spent. If *Cahiers* remains to non-French audiences at least much the better known, this is because so many of those who wrote for it went on to direct films in their own right. Chabrol, Godard, Rivette, Rohmer, Truffaut – the patron saints of the New Wave – all began as *Cahiers* critics in what remains the most striking mass migration from writing-about to writing-in film history has to offer. Their interest in low-budget American cinema led them to pursue with zeal the *politique des auteurs* – a pantheonisation of figures such as Howard Hawks and Samuel Fuller, whose individuality in making 'their' films in the teeth of studio-imposed constraints was lauded in a sometimes extravagant manner. *Positif*'s favourite sons, such as Otto Preminger and Raoul Walsh, have lasted somewhat less well by comparison.

The *Cahiers/Positif* antithesis is important for a number of reasons. It exemplifies a tendency in French cultural life – illustrated at very much the same time by the work of such 'new novelists' as Alain Robbe-Grillet and Nathalie Sarraute – for critical and theoretical reflection to stimulate and feed through into artistic production. It illustrates the importance of political loyalties, or their absence, already marked in the cinema of the Popular Front era, in informing aesthetic and cultural debate. Finally, it stages the love/hate relationship with the United States that has been so crucial a factor in French artistic and cultural as well as political and economic life throughout the post-war years. For reasons we shall now explore, 1959 was the year in which all these trends converged to inaugurate what was rapidly recognised as a new era for the French cinema.

1959–1968: THE NEW WAVE

The New Wave never formally constituted itself as a movement (the term was coined by the journalist Françoise Giroud), so that 'membership' of it is to a large extent a matter of opinion. The five 'core' directors – Claude Chabrol, François Truffaut, Jean-Luc Godard, Éric Rohmer and Jacques Rivette – had met at the Paris *Cinémathèque* in the late 1940s or early 1950s and had graduated to film-making by way of the influential journal *Cahiers du cinéma*. The major intellectual and personal influence on them was the critic André Bazin, a passionate advocate of 'realism, mise-en-scène, and deep focus (which he saw in opposition to montage)' (Monaco, 1976: 6), and of the *politique des auteurs*. European art-house directors, such as Renoir or Rossellini, had traditionally been treated as the 'authors' of their films, in much the same way as Balzac or Baudelaire were of the literary texts they signed. The American low-budget cinema, on the other hand, tended to be thought of as a commercial and studio-based product, to which Godard pays homage in his dedication of *A bout de souffle* (1959) to Monogram Pictures. *Cahiers'* innovation was to treat film-makers such as Hawks or Fuller as the authors of their films in much the same way as their more 'respectable' European counterparts.

The New Wave directors, like their Hollywood predecessors, worked individually and creatively within often severe budgetary constraints and the conventions of studio genre. Their films were frequently self-referential (Godard making a brief Hitchcock-like appearance in his own *A bout de souffle*, Truffaut's *Les 400 Coups* (1959) containing an obvious visual quotation from Vigo's *Zéro de conduite*), as though to assert the value of film as a form of artistic expression on a par with the novel or the theatre. Allusions to art cinema and Hollywood action film sat side by side in a manner that, nowadays, with the erosion of the barrier between 'high' and 'popular' culture, seems unremarkable, but was extremely innovative at the time. The literary adaptation and the costly studio set-up were anathema to these film-makers, whose use of hand-held cameras and location filming gave their work a constant charge of the unexpected. They were also greatly helped by the introduction, in 1960, of the *avance sur recettes*, a system of government loans, granted on the basis of a working script, to enable films to be produced. One in five French films benefits from this funding, though only one in ten of these has been sufficiently successful at the box office to pay off the loan in full (Hayward, 1993: 46). The system thus effectively works as a source of subsidy, another reason for the often-remarked thriving independent and experimental sector (known as *art et essai*) of the French industry.

Chronologically, the first New Wave film was Chabrol's *Le Beau Serge* of 1959, followed in the same year by his *Les Cousins*. The influence of Hitchcock is marked in the exchange of roles between the central characters (in both films played by Gérard Blain and Jean-Claude Brialy), the latter of whom represents Parisian would-be sophistication against the provincial benightedness of the other. Chabrol has had a wildly uneven career, often filming neither wisely nor too well, but at his best he is the master denouncer of the hypocrisy and pretentions of the bourgeoisie. Misanthropy and misogyny are other components of his work and both are plain in *Les Bonnes Femmes* (1960), about the varying fortunes and ambitions of four young women who work in an electrical shop, an emblem of the modernisation of French society. *Les Biches* (1966) features a bisexual love triangle in Saint-Tropez, probably the first major French film to deal overtly with lesbianism, albeit in a manner that changes in sexual politics have caused to appear dubious.

The year 1959 – *annus mirabilis* of post-war cinema – also saw the feature debuts of Truffaut and Godard. The former's *Les 400 Coups* remains among the cinema's most touching evocations of a less-then-happy childhood, modelled in many ways on Truffaut's own. Film here is the medium at once for autobiographical essay and for formal audacity, as in the celebrated final shot in which the young Antoine Doinel/Jean-Pierre Léaud runs away from reform school and is frozen by the camera, half-fearful and half-exhilarated, as he catches his first glimpse of the sea. Truffaut wisely left Doinel to fend for himself for the best part of a decade, during which he broadened his experimental use of the medium with the bitter-sweet gangster parody *Tirez sur le pianiste* (1960), starring Charles Aznavour, and the prolonged triangular love story between a Frenchman, a German and the capricious Catherine/Jeanne Moreau, *Jules et Jim* (1962). This earned an unprecedented standing innovation at the Cannes festival, from which Truffaut had a few years before been banned, and the all-but-envious homage of Renoir. The homoerotic intensity of the relationship between Jules and Jim, mediated it would be possible to argue through their shared passion for Catherine, now gives the film a strikingly modern feel. The theme of tragic or impossible love, and its close linkage with death, recurs in more conventional format with *La Peau douce* (1964), generally regarded as Truffaut's most Chabrolesque work.

A bout de souffle remains probably the best-loved of New Wave films, its innovative use of jump-cuts, location filming of a non-touristic Paris and *mise-en-scène* of the love/hate relationship between French and American culture remaining as fresh now as when it was released. The fecundity of Godard's experiments with sound-image relationships and filmic genre is a constant in his work throughout the decade, which spanned the musical (*Une femme est une femme*, 1961), science fiction (*Alphaville*, 1965) and the sociological treatise (*Deux ou trois choses que je sais d'elle*, 1966). *Le Mépris* (1963) gives Brigitte Bardot her major serious dramatic role, and stages an eloquent enactment of the contradictory pressures on the film-maker to make money and produce significant art. Much of Godard's work during this decade displays an unnerving prescience. *Bande à part* (1964) alludes to the genocidal conflict in Rwanda 30 years before it came to widespread attention. *Masculin féminin* (1966) pre-echoes the debates about gender and sex roles that were to achieve such importance in succeeding decades. The cultural and institutional upheaval of May 1968 has a very good claim to being the most unexpected major event in post-war European history; yet Godard's two 1967 films, *La Chinoise* and *Weekend*, are extraordinary straws in the wind, the former foreshadowing the leftist agitation at the University of Nanterre that was to spark the events off, the latter a Surrealist, cartoon-like dramatisation of the consumerism so characteristic of French society in the 1960s and of the 1968 reaction against it.

The political strain in Godard's work becomes evident as early as *Pierrot le fou* (1965), which features Jean-Paul Belmondo from *A bout de souffle* in a doomed love affair with Godard's then wife Anna Karina, his inspiration for much of this period. *Pierrot le fou* suggests much of what was to follow in Godard's subsequent work, with its strikingly poetic use of colour, its use of mockingly didactic, quasi-Brechtian tableaux and its references to the Vietnam War.

Rohmer's work remains, certainly in French and probably in world cinema, unique in that he has never lost money on a film in a 40-year career. His low-budget approach, reliance on highly crafted dialogue and fondness for ironic philosophising make a 'Rohmer film' instantly recognisable, and in these respects he can, even by those not uniformly enthusiastic about his work, be seen as the supreme *auteur*. *Le Signe du lion* (1959) is his most savage work, about an over-trusting bohemian's destitute summer in Paris. His work for the remainder of this period took the form of short films, often made for television, a further illustration of the economic awareness that informs his work.

Rivette's love for lengthy, intricate narratives was apparent from his first feature, *Paris nous appartient* (1961), and has caused him to have a rather chequered career. *La Religieuse* (1966), his only other feature of the period, was briefly banned by the censor for its supposedly scandalous evocation of convent life, and authorised to be exported only under the distancing title of *Suzanne Simonin, la religieuse de Diderot*, much as Godard's 1964 *La Femme mariée* had to be retitled *Une femme mariée* before it got past the censor.

Other film-makers closely associated with the New Wave, though not with *Cahiers du cinéma*, were Alain Resnais, Agnès Varda and Jacques Demy. Resnais, the great cineast of memory, remains unique in his exclusive use of pre-written scripts, the basis for the most extensive formal experimentation with montage among contemporary film-makers. Novelists Marguerite Duras and Alain Robbe-Grillet, both themselves to go on to direct films, scripted respectively *Hiroshima mon amour* (1959) and *L'Année dernière à Marienbad* (1961). *Hiroshima* intertwines the horrors of the nuclear bomb and its central female character's love affairs with a German during the war and a Japanese afterwards, broaching at once political and ethnic taboos. Nowadays, with a more widespread awareness that 'the personal is political', its 'dime-store novel' plot (as the central character, played by Emmanuelle Riva, herself describes it) appears less audacious than it did at the time, when its sympathetic evocation of a love affair with the enemy was moving into largely uncharted territory. The film, as important a first feature as *A bout de souffle*, makes vivid, often startling use of subjective visual flashbacks, cutting back and forth between the Hiroshima of 1958 and the French provincial town of Nevers under the Occupation.

L'Année dernière à Marienbad (see Figure 1.2) is a virtuoso essay in the 'eternal present' of the filmic image. It is impossible to tell whether its love story, with Delphine Seyrig as the object of two men's desire, is past, present, future, fantasy, or all or none of these. In this respect the film is analogous to the experiments of the 'new novelists' – including Robbe-Grillet – with subjective, fragmented or even contradictory narration. A strikingly, even flamboyantly, modern work, it is also an evocation of and homage to the golden age of black and white film-making; there is scarcely another film it would be so difficult to imagine in colour. *Muriel* (1963), also starring Delphine Seyrig, ran into censorship difficulties because of its references to torture in the Algerian war, much as Godard's *Le Petit Soldat* had done three years earlier. Censorship of film was rife in the Gaullist era – the downside perhaps of the state's interest in the medium. Officially instituted for the first time during the Occupation, it continued in force thereafter, to such an extent that during the eight years of the Algerian War (1954–1962) 'not a single film on the Algerian question was granted a visa' (Hayward, 1993: 40). Not until Giscard d'Estaing became president in 1974 did it all but disappear.

The *succès de scandale* enjoyed by Louis Malle's second feature, *Les Amants* (1958), is there to remind us that sexual censorship was scarcely less to be reckoned with (though less specific to France) in this period than its political counterpart. *Les Amants* stars Jeanne Moreau as a bored bourgeois trophy wife who leaves her family and lover behind after a night of love with a young student she met on the road. The aforementioned *succès de scandale* pertained to the film's (inevitably) discreet depiction – or evocation – of cunnilingus, but more profoundly shocking than this might be the wife's seeming abandonment of not only her husband, but her young daughter. Malle's role as starmaker was reinforced by *Vie privée* of 1962, with its barely disguised references to the real life of its star, Brigitte Bardot.

Varda is beyond doubt French cinema's leading woman director. The number of films directed by women in France has increased exponentially over the past decade in particular, but until the post-war period a woman director was a rarity,

Figure 1.2 L'Année dernière à Marienbad

and Varda for a very long time was – certainly so far as non-French audiences were concerned – seemingly the only one of her kind. *Cléo de 5 à 7* (1962) tells in real time the story of a singer who suspects she may have cancer. Hope and encouragement are given to her by a young conscript soldier she meets in the Parc Montsouris while waiting for the result of hospital tests – a scene given particular poignancy by the fact that he is at the end of a period of leave from Algeria. The counterposing of a life under threat from within and one under threat from without figures the interplay of the personal and the political we have already seen at work in *Hiroshima mon amour*, as well as suggesting how film-makers found ways of incorporating references to the Algerian War into their work without falling foul of the censor. Varda's other work in this period was in the short or documentary format, apart from the ironic love triangle *Le Bonheur* of 1965.

Demy (Varda's husband) made two major films during this period, *Lola* (1961) and *Les Parapluies de Cherbourg* (1964). Set in western French seaports (Nantes and Cherbourg respectively), they refer, in a perhaps deceptively lighthearted way, to the twofold processes of modernisation and decolonisation under way in the France of the time (see Ross, 1995, for a masterly analysis of these). *Lola*'s eponymous heroine, played by Anouk Aimée, oscillates between a French and an American lover before her first love returns (driving a vast American car) to reclaim her at the end. *Les Parapluies de Cherbourg*, for all the frothiness of its entirely sung dialogue (to music by Michel Legrand), actually offers a serious treatment of the effects of modernisation along with those of the Algerian War. Catherine Deneuve, in her first major role, becomes pregnant by the man she loves the night before he leaves for Algeria; on his return he finds her married off to a wealthy local jeweller, in part because her mother does not believe that a garage mechanic would be an acceptable match for her. The irony of this, in the increasingly motorised French society of the time, becomes manifest in the film's final sequence, where we see Michel as the proud owner of a large and gleaming garage.

Bresson, Tati and Melville, all of whom had come to the fore in the war years, produced arguably their finest work during this period. Bresson's *Pickpocket* (1959) and *Au hasard Balthazar* (1966) refine his elliptical precision still further; editing here becomes a spiritual quest. *Pickpocket*'s anguished Dostoevskyan hero is never 'analysed' (a term anathema to Bresson) in any detail. His compulsive thieving is observed in tight phenomenological detail, and only in the film's final sequence, where in prison he is visited by Jeanne for whom he realises the depth of his love, does it dawn on him (and the audience) that it has represented his way to redemption. *Au hasard Balthazar* realises the *tour de force* of making the tribulations of a donkey (its central 'character') into a spiritual odyssey – Bresson's rejection of the very idea of the actor carried to its furthest extent – while also offering a surprisingly barbed view of modernised France through the presence of the villainous *blouson noir* Gérard. Tati's only feature of the period, *Playtime* (1967), is a prodigiously choreographed near-silent comedy, which lost a vast amount of money and all but ended his career. Nowadays, it appears not only as his finest work, extraordinarily intricate in its complexity of visual organisation, but also as a striking prefiguration of the postmodern era in which everywhere looks like everywhere else. The film follows a group of tourists as they journey round a concrete and glass Paris whose iconic landmarks, such as the Eiffel Tower, are visible only in travel agency posters. Melville's masterpiece *Le Samouraï* (1967) carries his stylisation of the gangster movie to iconographic lengths, in a pared-down narrative with minimal dialogue sustained largely by the androgynous performance, by turns violent and vulnerable, of Alain Delon.

By the end of our period the New Wave as any kind of unified movement or entity had ceased to exist (some would situate its demise as early as 1963). The film-makers associated with it were pursuing widely divergent paths – from the increasingly politicised experimentation of Godard to the more commercial work of Truffaut or Chabrol – all with significant success. Part at least of the reason for this had to do with the actors and actresses their work brought to the fore. *Le Mépris* notwithstanding, Brigitte Bardot is not normally associated with the New Wave (her most celebrated role remains Roger Vadim's *Et Dieu créa la femme*, 1956), but the sexual openness and freedom with which she was for long synonymous struck a chord with the New Wave generation, echoes of which can be traced in Jean Seberg/Patricia in *A bout de souffle* and the early roles of Catherine Deneuve. Jeanne Moreau has tended to evoke a more sophisticated, upmarket sex appeal, exemplified not only by her roles in *Les Amants* and *Jules et Jim* but also by her periodic forays into independent and avant-garde cinema, such as Peter Brook's Duras adaptation *Moderato cantabile* (1960).

The key icons of masculinity during this period were Delon and Belmondo. The former's 'demonic presence beneath the disguise of an angel' (Passek, 1987: 113) was not to be deployed by a New Wave film-maker until 1990 and Godard's *Nouvelle vague*, but his work for Melville, René Clément (*Plein soleil*, 1959) and the Italian directors Visconti and Antonioni made him an international art-house superstar. Belmondo's craggy vulnerability made him the ideal interpreter for the two key Godard roles already referred to. He was to oscillate throughout his career between overtly commercial roles (in which his credibility was vastly enhanced by the fact that he insisted on doing all his own stunts) and appearances for 'respectable' directors including – as well as Godard – Chabrol, Resnais and Truffaut.

In 1968, French cinema, like the society in which it was rooted and which it represented, appeared to be quietly prosperous and securely grounded. Yet a crisis that occurred in February of that year suggested that this impression might not altogether conform to reality. The Paris *Cinémathèque*, co-founded in 1936 by Georges Franju and Henri Langlois, had during the 30 or more years of its existence become one of the world's leading film archives, where as we have seen the New Wave directors and many others received much of their cinematic education. Langlois's energy and commitment were immensely important in its success, despite his often anarchic curatorial methods. It was these latter that led, in February 1968, to his dismissal by the Culture Minister, André Malraux, in an attempt at increasing already pronounced governmental control over the world of culture, which sparked off a massive wave of protest. The *Cinémathèque* was effectively closed down by demonstrations until Langlois's reinstatement at the end of April. The 'Langlois affair' now appears as an obvious precursor of the 'events' that were to shake France to the core the following month – events that, as we shall see, were to have a major cultural and political impact in which the cinema would have its part to play.

1968–1981: THE NEW WAVE (POSTSCRIPT), REALISM AND COMEDY

The May 1968 events – a student protest leading to a general strike on a massive scale and briefly seeming to menace the whole institutional structure of French society – appear in retrospect as the moment when culture assumed a major importance in the political arena. The Langlois affair, as we have seen, was a prefiguration of this, and the 'Estates-General of the Cinema', set up during the events by the film technicians' union, discussed various possibilities for the restructuring of the cinema industry in the revolutionary perspective dominant at the time.

For all this involvement, however, May 1968's effect on film-making was in the end slight. More significant for the industry, though not necessarily for film as an art form, was Giscard's abolition of censorship, spearheaded by his Culture Minister, Michel Guy. This led to a burgeoning of pornographic films, which were more heavily taxed than other films and thus cross-subsidised the 'legitimate' industry. They to some extent helped to stem a decline in cinema attendance which nevertheless, as everywhere else, proved to be inexorable, owing above all to the pervasiveness of television. Even so, the French industry was to prove, as it has done ever since, the envy of many others in its ability, thanks to state intervention, to keep its head above water, instanced during this period by the continuing success of the major directors from earlier years and the coming to the fore of new film-makers.

The major impact of May 1968 on film-making practice is undoubtedly to be found in the work of Godard. We have seen that *La Chinoise* and *Weekend*, made the year before the events, were a striking prefiguration of them. Godard became heavily involved in far-Left politics, working with Maoist groups and plunging himself into the making of *ciné-tracts* – revolutionary propagandist collages – before disowning his earlier work, 'claiming that it functioned only at the level of theoretical experiment rather than of social and political struggle' (Williams in Hughes and Reader, 1998: 273–4). His work in the rest of this period was marked by a politically inflected investigation of the image/sound relationship, across a variety of genres – from political shorts, via a subversive return to the 'commercial' cinema with 1972's *Tout va bien* (starring Yves Montand and Jane Fonda), to experimentation with video in *Numéro deux* (1975), which returns to the theme of gender relationships he had adumbrated as early as *Masculin-féminin* in 1966.

Godard also worked for television, unsurprisingly encountering problems with its state-dominated apparatus, before returning to his country of citizenship, Switzerland, in the late 1970s. *Sauve qui peut (la vie)* (1979) was his most 'mainstream' film for some considerable time, situating its political involvement at the level of interpersonal and particularly gender relations rather than of the class struggle. In its diversity of institutional contexts, its engagement with video and television, its passage through a vehemently committed Marxism to a more diffuse and labile view of what constituted the political, Godard's work of this period serves as a remarkable crystallisation of the wider cultural and ideological evolution of the France of these years. That evolution, we shall see, was to culminate in the election of a Socialist president – François Mitterrand – in 1981 and the dwindling of May's revolutionary optimism into diverse movements for other forms, notably ethnic- and gender-based, of social change.

Among New Wave figures, Truffaut rejoined Doinel/Léaud for three autobiographical features: *Baisers volés* (1968), *Domicile conjugal* (1970) and *L'Amour en fuite* (1979). He won an Oscar for *La Nuit américaine* (1973), a comedy about the making of a film, and enjoyed his major commercial success with the Occupation-set theatre drama, *Le Dernier Métro* (1980), giving starring roles to Catherine Deneuve and the mountainously extravagant Gérard Depardieu. There was a tendency, in this period characterised by arduous political commitment and formal experimentation, to dismiss his films as lightweight, especially in the light of *Cahiers du cinéma*'s Marxist position of the 1970s (see the section on 'ideology and suture' in Chapter 2 of this volume). Yet the exploration – ambiguously complicit or critical – of 'Donjuanism' and gender relations in *L'Homme qui aimait les femmes* (1977), and the death-haunted central character of *La Chambre verte* (1978), played by Truffaut himself, in different ways give the lie to this view. *La Chambre verte* appears particularly poignant in the light of Truffaut's tragically early death from a brain tumour in 1984.

Chabrol went at the provincial bourgeoisie with a will in *Le Boucher* (1970) and *Les Noces rouges* (1973), among more ephemeral ventures. *Le Boucher* shows the influence of Hitchcock in its metaphysical echoes, notably the possible transference of guilt for the village butcher's murders on to the school teacher Hélène (played by Chabrol's then wife Stéphane Audran), who has rejected, or at least refused to confront her love for, him. The previous year's *Que la bête meure!* likewise suggests a disturbing transference, here between the father seeking to avenge his son's death and the monstrous hit-and-run driver – played by Jean Yanne in a prefiguration of his title role in *Le Boucher* – responsible for it. Rivette enjoyed the biggest success of his career with the screwball-influenced *Céline et Julie vont en bateau* (1974), while making almost certainly the longest French feature film ever, *Out One* of the same year, which ran for 12 hours and 40 minutes and was understandably only ever screened once in the full-length version.

Rohmer's *Ma nuit chez Maud* (1969), one of his 'Six Moral Tales' series, is probably his defining work, in its use of intellectualised irony (here rooted in a reading of the seventeenth-century philosopher Pascal) and investment in talk as alternative rather than preliminary to sex. *Le Genou de Claire* (1970) and *L'Amour l'après-midi* (1972), part of the same series, likewise deal with temptations to infidelity or sexual transgression that are resolved through language rather than action. At a time when Lacanian psychoanalysis, with its stress on the inextricable interplay of language and desire, was carrying all before it in French intellectual life, it is perhaps not fanciful to suggest that Rohmer's films, for all their evocation of the early Enlightenment world of Marivaux's comedies, were more in tune with their own period than might at first appear. Resnais enjoyed less success in this period than previously, though *Mon oncle d'Amérique* (1980) is a masterly *mise-en-scène* of the technocratic modernisation of France in the 1970s. The social transformations of the Giscard years, fuelled by growing Americanisation and issuing in measures ranging from the abolition of censorship to the 1975 legalisation of abortion, have tended to be somewhat overshadowed by the earlier hegemony of Gaullism and the (largely unrealised) hopes invested in the Socialist victory of 1981. Yet they were considerable, and Resnais's chronicle of the changing and intertwined fortunes of his three main characters traces them in fascinating detail.

Bresson used colour for the first time in the Dostoevsky adaptation *Une femme douce* (1969), though many find his colour work less starkly challenging than the black and white films. In *Lancelot du lac* (1974), he constructs a bleak and pitiless Middle Ages from which any sense of faith or purpose has been evacuated, and the same is true for his evocation of suicidal contemporary youth in *Le Diable, probablement* (1977). The redemptive possibilities of *Journal d'un curé de campagne* or *Pickpocket* seem definitively banished from an increasingly pessimistic body of work.

All in all, then, the New Wave's reputation for innovation did not long survive its first half-dozen or so years. Its swansong – by one not even considered a New Wave director – has to be Jean Eustache's *La Maman et la putain* (1973), three and a half hours of sexual and philosophical agonising, which take apart the aesthetic, emotional and political hopes of the 1959–68 generation (see Figure 1.3). The film stars Jean-Pierre Léaud in probably his greatest role, as a posturing (pseudo?-)intellectual dandy caught between the 'mother' and the 'whore' of the title – respectively, Bernadette Lafont (an early muse of Chabrol's) as the fashion shop owner with whom he lives and Françoise Lebrun as the unhappily promiscuous nurse with whom he begins an affair. The disillusionment that followed the extravagant hopes aroused by the events of May 1968 is matched and paralleled by the film's drawing out of New Wave stylistic trademarks – black and white location filming, dialogues that sound improvised (though they were not), the use of iconic actors – to something like a point of no return.

The 'New Wave generation' had been reared on first the myth of, then (in 1968) the reaction against, Gaullism – a cycle that only really came to an end in 1974 with the death of de Gaulle's *dauphin* and successor, Georges Pompidou. That also enabled the calling into question of the myth of omnipresent and heroic resistance to the Occupation on which Gaullism had been founded. Marcel Ophüls's documentary *Le Chagrin et la pitié* (1971) suggested the first stirrings of this. Commissioned by the state broadcasting system (the ORTF), it was not shown on television for more than a decade, its revelations of the extent of collaboration in Clermont-Ferrand, which could have been virtually any other French city, proving far too uncomfortable. The can of worms opened by the film was still alive and writhing in the 1990s, as illustrated by the 1994 revelations about President Mitterrand's collaborationist past and the imprisonment of former Giscard minister Maurice Papon for his part in the deportation of Paris Jews.

Where the documentary film had led the way, the feature was soon to follow. Louis Malle's *Lacombe Lucien* (1973) gave the first (moderately) sympathetic portrayal of a collaborator, in the person of its central character who joins the Milice only when

Figure 1.3   La Maman et la putain

rejected by the Resistance and helps to save the life of the Jewish girl with whom he falls in love (see Figure 1.4). The debate aroused by these and other films of the time centred less on their artistic qualities than on the legitimacy of calling the myth of the Resistance – hence, for many, the hard-won social and institutional stability of post-war France – into question. This was at the same time a debate around two divergent views of history – one the classic 'classroom' kind grounded in great names and dates, the other more popular, anecdotal and concerned with the study of attitudes and phenomena rather than landmark events. The second view, promoted first by the journal *Annales* in the post-war period, then by the immensely influential philosopher and historian of ideas Michel Foucault, became extremely influential in the aftermath of 1968, with its stress on the need to give excluded or marginalised voices a hearing. René Clément's 1966 *Paris brûle-t-il?*, whose main characters are major historical figures from the Occupation of Paris, can stand as an example of the heroic view of *les années noires* as battle between good and evil, which subsequent texts and debates, historical and cinematic, were relentlessly to undercut. Cinema was to have a greater impact on French society and (in the wider sense) politics through its role in these debates than through the politically fuelled formal innovations advocated by *Cahiers du cinéma* in the 1970s.

In part because of 1968's limited direct influence on film-making practice, but more significantly in response to the challenge of television and the increasing multinationalisation of the industry, the film-makers who began to build careers for themselves in the 1970s tended towards more conservative models and techniques than their predecessors. Bertrand Tavernier's low-key social realism, as in the Lyon-set *L'Horloger de Saint-Paul* (1974) and *Une semaine de vacances* (1980), is a good example of the resurgence of a kind of film-making the New Wave had fondly imagined dead and buried. That Tavernier's major scriptwriter is Jean Aurenche – he of the Aurenche and Bost reviled by Truffaut and others as epitomising the *cinéma de papa* – shows how tenacious such cinema was to prove, reaching its financial if not always artistic apotheosis in the 'heritage movies' of the 1980s and 1990s.

Maurice Pialat began to make his reputation with the terse realism of early works such as *L'Enfance nue* (1969) and *La Gueule ouverte* (1974), which established him as a venomously anarchistic dissector of the nuclear family and its discontents. Pialat's reputation as all but impossible to work with has never ceased to dog his relationships with producers and actors alike, at the same time as whetting audiences' appetites to see films whose on- and off-screen tensions are reputedly almost indistinguishable. *Loulou* (1980) was among the first films to bring Isabelle Huppert, arguably the key female star of that decade, to prominence, as well as giving a major role to Gérard Depardieu, who plays the layabout of the title, with Isabelle

Figure 1.4 Lacombe Lucien

34

Huppert as the middle-class girl who abandons everything for a turbulent sexual relationship with him.

Depardieu had become known a few years earlier for his work with Bertrand Blier. Blier's mixture of misogyny and carnivalesque parody was to make him, along with Tavernier and Pialat, the key director to emerge in the 1970s. In this he was greatly helped by the team of actors who worked with him, many of them coming from the world of *café-théâtre*. *Les Valseuses* (1974) is a road movie, but breaks with one key convention of that genre in that its central characters (played by Depardieu and Patrick Dewaere) are in no sense concerned with self-discovery through travel. Their sole concern is sexual and material self-indulgence, in which they are helped by major actresses from different generations – Jeanne Moreau and Miou-Miou. Blier had in 1978 won the Best Foreign Film Oscar for *Préparez vos mouchoirs*, again starring Depardieu and Dewaere.

The entirely male focus of this chapter – at least so far as directors are concerned – will not have escaped the reader, the more so since Blier's sexual politics have been the target of frequent, and sometimes well-justified, criticism. It was not until the 1980s and 1990s that women directors were to become an everyday phenomenon in the French cinema, but significant figures began to make their mark in the previous decade. Coline Serreau's love triangle comedy *Pourquoi pas?* (1977), and Diane Kurys's autobiographical *Diabolo menthe* (1977) were early works by filmmakers who were to go on to lasting prominence.

The films discussed here were not, of course, the French productions actually watched by most French people during the period under discussion. That distinction went to Just Jaeckin's *Emmanuelle* (1974), most notorious of the soft-porn features that followed the disappearance of censorship, and Gérard Oury's *Les Aventures du Rabbi Jacob* (1973). Oury had enjoyed even greater success in 1966 with *La Grande Vadrouille*, like *Les Aventures du Rabbi Jacob* starring two of France's best-loved screen comedians of the time, Bourvil and Louis de Funès. Both, like the more internationally known Dewaere and Depardieu later on, came from the world of the stage and the music hall – evidence that for all the specificity of film as art form so vaunted by the New Wave, the French cinema remained profoundly dependent on other types of popular performance art, not always of a kind that travel well.

Despite the steady decline in cinema attendance over this period, the French industry continued to fare better than its main competitors, thanks to co-production deals, with television and other European countries, and the constant – some would say protectionist – vigilance of successive governments. The 'Mitterrand years', as we shall now see, were to develop and extend that vigilance, even if it was often to be a question of running fast to stay in the same place.

1981–2001: HERITAGE, THE LOOK, WOMEN, BEURS, BANLIEUE, LE JEUNE CINÉMA

There were major changes in the production and distribution of films during the late 1970s and early 1980s, which had a significant impact on the cinema. Some of these changes were common to other developed countries in Europe. Amongst these, there was the rise of TV co-productions, in particular with the encrypted channel Canal+, which unlike its counterpart in the UK, Channel 4, was almost exclusively devoted to films; other major channels such as TF1 and FR3 became associated with film production, alongside Canal+. The effect on films was that an increasing number of them were conceived from the outset for screening on the small rather than the big screen, leading to what was called a 'televisualisation' of the cinema.

A second major change, which occurred in other countries as well, was the rise of the multiplex. This had started as early as the beginning of the 1970s, supported by state funding. However, in the mid-1980s, Pathé and Gaumont, the main distributors in France, came to an agreement that led to the expansion of such complexes. A greater number of film theatres meant that distributors were less likely to take risks, and would screen the same film throughout the country with a vast advertising campaign, leading to ever more expensive films. This at least had the merit of concentrating resources in the national products, which were then, arguably, in a better position to vie with Hollywood films.

The third major change was the shift by French audiences away from the national product to the increasingly globalised and even more heavily marketed Hollywood product. In 1986/87, for the first time in the history of the French cinema, there were more French audiences watching Hollywood films than French films. Unsurprisingly, this led to the gradual waning of the more popular French genres such as the police thriller and the comedy. In their place came new genres in the 1980s, which, with the exception of mainstream heritage films, one could call the 'cinemas of the marginal', suggesting that French cinema, much like the French press, was diversifying in an attempt to find niche audiences, at the very same time as it was being absorbed, one might argue, by the curious phenomenon of the Hollywood remake. Remakes are of course a frequent phenomenon in the history of the French cinema. However, whereas there are some 20 Hollywood remakes in the period 1930–1950, dropping even more in the next 30 years when there were only six, there was a marked increase in the last 20 years of the century, with some 34 remakes, most of them being comedies. This led many commentators, on both sides of the Atlantic, to talk about the inferior quality of the remakes as well as the paucity of the industries that somehow could not manage to find outlets in any other way. What it signals, rather more importantly perhaps, is the increasingly globalised nature of some film-making, as we shall see when we allude to particular directors such as Besson and Jeunet, although it would be equally important to recognise the attempts by certain French stars to make a career in the USA. Isabelle Adjani began early in *The Driver* (Hill, 1978), returning to the USA for *Ishtar* (May, 1987). The other major star, Gérard Depardieu, just failed to get an Oscar nomination for *Green Card* (Weir, 1990), but reprised his role as the father in Veber's *Mon Père ce héros* (1991) in the Hollywood remake, *My Father the Hero* (Miner, 1994), as well as acting in a number of other translatlantic films, such as playing Columbus in Ridley Scott's *1492: Conquest of Paradise* (1992) or Porthos in *The Man in the Iron Mask* (Wallace, 1998). The move across to the USA was not confined to the two major stars, however. Emmanuelle Béart had a significant part in *Mission Impossible* (de Palma, 1996), Sophie Marceau was the French Princess in *Braveheart* (Gibson, 1995) and, more recently, Juliette Binoche starred alongside Johnny Depp as a mixer of heady chocolate potions in *Chocolat* (Hallström, 2000).

Despite these moves by stars in the last decade of the century, suggesting the increasing visibility of the French industry abroad, directors associated with the New Wave or with the 1970s continued to produce films of great interest and quality, and it is worth reviewing their output before turning to the new types of cinema more readily associated with the 1980s and 1990s.

The most emblematic director of the New Wave, Truffaut, died in 1984, but not before producing several major films, one of which heralds the mid-1980s emergence of what has come to be called heritage cinema, *Le Dernier métro* (1980). Godard's films during the 1980s were frequently deconstructions of well-known stories or genres: the Carmen story in *Prénom: Carmen* (1983); the myth of the Virgin Mary in *Je vous salue Marie* (1983); the police thriller in *Détective* (1984); and King Lear in the film of the same name (1987). If these films seemed increasingly hermetic, his ten-year documentary project on the history of the cinema (*Histoire(s) du cinéma*, 1989/1998) is one of the more remarkable outputs by a film director who is perhaps less a film director than a cultural critic or, as he has often put it, an essayist in film. Varda continued to make largely short films, though *Sans toit ni loi* (1983) features one of the period's most remarkable female performances, from Sandrine Bonnaire, who also features in two of Rivette's more recent films, the two-part story of Joan of Arc, *Jeanne la Pucelle* (1994), and the corporate crime drama

Secret Défense (1998). Rivette's more remarkable achievement in this period, however, is the long film about the creative process, *La Belle Noiseuse* (1991), starring Emmanuelle Béart and Michel Piccoli, which won several prizes, including the Grand Jury Prize at Cannes that year.

Rohmer, perhaps the most literary of the old New Wave directors, continued the light touch with heavy dialogue in a number of award-winning films concentrating on relationships, usually between young people. These sometimes irritate, particularly when Rohmer allows his actors to improvise, as in the case of *Pauline à la plage* (1983) or *Le Rayon Vert* (1986), but more often than not elicit remarkable performances, as was the case with Pascale Ogier in *Les Nuits de la pleine lune* (1984). During the 1990s, Rohmer completed a cycle of four films, the *Contes des quatre saisons*.

During the 1980s and 1990s, Resnais worked with what was essentially a repertory group of actors – Fanny Ardant, Pierre Arditi, Sabine Azéma and André Dussollier – in a number of films scripted by Jean Gruault (who had scripted many of the great films of the New Wave directors): *La Vie est un roman* (1983), *L'Amour à mort* (1984), *Mélo* (1986). The last of these was the adaptation of a stage play, as were Resnais's major films of the 1990s, the Alan Ayckbourn adaptations *Smoking/No Smoking* (1993). His most talked-about film of the 1990s was the comedy musical tribute to UK playwright Dennis Potter, *On connaît la chanson* (1977), scripted by one of the key partnerships of then current French cinema, Jean-Pierre Bacri and Agnès Jaoui.

If we turn to directors who came to prominence in the 1970s, Maurice Pialat's career took off after *Loulou* (1980). This was followed by what is perhaps one of the key films of the 1980s, *A nos amours* (1983), the analysis of a dysfunctional family, headed by a father, played by Pialat himself, and focusing on his daughter, played by Sandrine Bonnaire, who has many transient sexual encounters. As with his previous film, this is a trenchant critique of the amoralism of French society, and in particular of French youth, acting as an interesting counterpoint to similar concerns, at least narratively, in the *cinéma du look*, which we shall consider below. In *Police* (1985), Depardieu plays a cop who falls for a gangster's moll, the theme again being problematic identities in an increasingly amoral society. Bonnaire and Depardieu teamed up with Pialat in his hard-hitting adaptation of Bernanos's novel, *Sous le soleil de Satan* (1987), which won the Golden Palm at Cannes. His *Van Gogh* (1991) won the actor Jacques Dutronc a César award.

Blier, much like Pialat, produced two key films during the 1980s, both starring Depardieu. In *Tenue de soirée* (1986), Depardieu plays a gay burglar, and in *Trop belle pour toi* (1989), he plays a businessman happily married to a beautiful wife (played by Chanel model Carole Bouquet), who falls for his dumpy secretary, played by Josiane Balasko. If Pialat's 1980s films with their melodramatic realism questioned youth identities, Blier's films, founded, as his earlier films had been, on provocative black humour, questioned the fragility of male identity. His 1990s films, the first three of which star the woman who was to become his partner, Anouk Grinberg, and who is regularly abused in these films, did less well, their provocative misogyny now out of kilter with the times.

The other major 1970s director whose career took off in the 1980s was Tavernier. His solid craftsmanship was probably been best illustrated by the post-First World War drama *La Vie et rien d'autre* (1989), in which his work with Philippe Noiret reached an apotheosis and which figured one key development in the 1980s and 1990s, the tendency to evoke (some would say 'retreat into') the past. This has become known generically as the heritage film, one of the most dominant genres in the 1980s, as elsewhere in Europe (see Vincendeau, 2001). Period films with high production values and based on literary masterpieces (the more obvious hallmarks of the genre) had appeared before. This was particularly the case in the 1950s, in the *tradition de qualité* films so detested by Truffaut; but it was also the case in the early 1980s, as can be seen with Tavernier's homage to the *tradition de qualité*, *Un dimanche à la campagne* (1984), for example, based on a short novel by one of the main screenwriters of the *tradition de qualité*, Pierre Bost, or the European co-production *Un amour de Swann* (Schlöndorff, 1983), based on part of Proust's *A la recherche du temps perdu*. Nevertheless, the heritage genre proper could be said to have established itself with the immensely popular Claude Berri films *Jean de Florette* and *Manon des Sources*. Berri's films both appeared in 1986, based on a novel by Marcel Pagnol; another Pagnol pair appeared in 1990, Yves Robert's *La Gloire de mon père* and *Le Château de ma mere*. Much like Merchant and Ivory in the UK industry, however, it is Berri who stands out as the main director of heritage films in France, with *Uranus* (1990) and *Germinal* (1993) amongst others. Jean-Paul Rappeneau directed two popular heritage films, *Cyrano de Bergerac* (1990), an adaptation of Rostand's nineteenth-century verse play, which enjoyed immense worldwide success, and *Le Hussard sur le toit* (1995). The latter is based on a historical novel by the regionalist writer Jean Giono, whose fiction has frequently been adapted to the screen, especially by Marcel Pagnol during the 1930s. This nexus of authors and films shows how the early 1980s heritage films are imbued with nostalgia for the golden age of the cinema, as well as the golden age of a rural France untainted by rapid post-war industrialisation and the alienation of increasing urbanisation in the 1980s and 1990s.

That said, the heritage films of the 1990s, *Germinal* and *Le Hussard sur le toit* among them, seem much darker in tone than the earlier films, suggesting a distinctive evolution of the genre on a formal level, and, socially, a disaffection with Mitterrandism, which, as we shall see, surfaces differently in another key development of the 1980s, the *cinéma du look*. A key film here is *Germinal*, seen at the time as the epitome of French cinema, largely because its release coincided with the epitome of US cultural imperialism, Spielberg's *Jurassic Park*, as well as with the acrimonious GATT negotiations that ended with a victory for the French, who claimed that state support for the film industry was not unlawful protectionism, but essential to safeguard French cinema. Significantly in this respect, *Germinal*'s premiere was very publicly supported by political figures, turning it into an icon of 'Frenchness'. And yet, the film is curiously heavy and dour when compared with previous versions of the story. Grimy, exhausted miners with little hope of a decent life were as nothing, however, compared to the flavour of other early 1990s heritage films, such as Angelo's *Le Colonel Chabert* (1994), with its opening shots of piles of military corpses, or Chéreau's remake in 1994 of Dréville's *La Reine Margot* (1954) with its thousands of assassinated Protestants in sixteenth-century Paris, or *Le Hussard sur le toit* with its vomiting, raven-pecked plague victims.

The heritage film developed still further during the 1990s with, first, all in 1992, three very different films with one subject in common, French Indochina, suggesting a gradual working through of French sensibilities relating to the loss of empire. These were *L'Amant* (Annaud), a soft-porn rendering of an autobiographical text by Marguerite Duras; *Indochine* (Wargnier), a star vehicle for Catherine Deneuve; and *Diên Biên Phu* (Schoendoerffer), a well-meaning quasi-documentary on the last days of French Indochina, like *Germinal* publicly supported by high-profile political figures (in this case Mitterrand himself). Another development during the early 1990s is what one could call the ironic heritage film, the best example of this being Patrice Leconte's *Ridicule* (1996). Such inflections of the genre worked alongside a continuation of standard, and indeed high-quality heritage, such as the seventh film version of Dumas's swashbuckler *Le Bossu* (1997), this time by a director more associated with 1960s and 1970s comedies, Philippe Le Broca.

It was the heritage genre that launched the careers of two major 1980s and 1990s stars, Daniel Auteuil and Emmanuelle Béart, who appeared together in *Jean de Florette* and *Manon des Sources*, and who became one of the industry's better-known film couples. Both appeared again in another major heritage film, Wargnier's follow-up to *Indochine*, *Une femme française* (1995), which like Claude Sautet's more intimist *Un coeur en hiver* (1991), is about the breakdown of a couple, fact and fiction mirroring each other as the off-screen pair split up. Auteuil went on to star in a number of heritage films: *La Reine Margot*, *Lucie Aubrac* (1997, a plodding resistance story by Berri), *Le Bossu* and, his second film for Leconte after the stylish black and white *La Fille sur le pont* (1999), *La Veuve de Saint-Pierre* (2000), where he acted opposite Juliette Binoche. One of the other major female stars of this period, who had started her career in the mid-1970s, Isabelle Adjani, confirmed her status as a star in the heritage biopic, produced by her, *Camille Claudel* (1988), well before her star performance as the eponymous heroine of *La Reine Margot*. The heritage genre also confirmed Gérard Depardieu's status as the most popular French star, both at home and abroad, despite his association with auteur cinema (Duras, Resnais, Truffaut) and comedy (Blier, Veber) in the late 1970s and early 1980s. Juliette Binoche, however, the star of *Le Hussard sur le toit*, emerged from the second new genre of the 1980s, the *cinéma du look*.

Whereas heritage films can be seen as a resurgence of an older 1950s cinema, the *cinéma du look* signals a new turn. Inaugurated by Jean-Jacques Beineix's *Diva* (1981), about a young man's idolisation of an opera singer, this genre is usually seen as grouping together Beineix, Luc Besson, and Léos Carax. Binoche acted in two of Carax's films, *Mauvais Sang* (1986) and *Les Amants du Pont-Neuf* (1991), about an *amour fou* between a down-and-out and an artist who is going blind. The films in this group have in common, according to most critics, a preoccupation with style at the expense of narrative. Their most enduring feature, however, is the focus on young people, especially in the films of Besson, and it is this, as well as their preoccupation with colour and décor, that signals the new turn. They demonstrate the resurgence of a romanticism for which the realism of a Tavernier or the cynicism of a Pialat had left no place, and it is no doubt partly for this reason that they were so successful. They were seen as representing the marginalised youth class of the 1980s: their three central films, both in terms of the (French) careers of their directors, and in terms of the decade – Beineix's *37°2 le matin* (1986, more familiarly known as *Betty Blue*, see Figure 1.5), Besson's *Le Grand Bleu* (1988) and Carax's *Mauvais Sang* (1986) – all have alienated central characters, who in one way or another reject society. Just as *Diva* marks the beginning of this new style, so too does *Les Amants du Pont-Neuf* (see Figure 1.6), set during the bicentennial celebrations of 1989, mark the end of an era, the consumerist 1980s dominated by a gradual shift in political terms from Socialist hopes at the beginning of the decade to the gradual loss of those hopes as Mitterrand's governments moved to the right. This sense of loss is reflected in the *cinéma du look*, which, despite its concerns with contemporary youth, frequently, like heritage cinema, alludes to films from earlier periods of French cinema, especially the golden age of the 1930s, as if taking refuge nostalgically in a vanished past (see Greene, 1999). That is less the case with Luc Besson, whose films nevertheless show a turn away from present-day France in his

Figure 1.5 Betty Blue

Figure 1.6   Les Amants du Pont Neuf

successful move to Hollywood in his 1990s films, *Léon* (1994) and *Le Cinquième Elément* (1997). Beineix and Carax, however, who stayed in France, each produced only one feature after the above-mentioned films, *Pola X* (Carax, 1999) and *Mortel Transfert* (Beineix, 2001), neither of which seemed particularly in tune with audiences.

A third major development during this period, after heritage cinema and the *cinéma du look*, is the increasing number of films made by women directors. Apart from Agnès Varda, who has already been mentioned, but whose documentary *Les Glaneurs et la glaneuse* (2000) is worth mentioning as one of the major films of the new century, the women directors who emerged from the 1970s to develop substantial careers in the 1980s and 1990s are Coline Serreau, Diane Kurys and Josiane Balasko. Serreau is the director of one of the 1980s most popular comedies, *Trois hommes et un couffin* (1985), remade in Hollywood two years later. *Romuald et Juliette* (1989) starred Daniel Auteuil as the framed company president who finds help and love in the arms of the company's black cleaning woman. *La Crise* (1992) starred Vincent Lindon as a man who loses his job and his wife on the same day, is befriended by a loser, and comes to realise that his troubles are self-inflicted. All three of these comedies have an exploration of masculinity at their core. The other major woman director to emerge from the 1970s was Diane Kurys, whose major film of the 1980s is the endearing autobiographical analysis of a female friendship in *Coup de foudre* (1983); her subsequent films did less well, although *La Baule-les-pins* (1990), which takes up the autobiographical story where *Coup de foudre* left off, was the most successful of these. A third woman director to emerge from the 1970s was Josiane Balasko. Unlike the other two, Balasko was an actress who formed part of the main *café-théâtre* group, Le Splendid. After playing in a number of comedies originating from Le Splendid routines, such as *Le Père Noël est une ordure* (1982), she directed several comedies in the mid-1980s, before her popular hit, *Gazon Maudit* (1995), a gay/lesbian comedy, whose outed nature could not be more different from the wistfully muted heritage of Kurys's *Coup de foudre* a decade earlier. Finally, a major woman director of the 1980s and more particularly of the 1990s is Claire Denis. Her autobiographical début, *Chocolat* (1988), is an exploration of a colonial childhood, and focuses on the fascination of the young girl for the body of her black servant. That fascination for the male body resurfaces in one of the most important films of the 1990s, her adaptation of Herman Melville's novella *Billy Budd*, set in the Foreign Legion, *Beau Travail* (1999).

France's greatest social and political problem during the 1980s and 1990s has been immigration, or rather, the difficulty in coping with the tensions between multiculturalism on the US model, and the more favoured French approach of assimilation of second- and third-generation immigrants, particularly those from the Maghrebi communities. Unsurprisingly, then, a number of films have attempted to fictionalise the issue, by both white and Maghrebi directors. During the 1980s, these films were seen as a distinct trend in French cinema. The best example of this in the 1980s is Mehdi Charef's *Le Thé au harem d'Archimède* (1985), like many of the *beur* films (*beur* being backslang for Arab, and signifying second- and third-generation immigrants). However, it was not until 1994 that Chibane's *Hexagone* could be called a film by a *beur* for *beurs* in the French press. Generally speaking, such films focus on the difficulties faced by young *beurs*, with racism and unemployment amongst the more obvious. A number of directors emerged during the 1990s working in this area, such as Karim Dridi, whose *Bye-Bye* (1995) starred Sami Bouajila, along with Sami Naceri one of the few Maghrebi actors to have been accepted in white French cinema, as in the feel-good gay road movie *Drôle de Félix* (Ducastel and Martineau, 2000).

Heritage films and the *cinéma du look* are arguably the most significant developments during the 1980s, extending in the case of the former well into the 1990s. What these two genres have in common is an evasion of the increasingly harsh French social reality of their time, whether through a return to the past or, as with *Les Amants du Pont-Neuf*, an aestheticisation of that harshness. That last remark might, *mutatis mutandis*, also be applied to Cyril Collard's *Les Nuits fauves* of 1992, about a promiscuously bisexual photographer, which won notoriety inside and outside France when its director/scriptwriter/star died of an AIDS-related illness four days before the film went on to win four César awards. *Les Nuits fauves*, with its ostentation, seems to have been very much a one-off. If ostentation survives, it has been in the inheritors of the *cinéma du look*, the most obvious of these being Jeunet and Caro, who as a pair directed *Delicatessen* (1991) and *La Cité des enfants perdus* (1995), before Jeunet went to Hollywood to direct *Alien: The Resurrection* (1997), paralleling Besson's move to Hollywood and sci-fi with *Le Cinquième element*. Films with a similar aesthetic have included the Besson-produced and scripted *Taxi* (Pirès, 1998), followed by the even more successful *Taxi 2* (Krawczyk, 2000), and the rather more distasteful *Dobermann* (Kounen, 1997), which is like a nightmarish version of Besson's *Nikita*, a resemblance encouraged by the fact that *Nikita*'s Uncle Bob, Tchéky Karyo, has a lead role in both films.

Parallel to these popular films, arguably the key development during the 1990s was the renewed interest in marginalised social groups, but with a distanciation from aetheticisation, and in some cases a distinctive return to the kind of realism associated with Pialat in the 1970s. The films and the directors, after some hesitation over terminology, are now usually referred to as *le jeune cinéma*. As is usually the case with catch-all terms, this description is not particularly enlightening as it encompasses directors who are not young (Robert Guédiguian, for example, whose films are always set in Marseille), as well as those who are. The more important issue, rather, is the focus on contemporary social problems, with a tendency to focus on the young, on women and on rural communities as much as on the city. This turn is not confined to a younger group of directors, of course. Tavernier, for example, has emerged as a significant director of socially aware films. Apart from his documentaries for French TV on the problem of the *banlieues* ('De l'autre côté du périph', 1998), he has made a number of films focusing on knotty social issues. In the same year as an extraordinary documentary on the Algerian War (*La Guerre sans nom*, 1992) – similar in many respects to Lanzmann's influential documentary on the Holocaust, *Shoah* (1985), using interviews rather than documentary footage – Tavernier directed *L627* (1992), a gritty drama about inner-city policing, and, after a number of rather different films, a film focusing on the difficulties of being a teacher in a depressed town of northern France (*Ça commence aujourd'hui*, 1999).

The shift to rural locations is an interesting feature of the new cinema, although as we shall see, this has to be set next to a continuing engagement, as Tavernier's two films might suggest, with the city. Nevertheless, several films focused, towards the end of the century, on small provincial towns or rural locations. Apart from *Ça commence aujourd'hui*, there are the films of Bruno Dumont, set in northern France: *La Vie de Jésus* (1997), which won the Golden Camera award at Cannes, is set near the Belgian border and focuses on the empty lives of out-of-work youngsters who ride their noisy mobylettes frantically round the countryside in a vain attempt to escape boredom; the controversial *L'Humanité* (1999), set in the same region, is about a detective investigating the rape and murder of a schoolgirl, sex, violence and despair mingling turbulently in what used to be synonymous with nostalgic escape from the city, the countryside.

The key film of this new turn, however, is Matthieu Kassovitz's *La Haine* (1995), about police brutality and the hopeless lives of young people culturally marooned on estates on the edge of Paris. Its black and white location filming, and the obvious influence of the American cinema (Martin Scorsese, Spike Lee), were an evident reaction against both heritage cinema and the *cinéma du look*, much as the New Wave had been against the *tradition de qualité*. *La Haine* quickly became recognised as the 'flagship' film of a genre within *le jeune cinéma*, the *cinéma de banlieue*, a genre represented also by such directors as Jean-François Richet (*État des lieux*, 1995) and Malik Chibane (*Douce France*, 1995). Film-makers' growing engagement with the problems of social exclusion and marginalisation in late 1990s France became particularly marked with the *mouvement des sans-papiers* of 1996–1997. The protests

Figure 1.7 L'Humanité

against the threatened deportation of some 300 Malian 'illegal immigrants' and against proposed legislation – in the event withdrawn – requiring French citizens to notify the police of non-EU citizens staying with them were largely led by figures from the cinema world, including Tavernier and Emmanuelle Béart. The importance of this event is that it was the first time that film-makers as a group had stood together over a political issue. If in practice the solidarity did not last long, as was almost bound to be the case with a single issue of this type, it can now be seen as part of a more general politicisation of the industry, not in terms of party-political politics, nor even in terms of single-issue pressure groups, but in the interest of a new generation of film-makers in social conditions. In the films themselves, this was frequently couched in the kind of realism associated with the Pialat of the 1970s, although it is important to realise that this does not characterise all of the films that have been linked to *le jeune cinéma*. If Veysset's *Y aura-t-il de la neige à Noël?* of 1996 does, in its documentary style and grainy camerawork, suggest Pialat's 1970s films, *La Haine*, by contrast, despite the fact that it is in black and white and focuses on young people in the *banlieues*, is a much more dramatic, if not melodramatic, film, whose American influences are very explicit, as for example when Vinz acts out Robert de Niro's 'are you looking at me' monologue as the character Travis Bickle in Scorsese's *Taxi Driver* (1976; see the sequence analysis in Chapter 4). Arguably it is *Y aura-t-il de la neige à Noël?* that can stand as the more emblematic of recent tendencies in the French cinema; it is the tale of a large, and largely single-parent, family on a Provençal farm, whose harshness is more powerful than that of *Jean de Florette* because it lacks the distanciation of the heritage genre. It won its young female director the Prix Jean Vigo for the best first feature of its year.

Also prominent in *le jeune cinéma*, which now appears as a foreshadowing of the fall of the Gaullist government the following year, were younger directors such as Laurence Ferreira Barbosa (*J'ai horreur de l'amour*, 1997) and Brigitte Roüan (*Post coitum, animal triste*, 1997). These names suggest the greater prominence than at any previous time of woman directors in the industry. Nicole Garcia, Marion Vernoux, Sandrine Veysset, Agnès Merlet and Anne Fontaine are other woman film-makers whose work has attracted widespread attention.

The focus over the last few paragraphs on social-issue films should be recognised as only one of a number of strands making up French cinema at the turn of the century. The heritage film is still a major feature of the industry; recent examples are the rather stodgy *Les Enfants du siècle* (Kurys, 1999), charting the turbulent relationship between the nineteenth-century novelist George Sand (Juliette Binoche) and her playwright lover, Alfred de Musset (Benôit Magimel, her real-life partner); and Binoche again, with Daniel Auteuil, in Leconte's later heritage film, *La Veuve de*

Saint-Pierre (2000), in which Binoche plays the wife of the garrison captain who befriends a murderer condemned to death, a friendship that causes the couple's ostracisation and the eventual execution of the captain, who is more committed to his wife than to his duty. There is a further group of films more readily recognisable over the years as 'typically French' intimist analyses of couple or, increasingly, family relationships. Claude Sautet's is an example of this kind of film-making. His career was revived in the 1990s in two films exploring close heterosexual relationships, and both starring Emmanuelle Béart: *Un coeur en hiver* (1992), which we have already mentioned, and *Nelly et Monsieur Arnaud* (1995). If the films of Téchiné also often focus on couple relationships (for example, *Alice et Martin*, 1999, with Juliette Binoche) even when they seem to focus on the family (the incestuous relationship between brother and sister in *Ma saison préférée*, 1993), there have been a number of films that deal with the extended family; examples are Klapisch's *Un air de famille* (1996), starring Bacri and Jaoui, and based on a play by the latter, and Chéreau's *Ceux qui m'aiment prendront le train* (1999), which explores what happens when the family of a dead man are forced to spend time together at his funeral.

We have covered several genres: the social conscience films, the heritage films, and what are called 'intimist' films. To finish, however, we shall briefly chronicle the success of the popular comedy. Increasingly during the 1990s this genre did less well in the cinema as its popularity increased on the small screen, *Les Visiteurs* (Poiré, 1993) and its 13 million spectators being something of an exception (see Figure 1.8). However, 2001 marked the first year since 1986 that French audiences went to see more French films than Hollywood films, following a spate of highly successful popular comedies. A Bacri-Jaoui collaboration, *Le Goût des autres* (2000), an almost perfect illustration of the way in which different classes mark themselves as different through taste, had 3.8 million spectators. *La Vérité si je mens 2* (Gilou, 2001), which had 7.8 million spectators, is the sequel to *La Vérité si je mens* (Gilou, 1997), both films focusing on a Jewish textile community in Paris, 'infiltrated' by a non-Jew in the first film, and focusing on the group of friends and their fight against a supermarket chain in the second. Another sequel, *Taxi 2* (Krawczyk, 2000), garnered a staggering 10.3 million spectators, and, finally, there were 9 million spectators for seasoned comedy director Francis Veber's *Le Dîner de cons* (1998), about a group of friends who meet regularly for dinner with the rule that each must take it in turn to invite an idiot (*con*) whom the others can make fun of. These films only prove the dictum that the most popular genre in French cinema is the comedy. In 2001, Jeunet's sentimental and nostalgic comedy about a naive girl who decides to take it upon herself to help those around her, *Le Fabuleux Destin d'Amélie Poulain* (aka *Amélie*) took France by storm, with some 6.5 million spectators

Figure 1.8   Les Visiteurs

by the summer of 2001, 6 million of those seeing it in its first seven weeks. Its success was rapidly repeated world-wide (see Figure 1.9).

The resurgence of the popular comedy raises interesting methodological questions. In this historical review, we have tended to adopt the canonical approach to French cinema, which privileges the director as 'auteur'. In the French context there are good reasons for doing this, not least because it is an approach established by the French themselves during the 1950s. Moreover, it is an approach favoured by many university courses, whether in France, the UK or the USA. Increasingly during the late 1980s and 1990s, however, Film Studies in general has been permeated by Cultural Studies, which favours the popular, whether the popular genres of comedy and police thriller, or stars. This approach is beginning to find favour in those parts of the academy that habitually teach French cinema, namely French or Modern Languages departments, but perhaps not so pronouncedly that we have felt it reasonable to jettison the canonical auteurist approach. Nevertheless, as even a cursory glance at the list of best-selling films in the appendices will show, 'French cinema' is just as much about popular films and stars as it is more 'difficult' 'art-house' films. (This point is made more problematic by the fact that what Anglo-American audiences often consider to be 'art-house' films, such as the heritage films of the 1980s and 1990s in France, are in France itself resolutely *popular* films.) Thus, for the bulk of French audiences, the box office is dominated by specific genres and stars rather than directors. Indeed, it is more the stars than the genres. The names that return time and again at the top of the box office, as can be seen from our list of best-sellers in the Appendices, are stars who on the whole are associated with specific genres: Gérard Philipe (period of dominance mid-1940s to mid-1950s) is associated with historical dramas; Jean Marais, known to Anglophone art-house audiences for his films with Cocteau in the 1940s, is better known in France for his historical epics in the 1960s. The popular genre par excellence, the comedy, has a number of major stars: Fernandel and Jacques Tati (1950s), Louis de Funès (1960s to 1970s), Pierre Richard (1960s to 1980s), Jean Rochefort and Jean-Pierre Marielle (1970s), Coluche (mid-1970s to mid-1980s), Josiane Balasko, and Christian Clavier and Thierry Lhermitte (1980s to 1990s). The second most popular genre in France, the police thriller or *polar*, similarly has a number of major stars, all male. Jean Gabin, after the films with Carné in the 1930s that typify the classic cinema of that period, and for which Anglophone audiences are likely to know him best, is in fact better known in France for his second career in the police thriller during the 1960s and early 1970s. There are also, in the same period, Alain Delon and Lino Ventura, the three stars famously appearing in one of the great popular thrillers of the 1960s, Verneuil's *Le Clan des Siciliens* (1969).

Figure 1.9   Amélie

There are also superstars who cross over the genres, such as Jean-Paul Belmondo, who after his early career in the New Wave, went on to become one of the longest-lasting French stars, associated mainly but not exclusively with the thriller, and dominating the box office from the early 1960s through to the late 1980s. Female stars have tended not to dominate the box office in quite the same way. Yet Catherine Deneuve is very much a superstar, her bust being until recently the image of the French state ('Marianne', the statuette in all French town halls); and Isabelle Adjani was one of the first stars to work in Hollywood, followed in the 1990s by Emmanuelle Béart and Sophie Marceau, and well before Depardieu. Nevertheless, it is perhaps most quintessentially for many, both French and Anglophone, Gérard Depardieu who is the French superstar *par excellence*, at home in art-house films, in broad comedy, in heritage films and in thrillers, and who has dominated the box office since the mid-1970s.

CONCLUSION

French cinema, through state encouragement, co-production and accommodation with television, is continuing to produce a varied and interesting body of work. The dichotomy that began with 'Lumière' and 'Méliès', between 'reality' and 'fantasy', is at once an unsustainable and an ever-present one. The *cinéma du look* fantasies are rooted in the realities of post-industrial France, much as the careful attention to period detail of the heritage film is a latter-day variant of poetic realism, a fantasy of history. *La Haine*'s central characters 'escape' to urban Paris for much of the film, but it is a fantasy that turns to nightmare when they are brutalised at the police station, and even the most traditionally beautiful province of all, *Y aura-t-il de la neige à Noël?* shows, can be no less brutalising in its way. In that interplay, if anywhere, the continuity, and thus the sense, of 'French national cinema' – and doubtless of any cinema at all – can be seen to reside.

Chapter Two

☐ THEORY

Why devote a chapter of this book to the specific ways in which film has been theorised in France? The importance of theory in writing about film has been long and widely recognised, as the number of books devoted to the topic will attest (among the best introductions are Tudor, 1974; Lapsley and Westlake, 1988). The reasons for this were at first largely polemical. Andrew Sarris – a critic who developed into a kind of theorist – wrote some 40 years ago: 'Since it has not been firmly established that the cinema is an art at all, it requires cultural audacity to establish a pantheon for film directors. Without such audacity, I see little point in being a film critic' (quoted in Wollen, 1969: 166).

The establishment of such a pantheon, or even rival pantheons – in which Sarris and, even more as we shall see, the writers associated with *Cahiers du cinéma* and *Positif* played crucial roles – was an important step along the road to getting the cinema accepted as a 'legitimate' art form on a par with literature. Nowadays, when Renoir and Hitchcock are almost as widely recognised and studied as Balzac or Faulkner, it is easy to forget that it was still possible for the prominent literary theoretician I.A. Richards to write of 'bad literature, bad art and the cinema' (Richards, 1948: 202–3). The selection of a pantheon required, in the broadest sense, some theoretical criteria. As Terry Eagleton says of literature, 'without some kind of theory, however unreflective and implicit, we would not know what a "literary work" was in the first place, or how we were to read it' (Eagleton, 1983: viii).

The expansion of Film Studies that began in the 1970s, and which has continued virtually unabated since, contributed significantly to the importance of film theory. This is largely because it coincided with a broader upsurge of interest in literary and cultural theories, often (and abusively) lumped together under the label of 'structuralism'. The cultural analyses of Roland Barthes, Michel Foucault's pioneering rewriting of the history of ideas, Louis Althusser's re-reading of Marx and Jacques Lacan's of Freud, and Jacques Derrida's linguistic philosophy, were immensely influential and the sources of much controversy, initially in English departments, but soon spreading to the rest of the humanities. What texts could and should be read, and how it was necessary or possible to read them, appeared as burningly important questions to which theory – as the above list of names makes clear, often coming from France – suggested a wide range of answers. The 'curricular revolution' to which this gave rise had the study of film as one of its most significant components. The importance of what was variously called the look or the gaze in cinema drew upon, as it contributed to, Lacanian and post-Lacanian readings of Freud, and contributions to gender studies, at the same time as mining a rich new seam of ways to read, for example, the western genre or the performances of Marilyn Monroe. The burgeoning of theory converged symbiotically with the growing importance of popular cultural studies, and film was a – perhaps *the* – key meeting place of the two.

The Frenchness of the key writers listed above is not entirely coincidental. The Paris of the years around 1968 was uniquely well placed to foster the radical intellectual tumult their names evoke. Intellectually and culturally dominant over the rest of the country to an extent unparallelled by any other European capital – the only city, indeed, that could lay any kind of meaningful claim to the title of intellectual capital of Europe – it was the epicentre of the 'May events' that had shaken French society to its foundations and suggested new approaches to Left-wing politics in which the cultural sphere assumed a crucial, possibly even a determinant, role. Even after the revolutionary political hopes had faded from view, the cultural and intellectual legacy of this period remained of vital importance.

This theoretical ferment took place in the country that had invented cinema, which has ever since held a place of particular importance as 'the seventh art' in its cultural affections. As we mentioned in our introduction, there is almost certainly no city anywhere in the world where it is possible to see a wider range of films than in Paris, a fact of which, as we have seen, the New Wave directors, largely but not solely through the *Cinémathèque*, took full advantage. Those directors began life as critics, and one major strand in French theorisation of film has been the writings of those who are themselves film-makers, from the beginnings of film theory in the silent period, through the Surrealists at the end of that period, to Bresson and Godard.

France's thriving film-making culture has earned her cinema its now unchallenged place on college and university French syllabuses; her theoretical volubility has ensured that there can be no literary or cultural studies course on which the contributions of French theory are not taken into account. The convergence of the two is what we shall be attempting to trace, in its historical and institutional specificity, in the pages that follow.

1900–1945: EARLY FILM THEORY

The first theorists of the cinema were mainly the directors themselves, and their critics, in the increasing number of publications devoted to the cinema, whether the daily press, fan magazines or the more serious journals. The latter had started appearing before the First World War and had spread rapidly in the early 1920s, making France, and more especially Paris, one of the world's centres of reflection on film. One of the earliest journals, *Le Film*, became the mouthpiece for one of the better-known theorists of the early period, Louis Delluc, originally a drama critic. Delluc was committed to cinema as a realist, popular medium. His view can be contrasted with that of Émile Vuillermoz, originally a music critic, whose avowed aim was to educate the public with a view to weaning it away from a view of cinema as a fairground attraction. It was Delluc who was the major impetus behind the establishment of film clubs, the *ciné-clubs*, which became a feature of French cinema from the early 1920s through to the 1950s, where they became an increasingly important feature as they were a place where enthusiasts could watch and debate films, and debate the various issues in film. It was Delluc, too, who began to talk of the director as a key force in the making of a film (his term was *cinéaste*), thus laying the ground for André Bazin's later *politique des auteurs*. It was Delluc again who addressed the spectator's relationship to the star, in work that foreshadows psychoanalytical film theory. Delluc, finally, coined the term *photogénie*, a much-debated concept in this period. The term was used to suggest the way in which reality was transformed by the camera through lighting, framing and so on – in other words, what made cinema special: 'The cinema was a *photogenic* or *revelatory* medium of absorption and defamiliarization, whether it focused on inanimate objects, faces, or landscapes' (Abel, 1988: 115; see also Aitken, 2001: 82–3 for a useful overview).

The other major theoretical term debated in the period was *cinégraphie*, introduced by Vuillermoz before the war, but adopted by a number of writers who wished to pursue the idea of film as a language, at its most basic a set of codes. Like so many other ideas circulating in the silent period, it resurfaced in the work of later theorists, in this case Alexandre Astruc in the 1940s and Christian Metz in the 1960s. These ideas were at the heart of the theoretical work of two Impressionist filmmakers and writers, Germaine Dulac and Jean Epstein, who, with others, struggled to define the detailed ways in which film could function as a language. Epstein's theoretical work, like Metz's later, crossed over into psychoanalytical concerns, with his view of cinema as self-revelation. This was a position shared by the Surrealists, who felt that films could represent dreams as well as work in ways analogous to dreams. Their particular interest was to undermine rationality. They therefore argued for films that subverted the real, whether the comedies of Chaplin and Keaton, or the early horror films, such as Murnau's *Nosferatu* (1922), or anti-narrative films, such as Buñuel's classic avant-garde film *Un chien andalou* (1929) or, finally, films that attempted to convey the dream-state, a position forcefully supported by the Surrealist poet Antonin Artaud, who, like many of his avant-garde contemporaries, wrote poetic screenplays as well as theoretical tracts and, indeed, in his case, acted in a number of films.

In the second half of the 1920s, the high/low polarity hardened in the furious debate between advocates of a mainstream cinema on the one hand and advocates of a 'pure cinema', as it was called, on the other, a cinema completely divorced from narrative concerns and constructed along different lines, such as rhythm. The pure cinema debate lasted only a few years, but it serves to demonstrate how deeply rooted the polarity between 'realism' and high-art cinema was, and has to some extent remained in French theorising. During the 1930s, after a considerable but brief flurry of theoretical work on the advent of sound, realism dominated theoretical discourse in Europe (see Aitken, 2001: 84–5). Whereas French theorists had dominated theoretical work in the 1920s, it was theorists of realism published in German such as Arnheim and Balázs who dominated the 1930s; André Bazin took up the issue of realism after the war. During the 1930s in France, however, writing on film was closely associated with film-making, as directors and critics took up polarised political positions, with many shades of grey, of course, between the supporters of Fascism and the supporters of Communism. What was clearly at issue in these troubled times was the way in which film could represent a 'reality' that was increasingly being moulded by political perceptions. Symptomatic of this period was the creation in 1936 of the Louis Delluc prize for the most promising film by a group of independent critics anxious that Delluc should not be appropriated by the Right.

The early period is characterised by a wide variety of theoretical concepts, tossed around, often contradictorily, by the same writers. It would be wrong to assume that theorising in this period can be characterised by the handful of writers we have selected (Delluc, Vuillermoz, Dulac and Epstein), since what is characteristic is rather the multi-faceted debate around the new medium. Many of these debates foreshadowed future theorising, and can broadly be summarised as the opposition between realism and fantasy, the slow establishment of the director as the key figure for a film, and the attempt to outline the specificity of film not so much through narrative types (what later became known as genre study), but rather through attempts to determine a film language. These broad areas of concern remained vital to theory in the following periods.

1945–1960: ANDRÉ BAZIN AND THE *POLITIQUE DES AUTEURS*

As was the case in the period 1900–1945, there was no clear distinction between critical and theoretical debate on cinema in the France of the immediate post-war years. Subsequent references to 'the *auteur* theory' are effectively anachronistic; it was not until the 1970s, with the upsurge of interest in what might be termed theory in general and theoretical Marxism and psychoanalysis in particular, that film theory came into its own as a separate discursive domain in France.

This situation came about largely because film was not recognised – some might say mercifully – as an autonomous object of study in the highly centralised and conservative French academic world of the 1940s, 1950s and 1960s. As had been the case in the 1920s, serious discussion and criticism of films took place in the pages of journals – *Cahiers du cinéma*, *Positif* and, before either of them, *L'Écran français* – fostered by the *ciné-club* movement so important in the period immediately after the Liberation. The *ciné-clubs*, equivalents of the film societies once common in British towns and cities, existed not only to screen films often not viewable elsewhere, but also to foster discussion and debate after the screenings. One of the most important was founded by Jean-Pierre Chartier and his friend André Bazin in 1942, just after all American films were banned in France, which along with heavy censorship drastically reduced the diet of the hapless French cinephile.

The democratic openness of the *ciné-club* format was an important influence on Bazin's critical work, arguably still the most important by a single author in the history of French writing about film, even if he himself never wrote a single book of 'theory', his work being formed from a succession of essays eventually collected in the mid-1950s under the title *Qu'est-ce que le cinéma?*. Bazin was, more than has perhaps been widely acknowledged, very much a product of the post-Liberation period. His interest in the western testifies to the renewed availability of and interest in American culture. His championing of a cinema that respected the spectator's freedom as opposed to what he saw as the coerciveness of montage – Renoir and Rossellini rather than the German Expressionists or Eisenstein – had much to do with the horrors of the Occupation and the restoration of democracy to France at the Liberation. These historical factors had likewise been crucial in the post-war rise of Existentialism, with its stress on the lonely inevitability of individual responsibility. Bazin's major intellectual influence was the Catholic existentialist Emmanuel Mounier, whose philosophy of 'personalism' stressed the unique importance of each individual. This can be detected in Bazin's respect for the cinematic spectator, at work in the *ciné-club* movement and in his critical/theoretical writings alike.

Apart from the emphasis on the spectator's freedom through cinematographic devices such as composition in depth, or 'deep focus', the distinctive contribution made by Bazin and the *Cahiers du cinéma* critics to discourse on cinema in France resided above all in their stress on film as language. Bazin signs off one of his best-known essays, 'Ontologie de l'image photographique', with the provocative observation: 'On the other hand, of course, cinema is also a language' (Bazin, 1974a: 16). This is provocative because the essay, building on the awe in which it had been held in the 1920s, has hitherto been arguing that photography and cinema give a qualitatively unique, perhaps even unmediated, access to being ('The photographic image is the object itself'; Bazin, 1974a: 14), which might be thought incompatible with the codes and structures of language. The tension between these two approaches – realist plenitude and signifying system – was, we shall see, to inform not only Bazin's work, but many key debates on film theory right through to the present day.

An important precursor of Bazin's in this respect was the article 'La caméra-stylo', by the critic and film-maker Alexandre Astruc, which appeared in *L'Écran français* in 1948. Astruc proclaims that 'the cinema is in the process of becoming a means of expression, like all other art-forms before, in particular painting and the novel' (Astruc, 1948: 209) – a modest enough claim nowadays, but an audacious one at the time, like his assertion that if Descartes had been alive in the post-war years he would have written the *Discours de la méthode* in/on film. Astruc's article combines references to Welles, Renoir, Eisenstein and Bresson – Hollywood at its best, the auteur cinema of the pre-war years, self-consciously theoretical Soviet experimentation with montage and a new rising star side by side, emphasising the scope and variety of cinematic writing and claiming that the novels of Faulkner or Malraux, like the essays of Sartre or Camus, can now find their equivalents in the cinema. To a contemporary readership weaned on the narrative complexities of Altman or the conceptual cinema of Godard this will doubtless appear obvious, but it needs to be set in the context of its time. This was a time at which cinema all too often sought artistic respectability not through developing the possibilities of the 'camera-pen', but through the laboured literary and theatrical adaptations against which Astruc and, after him, Bazin and the New Wave, were to react.

Astruc's essay was an early manifestation of the emphasis on the individual director, relayed a few years later by Bazin in his 1957 essay 'La politique des auteurs', and developed by the young critics of the film journal established in 1951 by Bazin, *Cahiers du cinéma*. These critics, soon to become directors in their own right (Godard and Truffaut being the most prominent), amongst other things detested the reliance on literary adaptations. In 1954, the young Truffaut wrote a famously vitriolic, if at times incomprehensible, essay ('D'une certaine tendance du cinema français'), lambasting what he called 'cinéma de papa', exemplified in his eyes by literary adaptations. This was not so much because he was against adaptations as such, but because so many of the films concerned were scripted by scriptwriters who were not the directors. This, in the view of the *Cahiers du cinéma* critics, minimised, indeed downgraded, the creativity of the director. The *politique des auteurs*, a polemical stance as the word *politique* (meaning 'political position') suggests, later became hardened into the 'auteur theory', as it is usually called, or even more briefly, 'auteurism'. At its origins, it was an attempt to make films respectable artistically, first, by privileging the impact of the director in their *mise-en-scène*, that is, the strictly cinematographic side of the film (camerawork, lighting, colour and so on) and, second, by emphasising the director's work as part of a specific worldview, with a set of 'themes', for example, much like the very traditional literary-critical approach to 'great novelists'.

The *politique des auteurs* was paradoxical. First, it came at a time when most intellectual work in France was geared against what is essentially a very Romantic theory of authorship: great literature/films produced by great men (the use of the word 'men', which excludes women, is intentional). In a sense, then, the *politique des auteurs* can be seen as completely out of phase with the theories of film that were about to be developed in the 1960s. Second, despite this apparently regressive stance, matched as it happens by a political conservatism criticised by the other major journal *Positif*, it underpinned what most historians agree is the advent of modern film in France, as its name, the New Wave, suggests. Finally, and most piquant for many, the *politique des auteurs* survived the 30-year-long shifting sands of what was to become 'film theory' in the period 1960–1990 to emerge as the dominant type of theory in the study of the French cinema in the new millennium, mercifully becoming more gender-conscious than it was in the 1950s.

1950–1970: SOCIOLOGY AND STRUCTURALISM

Bazin, who died in 1958, had nothing to do with the university sector, and his acolytes, the young critics, soon to become directors of the New Wave, did not emerge from film school (the IDHEC, *Institut des Hautes Etudes Cinématographiques*, had been established in 1945). Bazin, like theorists before him, was an enthusiast, if not a film-maker himself. Film theory in France took a new turn around 1960 as academics began to take an interest in the medium, heavily influenced in the early 1960s by structuralism.

Academics had become interested in film during the late 1940s. An *Institut de Filmologie* with a ponderous journal had been established under Etienne Souriau, whose *La Correspondance des arts* of 1947 argued for a comparison between different art forms, thus attempting to legitimise the cinema, as did the young writers of the *Cahiers du cinéma* a decade later with their *politique des auteurs*. A number of academics produced substantial books, such as Gilbert Cohen-Séat's *Essai sur les principes d'une philosophie du cinema* (1946). Amongst these writers was a sociologist, Edgar Morin, who published two important books. The first of these, very much influenced by Cohen-Séat and Sartre, was *Le cinéma ou l'homme imaginaire* (1956) a socio-anthropological analysis that likened spectatorship to the dream (an analogy already developed in the 1920s) and to magic (a new concept). For Morin, the spectator is infantilised by being passive. He suggests that the spectator absorbs the screen-world in what he calls 'projection-identification', identifying not just with screen characters but with the activity of spectatorship itself – what he calls 'anthropo-cosmomorphism' – foreshadowing positions developed by Baudry and Metz in the 1970s.

Morin's *Les Stars* was published in 1957, the year before Bazin's death. Of all the books produced by the Filmology group, it is the one that has remained the most influential, quickly translated (1960), with several re-editions, and, as is the case with so much French theory, foreshadowing and influencing the work of others, in this case the British academic Richard Dyer some 20 years later. Morin established a taxonomy of star types: the virgin, the *femme fatale*, the *gamine* (of which Brigitte Bardot is the best example), the action hero, the '*homme fatale* with his feminized features and fiery glance' (Morin, 1961: 15), and more particularly the eroticised 'good–bad girl' (e.g. Marilyn Monroe) and 'good–bad boy' (e.g. Humphrey Bogart). He analysed the way in which the star and the role interact, the function of paratextual material and events such as fanzines, gossip columns, festivals ('the mystic site of [the] identification of the imaginary and the real'; Morin, 1961: 62), the importance of the close-up for identification, and of make-up for idealisation and distance from the spectator. He pointed out the way in which stars combine the exceptional and the ordinary, so that they are at one and the same time close to the spectator and yet out of reach: 'star-goddesses humanize themselves and become new mediators between the fantastic world of dreams and man's daily life on earth' (Morin, 1961: 34). Foreshadowing developments in star studies that rely on an ethnographic approach (such as Stacey, 1994), Morin prints fan letters to analyse types of identification with the star and, unlike Stacey, takes into consideration gender differences in star identification; thus, the male spectator may imitate the male star, but 'does not wish to know him' (Morin, 1961: 103), unlike the female spectator's relationship with the female star. Finally, Morin explains the way in which stars are not just consumer objects themselves, but help to sell merchandise. Morin's work, like Dyer's in the 1980s, focuses principally on Hollywood stars. For work on specifically French stars, we have to wait until Dyer's colleague at Warwick University, Ginette Vincendeau, published a rigorous analysis of Jean Gabin (Vincendeau and Gauteur, 1993), followed by a collection of essays (Vincendeau, 2000) covering a variety of stars, including the early comic genius Max Linder, and a defining essay on Depardieu, whom Vincendeau famously characterises as the 'suffering macho'.

A key transitional figure before the structuralist turn is Jean Mitry, who was, with Georges Franju and Henri Langlois, a co-founder in 1938 of the Cinémathèque Française, as well the first university film professor in France, teaching at the IDHEC from 1945. He was a historian of film, as well as a theorist. His major theoretical work is a massive two-volume treatise on the cinema, *Esthétique et psychologie du cinéma* (1963; 1965), which, although influenced by Bazin, has none of his passion. It is a very 'academic' work, comparing and contrasting different theories, striving for the balanced academic view, examining problems in minute and often tedious detail, whether these problems have to do with structures (the subtitle of Volume 1), by which is meant the image and editing, or forms (Volume 2), which considers style. Mitry's main point is that film hides reality from the spectator by framing it (Bazin's view), while also transforming it through stylistic effects. These make film a kind of language, a second-degree language he suggests, since there are rules and there is meaning; but for Mitry the language was more akin to poetry than to the linguistics which Metz was at the same time applying to film. Mitry's influence, however, depends less on what he said than how he said it. Although at heart an historian of film, his methodical attempts to categorise and systematise very different film practices, so different from Bazin's impressionistic broad-brush strokes, are the precursor of Metz's structuralism (see Andrew, 1984, for more detail on Mitry's work).

Bazin's theoretical position, as mentioned above, is regressive in the sense that it relied on a nineteenth-century view of the artist as origin of the discourse. By the 1960s, intellectual work in the social sciences had moved away from this position, under the influence of linguistics. Modern linguistics was founded by Ferdinand de Saussure at the turn of the century; he called it 'semiology', the science of signs. For social scientists, not just language but all signifying systems, such as social organisation for the anthropologist Claude Lévi-Strauss or film for Metz, were seen as just that and no more than that: signifying systems. They were structures whose elements, like language itself, 'mean' something only in relation to the other elements, rather than in relation to some essential transcendental meaning. Unsurprisingly, given the history of film theory we have outlined, the main issue for Metz was to define in what sense film might be a 'language', the question that had haunted film theorists since the 1920s. Metz was uninterested in whether a given film might be 'good' or 'bad'; he wanted to understand how a given film worked. It is difficult to underestimate the shift that this represents; it is a shift away from the impressionistic judgements that had dominated theoretical discourses since the origins of film – outgrowths, one might argue, of intelligent reviewers – to an objective scientific analysis undertaken by academics versed in very specific academic disciplines. Mitry had moved some way in this direction, but his theorising had been little more than an evaluation of other people's theorising; he had not developed his own tools. Metz, on the other hand, adopted and adapted linguistic paradigms with considerable rigour. Like Bazin, he published his work in essay form during the 1960s, collecting it in two important volumes: *Essais sur la signification au cinéma* (1968) and *Langage et cinéma* (1971). When considering the issue of film as language, Metz demolished the standard view that the shot was like a word and the sequence like a sentence. The analogy between film and language operates at a different level: both are systems where small units combine to form larger signifying units. These are sentences in the case of language, and 'syntagmas', as Metz called them, in the case of film.

Over a period of time Metz formulated the 'Grande Syntagmatique', which is a typology of the ways in which a narrative can be organised in sequences or syntagmas. Metz defined eight of these, organising them into syntagmas where the shots were achronological and those where they were chronological, the single shot forming a separate instance. We have detailed these in Table 2.1, because we shall discuss the Grande Syntagmatique in some detail, as well as applying it to film sequences as a pedagogic exercise. The examples given in the table are for the most part those given by Metz himself in the final formulation of the Grande Syntagmatique in 'Problems of denotation in the fiction film', one of the chapters of *Essais sur la signification au cinéma*.

Like all methods, Metz's system has advantages as well as disadvantages. First, it is often difficult to define syntagmas with precision. In our experience, the parallel and alternating syntagmas are often confused, as are the bracket and the descriptive syntagmas. The difference between them lies in the chronological or achronological nature of the shots within the syntagma, and the conceptual nature of the achronological syntagma. The scene, the ordinary sequence and the episodic sequence are not always easy to distinguish in practice, because of the weight attached to ellipses when distinguishing between the scene and the ordinary sequence, and the interference of the conceptual for the episodic sequence (when the 'conceptual' is more usually associated with an achronological syntagma). Second, because the emphasis of the system is on the image, problems can be

Table 2.1   **Metz's Grande Syntagmatique**

Autonomous shot

A single-shot sequence (e.g. early silent films) or an inserted shot, of which there are at least four types.

1 Non-diegetic insert: objects exterior to the fictional world of the action, e.g. a metaphoric shot.
2 Displaced diegetic insert: events from the diegesis, but temporally/spatially out of context, e.g. the single shot of a pursuer inserted into a sequence showing a pursuit.
3 Subjective insert: memories, dreams, fears, premonitions.
4 Explanatory insert: closer shots of letters, headlines, etc.

Syntagmas with more than one shot in an achronological sequence

Parallel syntagma

Alternating two motifs without spatial/temporal relationship: 'scenes of the life of the rich interwoven with scenes of the life of the poor, images of tranquillity alternating with images of disturbance, shots of the city and of the country, of the sea and of wheat fields'.

Bracket syntagma

'A series of very brief scenes representing occurrences that the film gives as typical samples of a same order of reality, without in any way chronologically locating them in relation to each other.' The syntagma functions like a parenthesis (hence its title) which establishes a concept: 'The first erotic images of *Une femme mariée* (Jean-Luc Godard, 1964) sketch a global picture of "modern love" through variations and partial repetitions'; 'in *The Scarlet Empress* (Joseph von Sternberg, 1935), the sequence that constructs the terrifying yet fascinating image of Tzarist Russia that the future empress imagines as a little girl (prisoners tied to giant bell clappers, the executioner with his axe, and so on).'

Syntagmas with more than one shot in a chronological sequence

Descriptive syntagma

Objects or actions that occur at the same time and in the same space: 'a tree, followed by a shot of a stream running next to the

Table 2.1 **Metz's Grande Syntagmatique** – continued

> tree, followed by a view of a hill in the distance'; 'views of the sheep, the shepherd, the sheepdog'.

Alternating syntagma

> Two series of intercut actions where what happens within each series is consecutive, but the two series are taken to occur at the same time: 'shot of the pursuers, followed by a shot of the pursued, and back to a shot of the pursuers'.

Scene

> The event is continuous, and breaks do not disrupt the impression of continuity, e.g. a conversation.

Ordinary sequence

> The event is continuous, but there are temporal ellipses to excise unimportant details, and there is more likely to be a change of location than in the scene, e.g. a sequence dealing with an escape.

Episodic sequence

> Brief episodes whose meaning lies in their juxtaposition; they function as 'the symbolic summary of one stage in the fairly long evolution condensed by the total sequence'. Metz gives the example of the breakdown of Kane's relationship with his wife in the breakfast sequence, where swish pans separate different moments in a long period of time. Another example might be episodes suggesting a character's 'rise to fame'.

encountered when considering the soundtrack, which can overlap between syntagmas, for example, or which, when used diegetically, can turn what might look like an ordinary sequence into something more akin to a scene.

A deeper issue was for many that this kind of system scratches at the surface of any given film. Not only is it too mechanical, imposing a structure on a film which leaves everything to be said, but, more importantly perhaps, it establishes a radical separation between the objectively scientific spectator/analyst and what really matters in the act of watching a film, the way in which we are implicated affectively. However, it remains the only film-specific typology of narrative. Its major advantages are that it can help identify unusual features in a film and, despite its problems, indeed perhaps because of them, forces close attention to detail. It is for this reason that we have included examples of sequence analysis using the Grande Syntagmatique later in this book. The problems of detail in the Grande Syntagmatique were never resolved, because theorists, Metz among them, became less interested in what had dominated film theory since the 1920s, issues of film language, than in what the Grande Syntagmatique, with its pseudo-scientific approach, could not address: the position of the spectator, and the effect of the film on the spectator. The major question to be addressed in the following period was not so much the key question of the first major period of film theory from 1920–1970, 'Does film have a language?', as 'What does a film do to the spectator?', a subject already explored by Morin in the 1956 *Le Cinéma ou l'homme imaginaire*, but about to become the dominant film theory in France, and even more so in the Anglo-American arena. Before such questions began to be asked in detail, there was a theoretical diversion caused by the Marxist turn in the wake of the events of May 1968.

1968–1970: IDEOLOGY AND SUTURE

The major socio-political event of the late 1960s in France was that of May 1968, as discussed in Chapter 1. This had a major impact on the film industry; Godard, for example, withdrew from mainstream cinema to concentrate on radical political cinema as part of a collective; artists and intellectuals, including many film-makers, grouped together to force the reinstatement of Henri Langlois, the director of the *Cinémathèque*, who had been sacked. In film theory, there was also a Leftist turn which, arguably, had more impact on British film theorists than in the French arena. All forms of domination, whether capitalist at the economic level or hierarchically individualist in the case of auteurism, were questioned. *Cahiers du cinéma*, heavily influenced by the radical literary-critical group *Tel Quel*, radicalised itself, and for a few heady years, Marxism was the flavour of some film theory. Using the work of political and cultural theorists such as Brecht and Althusser, as well as the work of the psychoanalyst Jacques Lacan, two interesting theoretical notions were developed.

The first of these was an exploration of the way in which film subjects spectators, forcing them to accept certain ideological positions, which the Left-leaning intellectuals and artists of May 1968 wished to demolish. Echoing Bazin, theorists argued that precisely because of its closeness to reality, dominant cinema persuades spectators that they are free subjects, omniscient and all-powerful. Whereas, for Bazin, this was part of a utopian vision of the free subject, for the intellectuals of 1968 it represented a dystopian vision. For them the freedom created by the film apparatus was merely an illusion; spectators are alienated by the very structures that suggest their freedom to choose, caught up in a bourgeois (a term of abuse in this period) worldview. Film theorists, as indeed other writers and thinkers, were very much influenced by the work of the political theorist Louis Althusser, for whom we are all caught up in ideology, unable to see beyond or outside it. Film, like any other cultural production, therefore reproduces 'things not as they really are but as they appear when refracted through the ideology', as Jean-Luc Comolli and Jean Narboni, editors of the *Cahiers du cinéma* put it in a famous article in 1969 (Comolli and Narboni, 1990: 61). For them, 'film is ideology presenting itself to itself, talking to itself, learning about itself' (Comolli and Narboni, 1990: 61).

One of the ways in which this worked was through the much-criticised notion of suture, or stitching, a Lacanian term taken up by Jean-Pierre Oudart, who used it to explain how procedures such as shot-reverse-shot in, say, a conversation, serve to hide the fragmentary nature of film. As spectators, we are encouraged to be, first, the subject of one interlocutor's look, then the object, as the shot reverses, thus giving us a sense of illusory wholeness and, moreover, binding us, stitching us in, to the fictional world of the film, preventing us from standing back. To put it another way, the Marxist theorists wished, like Brecht, to encourage spectators to be distanced from the film, to avoid (self-)absorption, not to suspend their disbelief, but to maintain a vigilant sceptical eye, suspicious of anything resembling uncritical pleasure.

To be fair, some of the *Cahiers du cinéma* theorists tried to avoid dismissing all 'dominant' cinema as inevitably and irremediably tainted by the bourgeois brush. Jean-Louis Comolli and Jean Narboni, the *Cahiers* editors, suggested that some mainstream films show what they called 'symptoms' or 'cracks'. Such films were 'splitting under an internal tension', they argued, and 'while being completely integrated in the system and the ideology, end up by partially dismantling the system from within' (Comolli and Narboni, 1990: 63). They went on the following year to explain how John Ford's *Young Mister Lincoln* (1939) managed, despite its liberal (and therefore 'bourgeois') attitudes, to show cracks in the liberal façade (*Cahiers du cinéma*, 1970). The analysis generated considerable debate in the academic film journals of the time (see Wollen, 1972; Brewster, 1973; Henderson, 1973; 1973/74; Nicholls, 1975). The *Cahiers* critics could therefore have their cake and eat it: they could maintain a pantheon of great directors and great films, much as *Cahiers* had done in the early 1960s, while showing that there was at least something wrong with those films, but not too much. They were vehicles for ideology, like so many other films, but because of the 'cracks' patiently uncovered by *Cahiers du cinéma* critics, those films could be said to criticise ideology from within. Clearly, though, any theory that tried to turn the ideal spectator into a Marxist-oriented ideological analyst took no more account of spectator pleasure than had Metz's Grande Syntagmatique.

1970–1980: PSYCHOANALYSIS AND POST-STRUCTURALISM

The Marxist approach was short-lived, partly because it was too monolithic, but partly too because the attempt to account for spectatorial positioning and pleasure had been in the air since at least Morin's 1956 *Le Cinéma ou l'homme imaginaire*. Indeed, strictly psychoanalytical approaches did not suddenly appear in the early 1970s: as early as the 1940s, there had been an attempt to analyse Buñuel's *Un chien andalou* using Freudian psychoanalysis (see Mondragon, 1949). The psychoanalytic turn of 1970 is considerably less like the psychologist approaches of earlier decades, however, and much more related to structuralist linguistics, mainly because of Jacques Lacan's version of Freud. Lacan famously said that the unconscious is structured like a language, so it is easy to see how someone like Metz was able to slip, in just a few years, from using linguistics in the analysis of film to psychoanalysis.

Nevertheless, it was not Metz but Jean-Louis Baudry who acted as the transitional figure between the theories of ideology outlined in the previous section and psychoanalysis, as the title of one of his more influential articles suggests: 'Cinéma: effets idéologiques produits pas l'appareil de base' (1971). In this article, Baudry argues that the illusion of reality constituted by a film is fundamentally ideological. Using (as Laura Mulvey was to do in 1975 in the UK) Lacan's theory of the 'mirror-stage', he showed how a film constitutes the spectator as an imaginary unity that confirms the world as it is, rather than pushing the spectator to question it. In his 1975 article, 'Le dispositif: approches métapsychologiques de l'effet de réalité', Baudry, picking up where Morin had left off in 1956, argued that the cinema returns spectators to a regressive infantile state; they become 'absorbed into the image', and the film functions analogically as a dream (a theory debated in the 1920s). Baudry's 1975 article was published in a ground-breaking issue of the journal *Communications* on psychoanalysis and cinema. The journal was published by an interdisciplinary research group of the prestigious *Centre National de la Recherche Scientifique* with the cumbersome title of 'Centre d'Etudes Transdisciplinaires (Sociologie Anthroplogie Politique)'. This particular issue, edited by Metz, Raymond Bellour and Thierry Kuntzel, who all published articles in it, also included pieces by Roland Barthes, Félix Guattari and Julia Kristeva, amongst others. Metz in fact published two articles in the issue, both of which were collected in his major contribution to the field, *Le Signifiant imaginaire* (1977). One of these two articles pursues Baudry's discussion of the film as dream. Metz systematically explores the analogies between the two, pointing out that the *illusion* of reality is confined to the dream, and that in the case of a film, where we know we are watching a film, an *impression*, not an illusion of reality, is created (Metz, 1975b).

The other article, which gives its title to *Le Signifiant imaginaire*, is a remarkable analysis of film through psychoanalysis (Metz, 1975a; translated in Metz, 1982). Countering the problem of the objectifying view of the (linguistic) scientist which we discussed above, Metz questions his own investment in the analysis of film, saying that 'to be a theoretician of the cinema, one should ideally no longer love the cinema and yet still love it: have loved it a lot and only have detached oneself from it by taking it up again from the other end, taking it as the target for the very same scopic drive which had made one love it' (Metz, 1982: 15). He discusses various ways in which psychoanalysis could be used to analyse films: psychoanalysis of the director working back from the films as 'symptoms'; of the film script, by which he means the narrative (as had been the case with Mondragon's analysis of *Un chien andalou*; see Mondragon, 1949); of the 'textual system' by which he means not just the script but *mise-en-scène* and cinematography.

The more important parts of the article, however, concern issues of identification. Like Baudry, he likens the screen to the Lacanian mirror, the point in the child's development between six and eighteen months when s/he misrecognises what s/he sees in the mirror as a more complete ideal self, an issue also coincidentally discussed by Laura Mulvey in the same year, 1975, in the British film journal *Screen*. Metz points out the differences too, of course, in that what spectators see on screen is not an image of themselves. Nevertheless, the analogy of the mirror allows Metz, again following Baudry (who himself was picking up on comments by Morin in 1956) to claim that there are two types of identification for the film spectator. Identification with characters on screen is merely secondary identification. What the spectator identifies with in the mirror-screen, termed 'primary identification', is the act of viewing itself, the apparatus (camera and projector). The spectator both 'projects' on to the screen by identifying with the camera/projector, and 'introjects' (psychoanalytic terms used by Melanie Klein) what is coming from the screen on to the screen of the retina. Watching a film is therefore like a play of mirrors: 'the film is what I receive, and it is also what I release, since it does not pre-exist my entering the auditorium and I only need close my eyes to suppress it. Releasing it, I am the projector, receiving it, I am the screen; in both these figures together, I am the camera, which points and yet which records' (Metz, 1982: 51). The narcissism that this play of mirrors involves goes a long way towards accounting for the pleasure of omnipotence that spectators may feel when watching a film.

Metz also explores other kinds of pleasure, such as scopophilia (a psychoanalytic term meaning the pleasure gained from watching), suggesting that watching a film is akin to voyeurism. Again, this was an issue also explored by Laura Mulvey in 1975. Metz goes so far as to suggest that the thrill of watching a film may be related to the guilty pleasure of the primal scene, when a child watches the parents making love. Indeed, for Metz, the cinema is a particularly eroticised environment. Specific techniques such as framing, fades and so on, because they reveal and hide, excite desire and lead Metz, famously, to compare cinema with striptease:

> The way the cinema, with its wandering framings (wandering like the look, like the caress), finds the means to reveal space has something to do with a kind of permanent undressing, a generalised strip-tease, a less direct but more perfected strip-tease, since it also makes it possible to dress space again, to remove from view what it has previously shown, to take back as well as to retain. (Metz, 1982: 77)

We have separated three strong currents in the preceding sections – linguistics, Marxism and psychoanalysis – but it is important to realise that when it came to the analysis of films the three often worked together, in an environment also influenced by Jacques Derrida's post-structuralist 'deconstruction' or Barthes' analysis of literary codes. As Stam suggests, this combination led to sceptical readings of films, to 'calling attention to the repressions and contradictions [of films], the assumption that no text takes a position that it does not at the same time undermine, the idea that all texts are constitutively contradictory' (Stam, 1999: 183). The same issue of *Communications* that had the texts by Baudry and Metz to which we have referred, also included lengthy analyses of film sequences. Kuntzel had 53 pages of a shot-by-shot analysis of the opening sequence of *The Most Dangerous Game* (USA: Shoedsack and Pichel, 1932), using Freud, Lacan, Barthes, Derrida and Metz, amongst others, to explore issues of repetition (Kuntzel, 1975). Bellour explored *North by Northwest* (USA: Hitchcock, 1959), in an even longer Lacanian analysis (115 pages), with complex tables, diagrams and equations (Bellour, 1975).

The theories of the cinema we have outlined so far correspond broadly to the standard histories of film theory. We have of course omitted important theorists who were not French, such as Arnheim and Balázs pre-war, or Kracauer in the 1960s, as well as detailed consideration of the various Anglo–American psychoanalytically inspired debates during the period 1975–1985. It is at this point – the late 1970s – that there is considerable divergence between the French context and the Anglo–American context. Whereas psychoanalysis became, at least until the mid-1980s, the dominant form of film theory in the Anglo–American context, largely because it was taken up by feminist theorists, in the French context, psychoanalysis was absorbed into the combination of approaches referred to above, without in any way being privileged. One of the curiosities of the French arena is the almost total blindness to issues of gender that characterise theoretical debate in the period 1975–1985. But it is perhaps also because of this emphasis on gender in Anglo–American discourse that some of the more interesting developments in French-specific discourses have not been visible until very recently.

In our final sections of this chapter, then, we will outline more recent important French-specific developments. The choice of writers in what follows is inevitably partial and selective. We have not covered some who might be considered to be major theorists by many, such as Pascal Bonitzer and Jacques Aumont (both associated with the journal *Cahiers du cinéma*), whose work in the 1980s in particular examined the relationship between painting and film; their purpose was at least partly to bolster the notion of the auteur in the face of the *cinéma du look* and other 1980s trends, such as the superproductions (see Aumont, 1989; Bonitzer, 1985; see also Darke, 1993: 374–5 for a brief discussion of this point; Aumont's better-known work in the Anglophone arena is his work on the image, see Aumont, 1990, translated in 1997). The fortunes of those theorists we shall examine in more detail have been variable. Daney's work has not appeared in translation, and despite his prominence in the French arena, he is relatively unknown to Anglophone film writers. The issue of space in the cinema is a recent development, although Gardies does not figure high as a theorist in such debates, since the approach to space in the cinema has been, by and large, pragmatic rather than theoretical. Burch's work is frequently anthologised in English translation, as is Chion's. Deleuze in particular has assumed increasing importance for Anglo–American as well as French theorists and critics.

THE SPACE(S) OF CINEMA: DANEY, BURCH AND GARDIES

The three writers to be dealt with in this section have in common a preoccupation with the spatial dimension of cinema. Clearly this forms part of any serious approach to the medium, but for the major figures considered thus far it is largely subsumed under ontology: cinema's relationship to the 'real world' (Bazin), cinema as signifying practice (Metz) or, as we shall see below, cinema as movement in/through time (Deleuze). Burch and Gardies in different ways articulate something like a theory of cinematic space, in which considerable importance is given to off-screen space in particular. Daney's theoretical remit is far more modest; indeed, it may be questioned whether he should be called a theoretician at all, since his books are in fact anthologies of journalistic reviews and articles, and he never produced a text with the overarching general pretensions habitually associated with the term 'theory'. Yet there is little doubt that for 20 years and more, renewing an earlier type of discourse we saw with writers such as Delluc as well as with Bazin, he was the most influential writer on film in France, as is attested by the gathering together of so many of his writings in book form, from *La Rampe* (1983) to the posthumous *L'Exercice a été profitable, Monsieur* (1993). That he speaks, in the Preface to *La Rampe*, of cinema as 'the place of the off-screen, of montage, of stitching-together, of the "spectator's position", in a word the opposite of theatre' (Daney, 1983: 10) is sufficient to indicate a concern with filmic space quite as thorough-going as that of the other two, more overtly theoretical writers.

La Rampe brings together many of the key texts Daney wrote for *Cahiers du cinéma* between 1970 and 1982. This was a period, as we have seen, of major change and self-scrutiny for the journal, and one in which 'embryos of theory lie side by side with now stale polemics, wild evaluations sit next to a little droning pedagogy, and so on' (Daney, 1983: 11). Perhaps as interesting as the individual reviews and articles are the historical comments and contextualisations with which Daney prefaces each section. The post-1968 *Cahiers* was almost obsessively concerned with what he calls 'representation as violence' (Daney, 1983: 16), seeing any representational cinema, which of course meant the vast majority of what was actually produced, as complicit with the capitalist system of illusion they sought to overthrow. The fascination with Godard typical of this period, and persisting to this day, becomes comprehensible in the light of his work's unceasing interrogation of the processes and mechanisms of representation; Daney was to be a major interlocutor for much of Godard's later, more experimental, film and video work. Perhaps Daney's greatest importance for the history of film theory, or at any rate serious writing on film, will turn out to have been the fact that he ceased to be primarily a film critic. Where a previous generation of *Cahiers* critics had moved from writing on to writing in film, Daney's evolution took him successively into the world of the non-specialised press (he wrote editorials and pieces on tennis as well as film reviews for the centre-left daily *Libération*), and thence to the foundation of a new independent journal, *Trafic*. The collections *Le Salaire du zappeur* (1988) and *Devant la recrudescence des vols de sacs à main* (1991), the latter subtitled '*cinéma, télévision, information*', represent a uniquely sustained attempt at interrogating the difference between watching a film in the cinema and on television or video, the latter of which ensures that 'coming generations will discover the cinema *at the same time as they lose it*' (Daney, 1991: 11). The mourning of a certain cinematic space (evoked in the title of *Devant la recrudescence des vols de sacs à main*, with its allusion to the warnings against thieves posted in French cinemas) is indissociable from the discovery and production of its successor. Daney's avowal that 'there was more pleasure for me in writing about an old film, even a lousy one, which was shown on television and seen by a great many people than about a worthy new one shown in an empty cinema' (Daney, 1991: 107) marks the simultaneous death and rebirth of 'cinema' which, in a manner reminiscent of Bazin in its concern with the role of the spectator and of psychoanalysis in its preoccupation with the importance of desire, his later work articulates and anatomises.

Burch's *Praxis du cinéma* (English translation: *Theory of Film Practice*, published in 1973) was published in 1967 and reissued in 1986 with a severely self-critical Foreword by the author, in which he accuses himself of responsibility for the epidemic of formalism in Film Studies, notably in the USA, and of 'ignorance of the whole theoretical space which was being developed at the time' (Burch, 1986: 15). It may seem surprising to devote space to a text branded by its begetter as at once excessively formalist and theoretically undernourished; but space, precisely, is what Burch's book emphasises and foregrounds as few theoretical texts had done before. The text deals successively with the different ways in which cinema articulates space and time (a question to be covered in much more detail by Deleuze), with the deployment of off-screen space, in which Renoir's silent classic *Nana* (1926) is seen as a pioneering work, with the importance of dialectic interplay between on- and off-screen and with the use of sound, until then taken largely for granted. Burch's use of the term 'dialectic' often verges on the all-embracing and the work generally seems, as he himself suggests, to inhabit a curiously self-enclosed conceptual bubble. Yet it remains of great historical importance in opening up areas of discussion that writers such as Chion, in his interrogation of the significance of sound, and Gardies, in his elaboration of different types of space in cinema, were to develop.

Gardies' *L'Espace au cinéma* (1993) not only offers a comprehensive analysis and typology of the different kinds and uses of cinematic space, but views that space as an active participant in the production of meaning in cinema. Its approach is centripetal, beginning with an analysis of cinematic space in its broadest sense, and moving via diegetic space (the 'world' of the film) and narrative space (the story or stories it tells), to a consideration of the construction of space by and for the spectator. Cinematic space, for Gardies, includes the physical parameters of the cinematic institution, the spatial reality of 'going to the cinema' that, as Daney recognised, is in the process of being irrevocably undermined by other modes of viewing, but remains of fundamental importance in any historical, or even biographical, perspective. The spectator is defined as being enclosed in what Gardies terms a 'spectatorial bowl' (Gardies, 1993: 29) made up of two conjoined semicircles: on the one hand the eye of the spectator, on the other the space of the diegesis, which Gardies then goes on to analyse. Off-screen space is important here because of its kinetic interplay with on-screen, into and out of which it constantly flows.

The space of the diegesis is seen as, in the first instance, the product of a contract with the spectator. There is a renewed emphasis on the view, important in filmic analysis since Bazin, that cinematic space always exists for someone, while, in a bold appropriation of Saussure's theory of language as a signifying system issuing in individual *paroles* or speech-acts, 'space' is defined as the 'language' of which the individual 'places' of/in (a) film are *paroles*. It is not only the visual perception of the spectator that determines his/her construction of cinematic space, but what Gardies calls 'cognitive perception' (Gardies, 1993: 98), by which he means the spectator's broad cultural competence and his/her recollection or evocation of other spaces not currently shown on screen. A filmic shot or sequence derives its sense from its combination with other shots or sequences, so that it is appropriate that Gardies then goes on to consider narrative space, using an analysis of the opening of Hawks' *Rio Bravo* to demonstrate that 'each story, in its particularity, deploys a spatial order, more often than not an essential factor in its coherence' (Gardies, 1993: 108). The final section in a sense, and appropriately, brings us back full circle to the spectator's space first constructed at the beginning when Gardies speaks of the 'cleavage in the subject' (Gardies, 1993: 18) produced as the spectator pays for his/her ticket and takes his/her place in (the) cinema. The work's final paragraph evokes this circularity along with the role of cinematic space in constructing the spectator as well as vice versa:

> In this way, just as in order to see the film I had to take my place in the space of the auditorium, rigorously controlled by the cinematic institution, so I now realize that to be able to read a film I have to take my place within the ludic space of textual enunciation. It is on this condition that I can become a 'good' spectatorial subject. (Gardies, 1993: 209)

Gardies, writing after the advent of video, is able to provide a plethora of close sequential or shot-by-shot readings far less readily accessible to Burch, one reason over and above those cited by Burch himself why *Praxis du cinéma* now appears in many respects dated. Daney's itinerary, as we have seen, is in a sense that of the supplanting-cum-renewal of cinema by other uses of the moving image, the reconfiguration, it could be said, of filmic space already figured by that space's ceaseless redefinition of itself from shot to shot and film to film. Other prominent non-French theorists, most notably perhaps Stephen Heath and feminist writers such as Susan Hayward and Teresa de Lauretis, have contributed to this, as virtually since its inception has Godard's work on/in the moving image. Space takes its place along with movement and time as one of the key axes in cinematic theory.

THE MOVEMENT(S) OF CINEMA: DELEUZE

Deleuze published his two volumes on the cinema in 1983 and 1985. Recognised by many at the time as key interventions, their impact had only begun to be felt in the late 1990s in Anglophone Film Studies. Keith Reader pointed out in the mid-1980s that 'Deleuze gazes from a place very different to that learnt by most of us' (Reader,

1987: 99), which could act as the leitmotif for the reasons lying behind Deleuze's late impact.

The first reason is that the volumes appeared at about the same time as the major controversy in film theory was debated in the mid-1980s, between theorists working in the psychoanalytical and feminist tradition on the one hand, and their opponents led by David Bordwell representing what has come to be known as Historical Poetics. Deleuze's work has very little to do with either side of that debate. If at times he seems to reprise some of the positions taken by Bordwell in relation to film history and ways of thinking about the film image, he has nothing to say about what was then the dominant theoretical paradigm, psychoanalysis, still less with what that tradition moved towards in the 1990s, and which might be said to hold sway currently in Anglophone French cinema studies, namely the combination of Gender Studies and Cultural Studies. This silence where psychoanalysis is concerned is all the more surprising given that Deleuze is probably best known for his influential volume written with Félix Guattari, *L'Anti-Oedipe: Capitalisme et schizophrénie* (1972), which criticised the two theorists used most frequently in French film theory at that time, Saussure and Lacan.

A second reason is that not only did his work seem out of touch with current debates, but it relied heavily on nineteenth-century theorists who have never been used in Film Studies, the French philosopher Henri Bergson (1859–1941) and the American logician Charles Sanders Pierce (1839–1914).

A third reason is what might appear to be Deleuze's very unfashionable high-culture view of cinema. Put at its most simple, he believes that there are 'great directors':

> The great directors of the cinema may be compared . . . not merely with painters, architects and musicians, but also with thinkers. They think with movement-images and time-images instead of concepts. One cannot object by pointing to the vast proportion of rubbish in cinematographic production – it is no worse than anywhere else. (Deleuze, 1992: xiv)

He adopts the point of view of the cultured cinephile, and a view of cinema resembling that of film critics in the 1960s at the height of European auteurist cinema. For Deleuze there are great directors and the rest is rubbish. The great directors are Welles, Hitchcock and Fellini, amongst others, and the French directors he speaks at length about are typically iconoclasts: Bresson, Clair, Dulac, Duras, Garrel, Godard, Grémillon, Resnais and Robbe-Grillet. He mentions many more, of course, some frequently, such as L'Herbier, or Rohmer. However, Deleuze is not interested in these directors as directors. He is interested in the way in which they have worked in cinema so as to advance cinema as a form; and his approach to this form is not empirical and cognitivist like Bordwell's, it is philosophical. As the quotation above suggests, Deleuze sees in cinema a way of thinking, in this case a way of thinking about the nature of time and how to represent time.

Indeed, the most striking thing about Deleuze's volumes for a student of Film Studies is the combination of philosophising and the acute sense of film history and film form. The discussion of film is highly philosophical, involving very abstract ideas and a plethora of neologisms: dicisigns, mnemosigns, noosigns, onirisigns, opsigns, qualisigns, soundsigns, synsigns and many more, frequently confusing in their multiplicity. And yet, Deleuze's analyses of the films themselves, and the ways in which they develop ways of seeing unconstrained by commercial imperatives, can be deeply absorbing.

One reason why Deleuze's work has increasingly been making an impact is related to the development of film theory more generally. Since the important mid-1980s debate between the psychoanalytical theorists on the one hand, working in what Bordwell dismissively calls 'Grand Theory', and, on the other hand, Bordwell's own Historical Poetics, combining a more pedagogical approach based in Formalism and historical contextualisation, film theory has moved in two variant directions. One of these is Cultural Studies, which privileges popular films and has attracted the psychoanalytical theorists, partly because it lends itself well to Gender Studies; the other is the development of 'film philosophy', to which the adherents of Historical Poetics have been drawn, mainly because it allows new sorts of questions to be asked of films. If anything, then, Deleuze is closer to this latter strand of film theory. And yet, paradoxically, Bordwell thinks that Deleuze's work is derivative (Bordwell, 1997: 116–17), and his staunchest defender has been a theorist associated with the psychoanalytical paradigm, David Rodowick (see Rodowick, 1997).

Trying to situate Deleuze within the development of general film theory, however, makes less sense than situating him within a very French tradition of film theorists. Those he cites most are, in chronological order, Epstein, Mitry, Burch, Bonitzer and Daney, as well as citing copiously from articles in *Cahiers du cinéma*. Metz's linguistics-oriented work is dismissed in a few pages, as Deleuze, running counter to the long-running attempt by the French to determine in what ways film might be a language, states baldly that film is not a language, but rather a pre-linguistic 'matter', a variety of 'signs' (hence the list of neologisms above), articulated around two major types of image: the movement-image, and the time-image.

The simplest definition of these two basic image types is to conceive of the first as an unquestioning forward movement and the second as an introspective meditation shot through with ambiguity. In his conclusion, Deleuze characterises the difference thus: '[The film character] has gained an ability to see what he has lost in action or reaction: he SEES so that the viewer's problem becomes "What is there to see in the image?" (and not now "What are we going to see in the next image?")' (Deleuze, 1989: 272). Deleuze's meditations, complex and illuminating though they are, thus correspond very much to the standard way of conceiving of the history of narrative forms, that between classical Hollywood cinema, with its seamless narrative, and the European art cinema, with its ambiguity, as established, for example, by David Bordwell.

Deleuze divides the movement-image into three basic types. The first is the perception-image, which resembles what film theory understands by the point-of-view shot (for example, a shot of a room followed or preceded by a shot of a person looking, which we then assume to be the room as seen by the character). However, Deleuze is interested in challenging that particular notion, and shows how the perception-image can be both clearly subjective in the manner described above, and also, following Mitry, semi-subjective, sometimes adopting the point of view of the characters, sometimes floating free. Adapting some of the ideas of the Italian director and theorist Pier Paolo Pasolini, Deleuze uses this combination of subjective and semi-subjective camera to suggest that where there is insistence on the semi-subjective (such as in constant reframing, empty frames and so on), it leads to a cinema where the spectator becomes more aware of film as film, a more 'poetic' cinema.

The second type of movement-image is the affection-image, more commonly known as the close-up. Deleuze's discussion of the affection-image, however, is provocative, because for him a close-up turns any object into the equivalent of a face, it 'faceifies' it, to use his neologism, abstracting the object or the face from space and time, and acting as a complex concentration of affects, such as desire, fear or wonder.

Deleuze's third type of movement-image is the action-image, which describes a narrative structure. Here Deleuze distinguishes two basic types of structure. The first is what he calls, following Burch, the 'large form', a situation modified by an action, leading to a new situation, typical of American realist and epic cinema (Ford and Griffith). The other type is the 'small form', where an action leads to another action via an intermediary situation, more typical of comedy (e.g. Lubitsch), or of some types of detective film where, for example, a careless action creates a situation.

Deleuze situates the crisis of the action-image in the post-war period. This led to a different conception of time in the films of the period going from the Second World War through to the late 1960s. The change is anchored in the socio-political, as Deleuze makes clear in his conclusion, without being preoccupied with the way in which film might 'reflect' historical change. He talks of:

> The rise of situations to which one can no longer react, of environments with which there are now only chance relations, of empty or disconnected any-space-whatevers replacing qualified extended space. It is here that situations no longer extend into action or reaction in accordance with the requirements of the movement-image. These are pure optical and sound situations, in which the character does not know how to respond, abandoned spaces in which he ceases to experience and to act so that he enters into a flight, goes on a trip, comes and goes, vaguely indifferent to what happens to him, undecided as to what must be done. (Deleuze, 1989: 272)

There are two types of time-image, one in the past and the other in the present. It might be thought that Deleuze is referring to flashbacks or dream-images, but he points out that these types of image occur in the pre-war cinema dominated by the movement-image. He is trying to capture the quality of particular types of reflective images, images that enter into a new relationship with time. The most important notion in the second volume is that of the crystal-image. By this he means an image that is double, its doubling consisting in a perpetual shuttling to and fro between the real and the imaginary:

> What we see in the crystal is no longer the empirical progression of time as succession of presents, nor its indirect representation as interval or as whole; it is its direct presentation, its constitutive dividing in two into a present which is passing and a past which is preserved, the strict contemporaneity of the present with the past that it will be, of the past with the present that it has been. It is time itself which arises in the crystal, and which is constantly recommending its dividing in two without completing it, since the indiscernible exchange is always renewed and reproduced. The direct time-image or the transcendental form of time is what we see in the crystal. (Deleuze, 1989: 274)

What Deleuze means in practice is particularly the mirror; he cites, for example, the famous mirror scenes in two of Orson Welles' films, Susan's departure in *Citizen Kane* (1941), and the hall of mirrors in *The Lady from Shanghai* (1948). He also considers that images of ships are crystal-images, because they are open to the sky but closed to the sea in a kind of mirror image. Similarly, *mises-en-abyme* or self-reflexive moments in film (or indeed whole film narratives that 'reflect' on themselves, such as Godard's *Passion*, 1982) constitute the crystal-image. The crystal-image, then, is a privileged moment in film for Deleuze. When we come across such an image, which seems to confuse the real and the imaginary, 'the two become confused in a process that both deepens our understanding of objects or events and widens our access to circuits of remembered experience in a mutual interpenetration of memory and matter' (Rodowick, 1997: 92).

It may seem that Deleuze's work is little more than a taxonomy, a list of image types, and therefore more concerned with film form, in much the same vein as Metz before him. In that respect, he may not seem very different from other European theorists, whether German, Soviet or French, who were attracted to systems and descriptive structures. It is important to remember, however, that Deleuze's work is not a history of film form, it is a philosophical enquiry into the potential of the film image. Even if many readers may find his overall conception of that development difficult, because no writer on film has worked in this fashion since perhaps the great Soviet film-maker and theorist Sergei Eisenstein (frequently quoted by Deleuze), his volumes can still yield surprisingly acute analyses of individual directors' films. For students of French cinema there are, for example, his intriguing comments on the role of water in 1930s cinema (in Chapter 5 of the first volume), or the 'thinking cinema' of Resnais (in Chapter 8 of the second volume), or the description of Rohmer's films of the 1980s and 1990s: 'It is the female body which suffers fragmentations, undoubtedly as fetishes, but also as pieces of a vase or an iridescent piece of pottery that has come out of the sea: the *Contes* are an archaeological collection of our time' (Deleuze, 1989: 244).

Deleuze's work remains a philosophy of the cinema rather than film theory in the normal sense. In that respect, it is difficult to see how one could use Deleuze's work *systematically* to illuminate specific films without falling into the trap of simply repeating Deleuze's categories, effectively ending up illustrating Deleuze by the film under investigation. That said, current practice seems to suggest that some terms will survive in common usage in French Film Studies, much as 'intellectual montage' is one of the few terms coined by Sergei Eisenstein in the 1920s to survive his own complex musings on the cinema. The most obvious of these is Deleuze's attractive notion of the crystal-image, as explained above.

The interest of Deleuze for contemporary Film Studies is principally that, like all good philosophy, his challenges us to think film anew, as Rodowick points out: 'Deleuze challenges contemporary film theory to confront its blind spots and dead ends, as well as to question its resistances to other philosophical perspectives on image, meaning, and spectatorship' (Rodowick, 1997: xi).

THE SOUND(S) OF CINEMA: CHION

Michel Chion is primarily known in Film Studies for his ground-breaking work on the soundtrack, but he is also a composer of electronic music, a film-maker and a university teacher in Paris. He has published some 18 books since the mid-1970s, either on music, film-makers (one on Jacques Tati in 1987 and one on David Lynch in 1992) or various aspects of the film soundtrack. In this last group, there are five key works: the first three, on voice (1982), on sound (1985) and on dialogue (1988), were all published by the *Cahiers du cinéma*, and form a triptych; his volumes on 'audio-vision' (1990) and, more recently, on music (1995), have systematised and refined the work of the triptych.

Chion's general approach is broad-minded enthusiasm. He detests value-judgements in soundtrack analysis, a frequent statement being that of course a film could have been made in a completely different way with different music, but what we have is the film as it is, with all its faults and its attractions. Chion is, like Deleuze, full of enthusiasm for the great auteurs, such as Hitchcock, Welles, Bresson or Duras, but is equally filled with admiration for particularly interesting soundtracks in obscure as well as very popular commercial films. He is similarly full of enthusiasm for technological developments. Whereas many critics deplored the advent of the Dolby sound system during the 1980s, suggesting that it turned films into depthless spectacle, Chion sees the advantages of such a system, arguing, for example in *L'Audio-Vision* (1990), that having Dolby is like the difference between a concert grand piano and a drawing-room upright.

Although several theorists addressed the soundtrack prior to Chion (Arnheim and Balász, for example), they did not do so systematically. Chion remains, with Rick Altman in the USA, the most important theorist in this area, not least because much of the interest in the soundtrack in recent years has focused on music to the detriment of other aspects, whereas Chion is concerned to investigate all aspects of the soundtrack, and to rehabilitate the soundtrack within Film Studies.

L'Audio-Vision, unlike his previous works, which often read more like collections of essays, attempts to do precisely this. It begins provocatively by showing the many ways in which the soundtrack affects the image-track. Dialogue frames the visual images we see, and gives them meaning that, in themselves, they do not have. Music supports or undermines what we see on screen. Sound is associated with movement and therefore helps to indicate the passage of time; Chion gives the example of a sequence of images that could be read as actions occurring either sequentially or simultaneously; sound will tend to suggest sequentiality by its very nature.

The second major point made by the volume is again expressed provocatively, and was first elaborated in *Le Son au cinéma* (Chapter 5): the 'soundtrack does not exist'. Chion means that the soundtrack is not organised autonomously like the image-track, it is, rather, 'disorganised' around it. He uses the musical analogy of counterpoint, which holds that notes (or in this case sounds) evolve horizontally in relation to each other, but can be seen vertically as harmony. Chion's point is that the soundtrack in film generally is less obviously horizontal counterpoint, and more vertical counterpoint in relation to the image-track; it is the latter which, despite the claims made in the first part of the volume, predominates. Put another way, he is suggesting that sounds are better understood as part of a complex including the image-track, rather than as something separate in which they are seen only in relation to other sounds. He then lists the various ways in which the soundtrack interacts with the image-track: it links images together (with sound-bridges, the creation of atmosphere, the use of non-diegetic film music); it punctuates in the grammatical sense (as might do commas and full stops); it creates anticipation (especially in the case of music); and, finally, silence, an extreme case of the soundtrack, separates. Amongst the many terms forged by Chion, and now generally accepted, is a particularly clear combination of the soundtrack and the image-track, such as the sound and image of someone hitting someone else. As Chion points out, in reality blows rarely make the noise we hear in films; that noise combined with the image constitutes what Chion calls the 'point of synchresis' (formed on 'synthesis' and 'synchronic').

The next major section of the volume, and perhaps its most powerful, are the chapters devoted to the 'audio-visual scene' (Chapters 4 to 6). Chion's major point here is that unlike images, which are either 'there' or 'not there' and thus constitute an observable space, sounds by their nature escape localisation; in other words, images rely on the frame of the screen but sounds do not. Counterbalancing his provocative comments in the first section of the volume, then, Chion shows how the soundtrack is spatialised by the image-track; if a character is walking off-screen, spectators will visualise the sound of the footsteps off-screen. A key notion raised by this example is the off-screen voice.

One of Chion's more original, indeed eccentric, notions is that of the *acousmêtre*, usually translated as 'acousmatic being', by which is meant an invisible source of speech, such as the wizard in the *Wizard of Oz* (Fleming, 1939) or the Peter Lorre character in *M* (Lang, 1930). The idea has much to do with a voice-over, of course, but Chion's discussion of it brings out the notion of patriarchal power (since the acousmatic being tends to be male), while at the same time highlighting the undermining of that power (since the acousmatic being is often revealed as considerably less powerful than he was when we first heard his voice).

Chion has tried to systematise the 'audio-visual scene', formulating, for example, the 'tri-circle' with its three overlapping areas of sound, in-screen sound (the source is on-screen), off-screen sound (the source is off-screen, 'acousmatic', either permanently or temporarily) and off-sound (where the sound or the music have nothing to do with the situation which can be seen on the screen, like a voice-over or accompanying music). Chion was much criticised for the over-simplification of the tri-circle when he first introduced it in 1982, and in *L'Audio-Vision*, while accepting that the analysis needed to be extended to include other cases, such as ambient sound (birds singing), internal sound (a character's heartbeat being an example of internal-objective sound, and his memories internal-subjective sounds), and on-the-air sound (the sounds emanating from a radio), he remains unrepentant, suggesting that the distinctions made in the tri-circle facilitate analysis.

Indeed, so unrepentant is he that he returns to the power of the soundtrack and the concerns of the first section of the volume, which the tri-circle can in a sense be seen to diminish by its emphasis on the image as the key determinant of the status of a sound. Off-screen sound affects our perception of the image; for example, a landscape can be extended off-screen with the sound of a car crash or the sound of the sea, and two very different landscapes will appear to the spectator.

Nevertheless, sound and image are intricately intertwined, as Chion's next discussion shows. In this discussion he demonstrates how he is at his best when he takes what might have seemed a simple idea, and shows that it is far from simple, such as his discussion of the *point d'écoute* (point of hearing), which he contrasts with the *point de vue* (point of view). As a result of his discussion, we become more attuned to the ways in which sound and dialogue relate to the visual image, such as, for example, the way in which many films do not try to represent sound in a realist fashion (a conversation in a car that we see from a distance).

Despite the emphasis on the soundtrack as a whole, it is hardly surprising that Chion, as a musician himself, should have devoted considerable attention to music in the cinema. Half of *Sound in the Cinema* is devoted to music, the key issues being where the music is located and what it does in relation to the image. Chion contrasts what he calls *musique de fosse* (pit music, or accompanying music with no screen representation) with *musique d'écran* (screen music, in the sense that the source of the music can be seen on-screen); his distinction is one frequently made, although the terms used in Anglophone Film Studies are non-diegetic and diegetic respectively. However, two other terms coined by Chion are regularly used: music is either 'empathetic', working to support the feelings of the characters and to make spectators identify themselves with those characters, or 'anempathetic', working against them by creating a sense of nature's indifference to the characters. In extreme cases, that music can be 'contrapuntal didactic', forcing the spectator to adopt a very distanced, indeed a critical position in relation to the characters (as with, for example, a happy tune that accompanies a tragic event).

More recently, Chion has published a major volume devoted entirely to music (Chion, 1995). The volume reprises some of the theoretical concerns discussed in previous volumes relating to the functions of the soundtrack more generally, such as unification (plugging gaps), anticipation, giving meaning and temporality to the image, extension of off-screen space or specifically of music, such as symbolisation, and the contrast between empathetic and anempathetic music. The first part of the volume, however, is a history of music in film. While some of this material is famil-iar from the work of Anglophone theorists such as Claudia Gorbman (whose work Chion admires and frequently quotes), the interest of the opening historical section is Chion's tracing of different types of music (classical, jazz, rock, pop, opera films, modern scoring for silent films, and so on) and, more obviously for our purposes, his occasional attention to French cinema, such as the comment on what might be a 'typically French' musical score contrasted with other national cinemas:

> French cinema is less keen on sweeping strings. It has its own musical
> traditions, for example a solo instrument, such as the saxophone, emerging
> from the orchestra; played in a way quite different from jazz, it has long
> been a speciality of our screens. Another tradition is French cinema's taste
> for a relatively clever and abstract musical form, which avoids imparting
> too obvious an emotional tonality. (Chion, 1995: 131)

Chion also discusses the eclectic use of music in the New Wave, with a close analy-sis of the opening sequence of Godard's *A bout de souffle* (Chion, 1995: 143–4), and is particularly enthusiastic (unlike many reviewers of the time) about Kieslowski's use of music (and Dolby stereo) in *Trois couleurs: Bleu* (Chion, 1995: 268–70) in a long section that deals with music as a subject of films or as a metaphor in films (particularly interesting here is his discussion of the song within a film, as a principle of circulation; see Chion, 1995: 280–3). A third of the volume is an encyclopaedia of directors and composers, emphasising their use of music. Relevant here are Chion's sketches of a number of French directors: Blier, Corneau, Demy, Deville, Duras, Epstein, Godard, Lelouch, Ophuls, Renoir,

Resnais, Rohmer, Sautet, Tati and Truffaut. Only three composers are dealt with: the American Bernard Herrmann (Welles' and Hitchcock's composer), and two French composers. Surprisingly, Chion does not include Michel Legrand. The first of his two French composers is Maurice Jaubert (1900–40; see Chion, 1995: 342–4), the composer of Vigo's *L'Atalante*, a film on which Chion concentrates, while explaining the importance of Jaubert as a supporter of popular and realist music. The second French composer is Georges Delerue (1925–90; see Chion, 1995: 313–16), who is best known for his New Wave scores, such as *Tirez sur le pianiste* (Truffaut, 1960) and *Le Mépris* (Godard, 1963). In fact, Delerue was prolific, composing for directors as diverse as Ken Russell and Oliver Stone; he was prolific too in his use of musical styles, preferring to avoid imposing his own style. Chion characterises Delerue's music thus: 'Unlike the lavish orchestration of the American cinema, he does not pile on the colours; he prefers to use a solo instrument to give the main atmosphere, the climate, the place (accordion, banjo, flute, clarinet) over a "carpet of strings". Because of this restraint he has been seen by some American critics as typically French' (Chion, 1995: 314).

Chion's legacy is considerable. First, in his extensive discussions of the soundtrack, he has formulated expressions that are now commonly used. For example, apart from the terms empathetic and anempathetic, there is the term 'vococentric', by which Chion means that soundscapes are organised hierarchically around the human voice. Second, he has brought rigour to the analysis of the soundtrack; why say a 'sound' when you could say a crackling, a rumbling, a tremolo, he says in *L'Audio-Vision* (Chion, 1990: 158). Third, his case analyses are always fascinating, and often lead to brilliant observations, such as his comments on the use of the telephone for suspense. This is not only because the telephone separates the voice from the body, he says, but more because the telephone 'has the effect of "suspending" a character we see from the voice of someone we don't see' (Chion 1999: 63). Another example is his fascinating discussion of the structural importance of the scream in a film, which acts as the dead centre around which much else revolves, the unsayable around which what is said is gathered: 'The screaming point is a point of the unthinkable inside the thought, of the indeterminate inside the spoken, of unrepresentability inside representation' (Chion, 1999: 77). Finally, he has always insisted that France is the most inventive country when it comes to the soundtrack (see Chion, 1994: 201; Chion, 1999: 85), while also deploring the poor use of available technology by the French.

Chapter Three

PRACTICE

In this chapter, we will outline the types of academic work which have been produced on the French cinema, with a particular emphasis on work in the 1990s and beyond.

In the 1990s, French cinema, in academic and film distribution circles, joined the ranks of 'everything-that-isn't-Hollywood', nesting in the catch-all category of 'World Cinema'. At the same time, the late 1990s saw an explosion, not just in French cinema itself, with the advent of a new generation of young film-makers, as we outlined above in Chapter 1, but also in major books on French cinema in the UK and the USA, special issues of major journals (*Screen* and *Nottingham French Studies*, both in 1993; *French Cultural Studies* in 1996; *Australian Journal of French Studies* in 1999), and in the establishment of a new journal and association devoted entirely to French cinema in 2001, *Studies in French Cinema*.

Partly as a result of the gradual increase in numbers of courses on French cinema in universities, there was an accompanying increase in particular in general histories, auteur studies, compendia and single-film studies. The first two in particular have dominated academic work on the French cinema from the 1960s. Where histories are concerned, there was Williams in English (1992) and, occasioned by the centenary of the cinema, two very large volumes in French (Billard, 1995; Frodon, 1995). Following on from Susan Hayward's rather different conceptualisation of the history of the French cinema in the opening volume of the Macmillan national cinema series she edits (Hayward, 1993), there were significant volumes in English focusing on specific periods. The interest of these volumes is that instead of mapping out a general history where individual films are lucky to get more than a few lines of text devoted to them (what one could characterise as the thumbnail approach), these works have critical agendas and develop new ways of thinking about periods of French cinema. In silent cinema there was the ground-breaking work of Richard Abel (1984; 1994), who has almost single-handedly put the earliest periods on the critical map. For classic French cinema, there were two major volumes in the mid- to late 1990s (Andrew, 1995; Crisp, 1993). For the New Wave, there was Jeff Kline's absorbing work on intertextuality (Kline, 1992). In the post-New Wave period, there were histories that do not try to be all-encompassing, but select specific genres, directors or approaches. Forbes (1992) has chapters on less well-known directors, such as Allio and Garrel, for example; Austin (1996) has a substantial chapter on the *cinéma du look*, an important but under-researched area of 1980s production; and Powrie (1997) focuses on the 1980s through the lens of Gender Studies.

The last 20 years or so of the twentieth century saw the publication in English, but more especially in French, of numerous auteur studies on the directors of the New Wave: Chabrol (Magny, 1987; Blanchet, 1989), Godard (Desbarats, 1989; Douin, 1989; Aumont, 1999; Bergala, 1999), Resnais (Prédal, 1996; Leperchey, 2000), Rivette (Deschamps, 2001; Frappat, 2001), Rohmer (Magny, 1986; Bonitzer, 1991; Tortajada, 1999; Serceau, 2000) and Truffaut (Gillain, 1991; Le Berre, 1993; Rabourdin, 1995). Anglophone studies on these directors, with the exception of Godard (Dixon, 1997; Silverman and Farocki, 1998; Sterritt, 1999; Temple and Williams, 2000), were rarer and earlier in that period (Monaco, 1978, on Resnais; Crisp, 1988, on Rohmer). This was the case too with other major French directors. There were major Anglophone studies on Abel Gance in the 1980s (King, 1984) and on Jean Renoir (Sesonske, 1980; Faulkner, 1986; Braudy, 1989), but later work on Renoir was French (Serceau, 1985; Haffner, 1988; Bessy, 1989; Bertin, 1994; Viry-Babel, 1994), with the exception of O'Shaughnessy (2000), as is the case with that other major director of the 1930s, Marcel Carné (Pérez, 1994), or on one of the major directors of the 1980s, Maurice Pialat (Magny, 1995). The Paris Bibliothèque du Film's commitment to public access led to a recent series, 'Ciné-regards', each volume serving as handbook with biography, filmography, bibliography and extensive documentation such as contemporary reviews. Although encompassing directors from a variety of national cinemas, there have so far been more volumes on French directors (Buñuel, Becker, Duvivier, Mocky).

Anglophone auteur studies took off again with the vibrant Manchester University Press 'French Director' series, the first volume of which was published in 1998. Not least amongst its merits is the coverage of directors who are not from the French classical period or the New Wave. At the time of writing there have been volumes on Besson (Hayward, 1998), Beineix (Powrie, 2001b), Blier (Harris, 2001), Bresson (Reader, 2000), Chabrol (Austin, 1999), Kurys (Tarr, 1999), Méliès (Ezra, 2000b), Renoir (O'Shaughnessy, 2000), Serreau (Rollet, 1998), Truffaut (Holmes and Ingram, 1998) and Varda (Smith, 1998), with volumes on Beineix, Blier, Carax, Cocteau, Duras, Godard, Leconte, Resnais, Tavernier, Téchiné and Vigo to appear in the next couple of years. An additional interest of this series is that in general the conceptual approach taken is a combination of what one might call the old-style auteurist approach, but placed in crisis, with the conceptual paradigms that developed during the 1970s in mainstream film theory, most importantly feminist film theory. Quite apart from the statement made by publishing three of the first six volumes on women film directors, the approach taken by authors on men directors such as Besson and Chabrol has been heavily influenced by feminist paradigms.

Single-film studies (whether chapters in books or monographs) began in earnest in the late 1980s in both France and the UK. They increased in the 1990s, complementing the general history approach with careful and sustained analysis of individual films. There were significant anthologies of essays on individual films, beginning with the influential *French Film: Texts and Contexts* (Hayward and Vincendeau, 1990, reprinted in 2000), covering films over the whole of the twentieth century, followed by two on 1990s films (Powrie, 1999; Mazdon, 2001). There were also short monographs devoted to individual films, some more research-led than others. For example, the British Film Institute's 'Classics' series – a 360-strong list of which 50 have so far been published – has (so far) seven French titles, more than any other European national cinema. Meanwhile, in France, there was a similar development of single-film studies for the university market, with some 12 out of 30 handbooks published by Nathan in its 'Synopsis' series on French films, the directors represented being mostly classic French cinema or New Wave (Carné, Demy, Godard, Ophuls, Pialat, Renoir, Resnais, Truffaut).

Histories, auteur studies, and single-film studies will no doubt continue, although the shift to 'World Cinema' meant that French cinema studies often rubs shoulders, often productively, with more general European cinema studies, as for example in Forbes and Street (2000). There were new developments, however, towards the millennium; these are the historical study of the silent period, audience study, star studies, the focus on historical crisis and trauma, and, finally, cultural identity with a strong emphasis on the Franco-American debate (remakes).

The emphasis on early cinema history and the related focus of audience reception took time to establish itself in French cinema studies. This is because the dominant paradigm in Anglophone French cinema was the Gender Studies focus emanating from psychoanalytically inspired and feminist-inspired spectatorship theory (a key volume exemplifying this trend is Sandy Flitterman-Lewis's 1990 study of the films of three women directors). More general Film Studies scholarship, however, moved significantly away from this paradigm towards the early history of (Hollywood) film and the analysis of specific audiences. This occurred as a result of the perceived impasses of spectatorship theory and the development during the 1980s of the empiricist and formalist Historical Poetics of the anti-'Grand Theory'

Wisconsin School (Bordwell, Carroll, Staiger and Thompson). Fifteen years on from the great debates between theorists and empiricists in the pages of *Screen*, there was evidence of a shift in this direction by scholars in French cinema studies, such as Darren Waldron and his work on *Gazon Maudit* (2001). As yet, though, there is no substantial work in this area, nor even a transitional study comparable to Jackie Stacey's Hollywood-based *Star-gazing* (1994). On the other hand, work on the early cinema was increasingly done, with the Association Française de Recherche sur l'Histoire du Cinéma and its periodical, *1895*, being a leading force. Two names in Anglophone French cinema studies stand out in this respect. Richard Abel, as mentioned above, and Elizabeth Ezra (see her work on Méliès: Ezra, 2000b; and the chapter on Josephine Baker's French films in Ezra, 2000a) have made sustained interventions in this area, which attracted an increasing number of younger scholars – for example, Alice McMahan on the first French woman director, Alice Guy (McMahan, 2000), or Paul Sutton, who investigated Feuillade's *Les Vampires* in relation to Assayas's 'remake' *Irma Vep*, and reconsidered early cinema spectatorship and its relation to trauma (2001).

Star studies is very much associated with the work of Richard Dyer of Warwick University, as mentioned in Chapter 2. His colleague Ginette Vincendeau, amongst other things, worked systematically on French stars during the 1990s, her work in this area culminating in *Stars and Stardom in French Cinema* (2000). This builds on her major work on Jean Gabin published in France in 1993. The two volumes taken together are a formidable intervention in a vigorous area of enquiry in scholarship in several national cinemas. The volume begins with a remarkable analysis of the French star system. Vincendeau points out the closeness of screen and stage in the history of stardom in France, one amongst several differences with the Hollywood star system outlined in the volume, another being its artisanal nature, due to the absence of vertically organised studios. The introduction also anchors the star system within other key promotional vehicles, such as the various fanzines and the relationship with television, and shows how, unsurprisingly, there is a gulf between what one could call the quantity and quality issues: the biggest stars historically are less well known than those who have been consecrated in academic and cinephile work. The most fascinating part of the Introduction, and the strength of the volume as a whole, deals with issues of stereotype and identity; more specifically, how particular stars 'embody' the French nation. Particular attention is paid to the appearance of the stars: Bardot's combination of *gamine* (the fringe) and mature womanliness (the beehive), Belmondo's drooping cigarette and the air of 'superior indifference' (Vincendeau, 2000: 166) it creates, fetishising shots of Delon that construct a 'cruel beauty' at the service of lifestyle advertising (Vincendeau, 2000: 176), showing the shift away from subject-oriented identification (with Gabin, say) to 'spectatorial desire for a commodity: a face, a body, locations, consumer goods' (Vincendeau, 2000: 184). There are many more insights, such as Vincendeau's analysis of Deneuve's image as 'the simultaneous representation of extreme beauty and its defilement, from reverence to rape rolled into one image' (Vincendeau, 2000: 203), or Binoche whose 'sexy melancholy' 'combines the sexual appeal of French female icons . . . with the anguish of male stars' (Vincendeau, 2000: 250), sexualising anguish, as Vincendeau so memorably puts it; or the characterisation of New Wave acting as a '*combination* of authenticity and *décalage*, which parallels the filmmakers' paradoxical drive to realism and personal expression' (Vincendeau, 2000: 118; her italics), and the teasing out of Jeanne Moreau's importance as the key New Wave actress who concentrated 'the values of romantic love, sensuality, sensitivity and modernity', and in so doing 'brought a feminized surface to the New Wave which superimposed itself on its male and misogynist foundations' (Vincendeau, 2000: 130). By contrast, Louis de Funès, 'born middle-aged', Poujadist 'hero of the *France profonde*' (Vincendeau, 2000: 150), represented the antithesis of the New Wave's youth culture, grounded in middle-class values, but is of interest precisely because those values were under attack; his rage and dysfunctional masculinity are as much symptoms of social change in the 1960s as Bardot's hairstyle.

Amongst others working in this area there is Arnaud Chapuy, with a major volume on Martine Carol published in France (Chapuy, 2001) and, with the same publisher, a volume on the vamps of the first half of the twentieth century, such as Viviane Romance, Ginette Leclerc and others (Azzopardi, 1997). There are a number of scholars who have produced conference papers on stars since 2000; for example, Graeme Hayes on Alain Delon (2001) and Powrie on the 1920s star Pierre Batcheff (2001a).

Two historical issues dominated French cinema scholarship in the 1990s: war and colonialism/post-colonialism. In the latter category, Sherzer (1996), Norindr (1996) and Ezra (2000a) explored colonial and post-colonial issues (and special mention should be made here of Carrie Tarr's consistent body of work, as yet uncollected in a volume, on Beur films). Dine (1994), like Atack (1999), is not entirely devoted to cinema, but is an important intervention in thinking through the Algerian crisis in film, as is Atack's volume in relation to May 1968, that ever-fertile ground for debate. French historians, and French society more widely, however, showed more interest in the Second World War during the 1990s than May 1968 or Algeria, with well-publicised affairs of collaborators such as Paul Touvier and Maurice Papon causing considerable navel-gazing; hardly surprising, then, that there should be a number of volumes on the Occupation and related issues, such as Colombat (1993) and Chateau (1996).

Of particular interest here is Naomi Greene's *Landscapes of Loss*, which examines what one might call, in a Proustian sense, the involuntary memorialisation of the traumatic past. Whereas the focus of Higgins (1996) is very period-specific (and includes some literary texts as well as the films of Resnais, Truffaut and Malle), Greene ranges wider. There is a chapter that explores the way in which Resnais focuses on amnesia and repression, and, given the dearth of work on Tavernier, a fascinating chapter on his historical films showing how they chronicle liminally the collapse of the Marxist 'Grand Narrative'. There is a final chapter, which shows how the films of the *cinéma du look* (*Diva*, *Les Amants du Pont-Neuf*, *Delicatessen*) have recycled nostalgically the community films of the 1930s. Two chapters in particular are articulated around broader themes and placed firmly in the context of contemporary debates in French historical writing. There is a chapter that explores what the French historian Henry Rousso called 'The Vichy syndrome' in film, the truth value of *Le Chagrin et la pitié* being contrasted with the myth of resistancialism in *Lacombe Lucien* and *Le Dernier métro*. Greene's placing of these films in the context of 'Jewish memory' vehicled through documentaries highlights the slippery nature of fiction only too well as a means of forgetting while seeming to remember. There is also a chapter devoted to colonial films, which focuses principally on two very contrasting films and their difficulty in 'representing a past both unforgettable and yet inadmissible' (Greene, 1999: 134), Schoendoerffer's *Le Crabe-tambour* and Roüan's *Outremer*. Greene illuminatingly shows how these films can be compared with the work of the historian Pierre Nora, whose *Les Lieux de mémoire* (1986–1992) has, along with Rousso's work, been a defining moment in French history-writing.

Whereas Greene explores trauma through contemporary French historians, Emma Wilson uses the work of the more psychoanalytically inspired Cathy Caruth, amongst others. Two volumes (Wilson, 1999; 2000) are particularly interesting for their application of 'trauma theory' to films concerning the Second World War and Kieślowski respectively. This, when taken with the work done by many on the French heritage film, suggests that revisiting the past in film was of increasing importance during the 1990s.

The final area we would like to explore also involves revisiting. It is work on the remake, to which two important volumes were devoted at the turn of the millennium. Both Lucy Mazdon and Carolyn Durham take issue with the standard view of remakes, whether by French or American reviewers, that somehow the remake must always be worse, a debased version of a high-art original. Mazdon's opening chapters on the context of production and the history of the remake show how many other factors need to be taken into account, not least the frequent exchanges of financing, personnel and themes between the French and American industries.

These suggest rather more interaction and cross-fertilisation than most reviewers would allow for. Mazdon is particularly good at explaining differences in 'original' and remake by locating films in the context of their production and reception; thus, for example, the Hays Production Code caused significant plot changes in the remake of *Pépé le Moko* (Carné, 1937; remade as *Algiers*, Cromwell, 1938).

Most of Mazdon's book, like Durham's, deals with remakes since 1980, however. There are illuminating discussions about *Trois hommes et un couffin* (Serreau, 1985) and *Three Men and a Baby* (Nimoy, 1987) (this pair is also dealt with by Durham), *Mon père ce héros* (Lauzier, 1991) and *My Father the Hero* (Miner, 1994), focusing on issues of gender and particularly paternity, and *Le Retour de Martin Guerre* (Vigne, 1982) and *Sommersby* (Amiel, 1993), a comparison of which shows how both 'enable representation and/or critique of national myths and the construction of national identities' (Mazdon, 2000: 78). Mazdon's choices of remakes are mostly comedies: *Un éléphant ça trompe énormément* (Robert, 1976) and *The Woman in Red* (Wilder, 1984); *Le Grand blond avec une chaussure noire* (Robert, 1972) and *The Man with One Red Shoe* (Dragoti, 1985); *La Totale* (Zidi, 1991) and *True Lies* (Cameron, 1994); and *La Cage aux folles* (Molinaro, 1978) and *The Birdcage* (Nichols, 1996). As she points out, the fact that it is mainly French comedies that are remade by Hollywood gives the lie to the standard view that the original connotes 'high art', since French comedies, in France at least, are not connoted as such.

Mazdon also looks at a few thrillers, principal amongst which are *Nikita* (Besson, 1990)/*The Assassin* (Badham, 1993), and *À bout de souffle* (Godard, 1959)/*Breathless* (McBride, 1983), a pair also analysed by Durham. Interestingly, whereas Durham points out how McBride works towards coherence and inclusiveness with his camera, with Godard preferring discontinuity and rupture in gender relations, Mazdon sees fragmentation and incoherence in the remake. Both agree, however, that *Three Men and a Baby* is more concerned to assert heterosexuality and masculinity than the French 'original'.

Durham's chapter on *Trois hommes et un couffin*, published originally in 1992, and here updated with material on *Three Men and a Little Lady* (Ardolino, 1990) is a remarkable piece of writing. It shows how there is incompatibility between the drugs plot (male) and the domesticity plot (female), a confusion erased by the US version, which masculinises the narrative by including sequences familiar in action films. Durham also shows how the ideologies of the two films are moulded by different feminist contexts: women in the French film are excluded, because French feminists promulgated radical differences between the sexes, while the US remake does not reject women, stressing rather the equality of parenting, as might be expected from the different Anglo-American feminist tradition. Similarly, with patient and detailed comparison of cinematography and *mise-en-scène*, Durham shows how cultural issues affect the remake; for example, in Schumacher's remake of *Cousin Cousine* (Tachella, 1975; remade as *Cousins*, 1989) the French emphasis on freedom gives way to a very American emphasis on happiness, a general point also made by Mazdon, who shows how French acceptance of infidelity (in this case in *Un éléphant ça trompe énormément/The Woman in Red*) becomes a moral lesson in the American remake.

Another view of the remake, advanced by Mazdon, but questioned by Durham, is that Hollywood chooses French films to minimise the risk factor. Much more interesting is her claim that Hollywood remakes films because they are consistent with the US cultural climate. Commenting on what she rightly says is 'the otherwise astonishing decision to remake *La Cage aux folles*', she suggests that '*The Birdcage* is in so many ways the logical continuation of Hollywood's ongoing exploration of the homoerotic subtext that both consistently underlies the development of male friendships on screen and accompanies changes in traditional masculine roles within the family' (Durham, 1998: 200). At a time when the French state successfully managed to argue for French 'cultural exception' in the 1993 GATT round, and carries on jealously guarding its cultural heritage, it is particularly useful to have two cogently argued and detailed volumes on the apparently raw nerve of the remake.

To conclude this brief review of trends in academic film analysis, although the academic genres of the film history and the auteur study are still dominant, if inflected by the paradigms mentioned, the new trends are towards the study of early cinema, star studies, historical trauma, and what one might call the crisis in cultural identity. Until now, a paradigm gulf seems to have existed between Anglophone and Francophone Film Studies. Schematically, one could say that the former seems to have been characterised by Gender Studies, while the latter seems to have been characterised by aesthetic concerns.[1] It is reassuring, then, that in the trends we have highlighted, the two academic cultures seem to be growing closer, with the possible exception (paradoxically, since it involves the bringing together of Anglophone and Francophone) of work on *le remake*.

---

1 For example, the work of Bonitzer and Aumont, whose more influential volumes were published in the 1980s (an honourable exception is Sellier and Burch, 1996).

Chapter Four

WRITING ABOUT □
FRENCH FILMS

In this section we include specimen essays by students on French cinema, and sequence analyses by Phil Powrie. The purpose is to show you how you can write on a film or on a topic. We have therefore commented on each piece from a variety of perspectives, whether the purely formal (the structure and argument of the piece), or conceptual (the way in which the author has used specific themes or ideas familiar in Film Studies). The choice of films is not intended to be representative, but to suggest a variety of types of writing on film in the Essays section, as well as a selection of approaches to sequence analysis. The one thing we have tried to do is to tie one of the sequence analyses closely to one of the essays, on the 1989 film *Monsieur Hire*.

ESSAYS

1. ON *L'ATALANTE* (JEAN VIGO, 1934), BY ELLEN PARKER

This is a short essay composed in examination conditions by Ellen Parker, who was responding to the question 'Evaluate the importance of décor and setting in *L'Atalante*'. The film tells the tale of two newlyweds on a barge captained by a fantastical old sailor, Père Jules, the pressure of space on their relationship, their brief separation and their return to each other.

The essay is built on a classical ternary structure that allows very clear understanding of the points made: point 1 + point 2 leading to point 3, which places the first two points together but notes that they are irreconcilable:

- point 1 – negative space on the barge ('reality')
- point 2 – positive space on the barge ('fantasy')
- point 1a – negative water ('reality')
- point 2a – positive water ('fantasy')
- point 3 – duality

Figure 4.1   L'Atalante

TEXT

The barge is the centrepiece of the film, the setting on which or around which the action of the film and the interaction between the characters take place. The relationships between the characters are affected by the place they live and work in, whether these relationships be of work, of love or of friendship. The barge is a doubly paradoxical space. First, it is at one and the same time a prosaic and spatially limited working space, as well as a limitless space of dreams. This is doubled by a second paradox: the barge is a space whose mobility suggests unlimited freedom, but this mobile space is contained within the linear constraints of a canal. The barge's journey is in fact a metaphor for idealism and the loss of idealism.

The limited physical space on the barge causes friction at times. Père Jules's multitude of cats annoy the other inhabitants as they get in the way and make living in such a small place even harder. Jean is infuriated by the clutter in Père Jules's room and so breaches what little privacy Père Jules has by destroying his things. For Juliette, the cramped physical space and the limited possibilities for excitement within the barge itself cause her to venture outside the world of the barge in search for fulfilment. While at times the confinement of the barge allows the relationship between Jean and Juliette to bloom, the physical constraints of the environment also cause emotional suffocation in their relationship.

The barge is also where work and recreation must coexist. At first, for Juliette, the barge represents possibilities for exploration. The mobility of the barge to her suggests travel, excitement and the opening up of the whole world before her. On her first morning on the barge she listens to the men's song and it lends an atmosphere of entertainment or holiday, even though it is a song about work. The reality is that they are here to work not play, and this starts to sink in before

COMMENTARY

The introduction emphasises very clearly the two major themes to be developed, the barge and the water, and places them in relation to each other using the structuring idea of the paradox.

1a) The first part of the essay is devoted to the barge. The first section of the first part takes the notion of 'limited space' as its focus, announced clearly in the first sentence, and moves to the consequence of that limitation, anger, the search for fulfilment elsewhere and the deterioration of a relationship.

1b) The second section of the first part develops the idea of limited space by explaining its function as a workspace, and also develops one strand from the previous paragraph, Juliette's frustration.

too long. The lack of domesticity frustrates her as does the fact that Jean must stay up every night working. The barge for Juliette ceases to be a means of exploration and discovery, and instead becomes a stifling and monotonous place of work. When they finally arrive in Paris she is frustrated because they stay on the barge, which has become too small for her, and she longs to escape from it. Eventually, though, the real world turns out to be too big and menacing, and she is relieved to return to the safe, closed world of the barge.

The world of work and diversion from work is one world on the barge, but other worlds do exist there too. The extended cat family show how the limited space can be broken up and multiplied. There is a whole population of cats who inhabit cupboards, nooks and crannies, and, unlike the human population, can find comfort and privacy just about anywhere. As Baudelaire's favourite animals, the cats show an independence and adaptability, indeed an indifference to the décor which they colonise; this indifference, clearly an ideal, is in sharp contrast to the eventual spleen felt by Juliette and Jean. The presence of the cats, which might be taken merely as yet another oddity associated with Père Jules, is in fact more significant; they are the proof, *a contrario*, that even a small space can generate fantasy, as is the case with Père Jules' cabin.

Père Jules' cabin, small and cramped though it may be, contains the whole world and a whole lifetime. The artefacts and souvenirs he has gathered in his travels make his cabin an Aladdin's cave of treasures and treats for Juliette's imagination. His body's decoration, his tattoos, are an extension of this. They suggest a seedy past and are a source of wonder for Juliette. Each tattoo, like each object, has a memory and a story attached to it, and if Jean had not interrupted them, his stories could have transported

1c) The third section of the first part acts as a transition to the notion of fantasy, and is anchored on an insistent image in the film: that of the cats. There is a reference to one of the major poets of the nineteenth century, which both helps to give depth to an otherwise possibly minor image, and also helps to introduce the idea of the duality between an ideal and the pain felt when that ideal cannot be attained.

1d) The final section of the first part of the essay develops the notion of freedom and imagination in opposition to the negative aspects of the barge treated in earlier sections, thus acting as a counterargument.

Juliette, in both senses of the word, taking her ecstatically all over the world. The contents of his cabin verge on the surreal and the grotesque, such as the pickled hands of his friend and the way he smokes through his bellybutton. This treasure trove of weird and exotic memorabilia is about as far removed from the mundane, day-to-day life of a barge in the north of France as anything could be. The visit to his cabin feeds Juliette's imagination, and she looks again for the same sort of escapism when she meets the pedlar and his similar assortment of gadgets and trinkets.

The water on which the barge and its inhabitants travel is equally vital; the waterway has the dual function of fluidity of fantasy and linearity of direction, or way. The water is what will take Juliette to far-away places, and she imagines it will take her to the Paris of her imagination. In reality, what she sees as a romantic waterway, an opening out, with the fluidity of fantasy, is in fact a working industrial canal, a closing in, merely a way to get from one point to the other with a burden; and the Paris it delivers her to is a grimy and threatening place. Moreover, the same water carries Jean away from her, and so leaves her stranded in this big, dangerous world.

2a) Having completed an analysis of the negative and positive aspects of the barge, the essay now moves in its second part to a consideration of the second major theme: that of water. In this paragraph, the same structure is reprised as in part 1: we have first the negative aspects of the water.

Water functions as a symbol of dreams. If the water on which the barge journeys is an industrial canal, it is also a place where the fantastical and the fairy-tale can happen. The early shot of Juliette in her wedding dress when she appears to be walking on water is a magical, surreal image, and the slow movement of the camera from her point of view of the barge creates a sense of being helpless, of floating wherever the water may go. It carries Juliette out of the lives of her villagers to go who knows where. Jean longs to see Juliette's face in the water and, when he throws himself into the canal, his dream comes true in one of the cinema's most potent fantasy sequences; the water shows her in her wedding dress, as she was when

2b) Negative aspects are followed by positive aspects, those that are linked to fantasy as opposed to daily reality.

everything was beautiful between them and all the possibilities for their life together were still real. The final shot, when the camera is high and travels along the sparkling water in slow motion, leaves the spectator with a sense that everything is still possible for Jean and Juliette, and this beautiful, endless stretch of water might yet carry them to the places of Juliette's dreams.

Throughout *L'Atalante*, dual emotions and situations co-exist, at times in conflict and at times in harmony. The barge and the river represent work; the barge is also a place of play and a place of fantasy and escapism. The water can be a working canal or a medium for dream and fantasy. The opening sequence in particular shows this dualism in a very visual way, with the dark clothes of the wedding guests and the bright daylight. The chiaroscuro effects of the dark clouds against the pale sky, the light on the faces of the women and children who watch the barge pass, and Juliette's almost phosphorescent dress against water so dark it cannot be distinguished from the barge. Another sequence that underlines duality is the extraordinary sequence of Jean moping on the ice block, as if Juliette's departure had caused his tears to freeze in an abstract ice statue, the opposite of the fantasy and freedom represented by unfrozen water, signifying loss and absence. Sequences of fantasy and surreal imagery are interspersed with sequences that return us to quotidian reality.

3) The paragraph announces itself as a new part, and in this final part of the essay the various themes are brought together. In this paragraph, there is an emphasis on duality, or the co-existence of fantasy and reality in each of the two major themes (barge and water). Thus, the essay has been structured in a typical ternary fashion (a + b = ab). The paragraph also shows considerable awareness of *mise-en-scène*, a flair for visual detail and analysis.

In conclusion, in both narrative and *mise-en-scène*, then, the film is an interplay between the real and the surreal, the ordinary and the fantastical, in which the principal settings of barge and water are central, always maintaining and never reconciling the paradoxes of human freedom and imagination that are at the heart of the film. The potency of this setting was not lost on Léos Carax some 60 years later. He

The conclusion, clearly announced as such, states once more the key ideas of the first paragraph, with the new twist of an unreconciled dualism (another argument could have attempted to

reprised parts of this film for *Les Amants du Pont-Neuf* (1991), his paean to the marginality of youth during the bicentennial celebrations of 1989, where similarly long-lost lovers float away from Paris towards a future that is not uncertain, but improbably fantastical.

reconcile the paradoxes outlined in the first paragraph). Finally, the essay looks forward to a modern film as well as looking back, and shows awareness of intertextual allusions.

FURTHER READING ON *L'ATALANTE*

Salles Gomes, P.E. (1972) *Jean Vigo* (London: Faber & Faber; 2nd edn 1998; first published in French in 1957), 149–94.

Warner, Marina (1993) *L'Atalante* (London: BFI 'Film Classics').

2. ON THE OPENING SEQUENCES OF *WEEKEND* (JEAN-LUC GODARD, 1967), BY JOHN WILLIAMS

This longer essay was written as a course assignment on what Godard called his last bourgeois film before retreating after the events of May 1968 into work in television as part of a group of film-makers. This film, a companion piece to *La Chinoise* (1967) is an analysis of consumerism and materialism. The very loose storyline has a materialistic couple, Corinne and Roland, who leave Paris for the weekend plotting to kill Roland's mother so as to inherit a fortune. They lose their car in a crash, manage to kill the mother, and meet a variety of strange characters, including, finally, a group of cannibalistic 'revolutionaries' who live in a forest, whom Corinne joins, eventually eating her husband.

The essay works through a number of illustrations of an over-arching point – the difficulty spectators have in identifying with the characters – through an investigation of *mise-en-scène* (décor, lighting, intertitles), framing and soundtrack (delivery, diegetic sounds, non-diegetic sounds/music). Unlike the previous essay, this one is particularly good in the way it backs up its points and illustrations with theoretical references, showing that considerable research has gone into its preparation. One might have expected references to standard Film Studies texts written by Bordwell and Thompson, or James Monaco; what is more impressive is the research into Brecht and even the reference to a venerable film manual, showing an inquisitive mind.

Note, too, how the reference system is organised. This is the reference-within-the-text system, often called the Harvard system. It can usefully be compared with the rather more cumbersome reference system used in the following essay, where it is not always clear to the reader what the reference is if it is signalled in notes by an 'op. cit'.

Figure 4.2 Weekend

TEXT

Weekend has been interpreted as a satire on bourgeois materialism, and an expression of Godard's 'feeling of profound despair at the spectacle of man's inhumanity to man' (MacBean, 1975: 47). The emotional nature of this comment seems to miss completely Godard's intention of creating a critical distance, both between the spectator and the characters, and the spectator and the themes. This intention is primarily achieved by extensive use of Brecht's *Verfremdungeffekt*, or the alienation effect. Wollen has drawn attention to a number of ways Godard's more avant-garde work has employed these techniques, particularly by using picaresque narrative techniques, and the related effect of estrangement between the spectator and the characters within a film (see Wollen, 1982). However, much of the power of *Weekend* is due to the fact that Godard was still working, albeit loosely, within the conventions of classical narrative cinema, and therefore his transgressions still had the ability to shock.

An analysis of the first three scenes of *Weekend* will demonstrate how Godard establishes the alienating/estranging techniques from the very beginning of the film. The first scene introduces the main characters, Roland and Corinne, and is set on the balcony and interior of an apartment. The second scene features an extended erotic monologue performed inside a room, while the third scene consists of a fight between the couple and their neighbours. I hope to show, with reference to standard definitions of such techniques as manipulation of *mise-en-scène*, cinematography, and diegetic and non-diegetic sound, how Godard uses Brechtian techniques to achieve a distanciation, after first appearing loosely to follow cinematic conventions.

COMMENTARY

The introduction is in two sections. In this first section, the film is introduced in broad terms, but sharply, because the text opens immediately on a questioning of a received view. As in the previous essay, the introduction works well because there is also the outlining of a familiar paradox: to shock people, you must adhere, if only negatively, to a set of rules.

The second section of the introduction relates the opening comments to the matter in hand, the rather tighter focus on the first three sequences of the film. These are helpfully thumbnailed for the reader, before a brief list of salient issues to be covered is given. Note how the paradox mentioned in the first paragraph is here reprised to remind the reader of one of the guiding threads of the essay, as well as acting as a transition to the following paragraph.

In terms of narrative, the opening scenes convey a great deal of story information, albeit in a compressed way. What is particularly striking about the first scene is the way that the spectator is privileged with more story information than the characters. This is a typical technique of 'classical' cinema, which Bordwell describes as 'unrestricted narration' when 'we know more, we see and hear more, than any or all of the characters can . . . such narration is often called *omniscient narration*' (Bordwell and Thompson, 1997: 102). Once Roland has left the room to take a phone call, Corinne reveals by her intimate tone that the other man is her lover, and has already attempted to kill Roland. She confidently explains that he is unsuspecting: 'I have to let him screw me from time to time so he thinks I love him', but it is then revealed that Roland is taking the phone call from his lover, and is in turn confidently proclaiming that Corinne does not realise he has twice tried to have her killed: 'I've got to be cautious after those sleeping pills and the gas.' Thus, a large amount of narrative cues have been skilfully conveyed, allowing the spectator to construct what the Russian Formalists described as the *fabula*, namely the 'result of picking up narrative cues, applying schemata, framing and testing hypotheses' (Bordwell, 1985a: 49). The information creates a degree of suspense about who will be killed and how, and a curiosity on the part of the spectator as to how the story will unfold.

1a) This paragraph's function is to explain the way in which the film begins conventionally. It ties description of content firmly to key ideas developed by theorists, such as 'classical narration', the *fabula*. The end of the paragraph completes the point, and creates its own suspense within the conventions of the essay itself, since the reader knows that the first point, conventional techniques, has been developed, and is now waiting for the second point, the way in which those conventional techniques are undermined.

The following scenes, however, deliberately undermine this establishing scene. Although it could be argued that Corinne's sexual monologue gives us further information about her lifestyle, and her relationship with Roland, its nine-minute length puts a strain on the narrative. This scene could be classed as retardatory material, i.e. that which delays: 'the revelation of some information [. . . to] arouse anticipation, curiosity, surprise and suspense' (Bordwell, 1985a: 54). Godard, though, is not trying to create

1b) This paragraph does not give the whole answer; indeed, very cleverly, it delays the answer by talking about Godard's own delaying techniques. The final sentence, however, acts as the cue and transition to the major points to be

suspense in the spectator. On the contrary, he is attempting to annoy, irritate and frustrate the spectator, with the insertion of material that is unclear in relation to the other scenes. This is an extreme example of Godard's 'continual foregrounding, constant deviations from any intrinsic narrational norm' (Bordwell, 1985a: 316). In this way, we see Godard alienating the spectator by his narrative method, something that is also achieved in his subversion of classical cinematic techniques.

made concerning the undermining of conventional techniques.

Godard sometimes uses the *mise-en-scène*, i.e. 'that part of the cinematic process to be found on the set' (Monaco, 1981: 441), in a classical manner, so as to introduce the obvious themes of the film. Roland and Corinne are revealed as a typically bourgeois couple. The furnishings, the table on the balcony for alfresco meals, and the stylish designer dress worn by Corinne all point to this fact. The objects within the scenes are associated with consumerism. Corinne breaks off her monologue for a cigarette, but refuses a Gitane as she will only smoke American cigarettes. America is an obvious symbol of the consumer culture, and in the 1960s and after, the brand of cigarette purchased was a significant statement about an individual's social status.

2a) The first section of the second part of the essay deals with *mise-en-scène*, showing how Godard uses typical techniques, but in such a way as to prevent identification with the characters, who become more akin to ciphers or signs for something else – in this case, the idea of bourgeois consumerism. The two paragraphs cover, first, relatively unimportant elements of décor for this film, costume and cigarettes, before moving on to a more extended discussion of one of the focal points of the film, the car.

An even greater index of status, and brand importance, is the car, which Godard also includes as an important item in the *mise-en-scène*. Cars have already been associated with violence, when Corinne's lover remarks on car deaths at the Evreux junction. Godard then emphasises the association by showing two separate incidents involving fights around cars. The first altercation is outside the apartment block, and is observed by Roland and Corinne. The second is also outside the block, but this time involves Roland and Corinne. If we view cars as an embodiment of the perfect consumer product, then these parallel scenes clearly identify bourgeois consumerism as being essentially violent. Godard has used the setting, and objects within the setting, to establish the themes of *Weekend*, but in such a way as to encourage identification of the characters and objects with ideas of consumerism, rather than letting the spectator identify with the characters themselves.

This is taken further by the use of figure expression and movement within these opening sequences. Lines are delivered in a robotic, emotionless way, while normal human reactions to news of murder plots, and sexually explicit revelations, are eschewed in favour of a flat monotone. The unusual delivery is seen most clearly at the end of the first scene, when Roland bids a 'fond' farewell to his lover. As the printed screenplay describes it: 'we hear his voice repeating, like a stuck gramophone record'. The lack of reaction by the 'friend' to Corinne's monologue in the second scene, also demonstrates the coldness of the characters. This could be seen as another illustration of the dark, amoral nature of the bourgeois lifestyle, but its main significance is as an application of Brecht's theories of acting. Brecht believed that: 'Spectator and actor ought not to approach one another but to move apart. . . . Otherwise the element of terror necessary to all recognition is lacking' (Brecht, 1978: 26), and Godard applies this technique to achieve 'a double distanciation, between the actor and the part, and between the actor and the spectator' (Stam, 1982: 199). It is by using distanciation that Godard can encourage the spectator to focus on the issues within the film.

Godard enhances this distanciation with his use of light. Corinne's sexual monologue to the 'friend' is marked by the use of a backlight as the single point of light. This is a standard method of creating silhouettes: 'Used with no other sources of light, backlighting tends to create silhouettes' (Bordwell and Thompson, 1997: 179). This prevents the viewer from

2b) Since it might appear odd to focus on objects rather than people, the essay explains how characters in the film are difficult to identify with because of their delivery. The point is backed up by extensive theoretical references.

2c) A second point is made with regard to characters: the use of light, which distances them from us. Again, clear explanations are given of the terms used

seeing Corinne clearly: 'In order to search out detail in the shot we have to work, which makes us feel, faced with the bright window, not unlike voyeurs' (Monaco, 1981: 169). Voyeurs, of course, are on the outside of the action, and the added inability to see Corinne's facial expression again serves to prevent audience identification. When combined with the unusual nature of her sexual confession/fantasy, and the 'alienated' style of acting, the overall effect is to encourage estrangement rather than identification.

This estrangement is amplified in the other opening scenes by Godard's use of natural light. This is contrary to the classical practice of using primary and secondary sources of light, and combining them to pick out particular characters: 'This in turn was desirable because it kept the eye from wandering to the set and away from the main narrative action' (Bordwell, 1985b: 226). Godard wants the spectator's eye to 'wander' over the screen, away from the actors, and therefore away from identification with the characters. In Brechtian terms, the spectator must be discouraged from engaging emotionally with the drama, so as to form a critical position: 'A critical attitude on the audience's part is a thoroughly artistic one' (Brecht, 1978: 140). Godard, though, tries to take this process further. Not only does he require the spectator to be alienated from the diegesis, he also uses devices to continually remind them of the film-making process.

As might be expected, this is attempted by using the non-diegetic aspect of the *mise-en-scène*, namely the intertitles. Some of these intertitles directly draw attention to the unusual form of the film: 'A FILM FOUND ON A SCRAP-HEAP', which suggests something thrown away or worthless. Intertitles are usually used to denote time and place to the spectator, but Godard uses them to deny simple location: 'A FILM ADRIFT IN THE COSMOS'. The effect of these titles

by reference to standard introductions to Film Studies, as well as to Brecht, showing that careful research has been done.

2d) This paragraph's linking technique is double. First there is the final sentence of the previous paragraph warning the reader to expect a new illustration of the point; second, there is a further

is to further distance the spectator from the material, this time by supplanting the images altogether. Again Godard is making use of a Brechtian device, this one known as literalisation:

> The screens on which the titles of each scene are projected are a primitive attempt at literalizing the theatre. . . . Literalizing entails punctuating 'representation' with 'formulation'; gives . . . the possibility of making contact with other institutions for intellectual activities. (Brecht, 1978: 43)

quotation from Brecht, who was the author of the last quotation supporting the previous illustration; the new illustration of the point to do with *mise-en-scène* is clearly announced in the first sentence of the paragraph.

This is particularly seen with the inserted intertitle during Corinne's sexual monologue: 'ANAL-YSIS', which contrasts the lack of analysis present in the scene, with the fashionable adherence to psychoanalysis prevalent in the bourgeois. The use of the intertitle as a direct form of address by Godard communicates the fact that the spectator is watching a film. But it is not just in the *mise-en-scène* that Godard draws attention to cinematic techniques.

Much has been written on the use of framing in *Weekend*, i.e. that aspect of cinematography which 'produces a certain vantage point onto the material within the image' (Bordwell and Thompson, 1997: 226). Henderson, particularly, has concentrated on Godard's use of 'a slow tracking shot that moves purely laterally' (Henderson 1976: 423), despite there being examples of the camera tracking forward and back in these opening scenes. I will concentrate on two aspects: the use of the long shot to depict the action, and Godard's subversion of the classical rules of reframing. Godard uses long shot almost unbrokenly in the first and third scene. This ignores 'the old adage that each scene should be covered in long shot, medium shot and close-up . . . a scene must be covered from more than one point of view' (Spottiswoode, 1951: 28). This is particularly evident

3a) The last sentence of the previous paragraph has signalled a new section, whose focus, once again, is made absolutely clear in the first sentence: framing. The paragraph explains what is meant by the term, before showing how important it is in Godard's work. A clear statement is made concerning the extent of the point: only two types of framing will be discussed. In this

in the fight sequences, when instead of using close-ups to emphasise the emotions of the participants, Godard chooses to remain aloof from the action. The placing of the camera puts the spectator at a physical distance from the characters, and by extension creates an emotional distance. The maintenance of this fixed camera distance is reminiscent of news documentary, and implies an objectivity that close-up and point-of-view shots would not provide. This is in keeping with Godard's didactic intentions with regard to his subject matter.

paragraph it is the use of the long shot and the refusal of close-ups.

The other aspect of framing occurs in the second scene, when Corinne breaks off her monologue to get a cigarette. As she is the central figure in the scene, it would be usual for the camera to reframe her as she retrieves the cigarette: 'If a character moves in relation to another character, very often the frame will pan or tilt to adjust to the movement' (Bordwell and Thompson, 1997: 249). Instead it remains in the same position, causing the spectator to lose sight of her. A similar incident occurs in the third scene, when Roland and Corinne escape in the car. Instead of following the main characters, the camera lingers on the peripheral neighbours. This fulfils a now familiar double function: Godard refuses to privilege the main characters, thus preventing spectator identification, while also making the spectator aware of the camera, which has its own agenda within the film.

3b) This paragraph discusses the second type of framing, what is known as 'reframing'. The final paragraph of this section will remind the reader of how important this apparently minor technical issue might be, as well as returning us to the main point of part 2, the difficulty of character identification, which is now sufficiently far away from us that we may have forgotten what major issues were being covered by this series of illustrations.

The film soundtrack similarly enhances this non-privileging of the characters. The external diegetic sound: 'sound represented as coming from a physical source within the story space . . . which we assume the characters to be aware of' (Stam, 1982: 60) features a constant stream of traffic noise. Unusually, this is allowed to almost drown out the dialogue on occasions, such

4a) We move to the final illustration of the overarching issue, the difficulty of identification with the characters, here by a focus on the film's soundtrack. As with the

as when Corinne is talking on the balcony, and when Roland is on the phone. This is contrary to the usual vococentrism manifested in the classical cinema, where 'all the phases of the sound production process are subordinated to the goal of showcasing the human voice and making it audible and comprehensible' (Stam, 1982: 61). Two things are happening here. The first is thematic: the car has been established by its presence in the *mise-en-scène* as thematically important, but when cars are not present on the screen they still dominate the spectator's attention. Second, the non-privileging of the human voice emphasises the point that Godard is not primarily interested in his characters, and that they are merely part of the intellectual aspect of the film.

> previous illustration, this is divided into two main areas. The first, in this paragraph, is external diegetic sound.

This is also invoked by the use of non-diegetic sound. There are two uses of music in the opening scenes. The first is after Corinne has witnessed the fight around the car. The spectator may well assume this is a use of 'redundant' or 'empathetic' music, that is: 'which participates in and conveys the emotions of the characters' (Stam, 1982: 63). The music is mournful, and seems to express revulsion at such a violent event. However, doubt is cast on this reading when compared to the use of music during Corinne's sexual monologue, where it acts as an aural masking effect: 'whereby a sudden noise ... strategically blocks out part of the soundtrack' (Stam, 1982: 62). There are two strategies being employed here. First, as in his use of diegetic sound, Godard is further alienating the spectator by preventing them from hearing the character's dialogue. Second, the use of music is foregrounded, so, as in the use of intertitles, the spectator is made strongly aware of a non-diegetic presence in the film. This is again contrary to classical film-making where: 'Music is ... subordinate to dialogue, entering during pauses in dialogue or effects' (Bordwell and Thompson, 1997: 321). Godard tricks the spectator into expecting empathetic use of music,

> 4b) The second is non-diegetic sound. Note how the final sentence reprises the over-arching issue, similar to the sentence used at the end of part 3, signalling the end of this section.

therefore causing the second use of music to be especially jarring and noticeable. This tactic is just another example of the consistent way that Godard effects emotional estrangement, and intellectual appreciation of cinematic form, on the part of the spectator.

The richness of these opening scenes is such that I have only touched on how the effects of alienation are achieved, rather than a further examination of what Godard is attempting to do once the spectator is estranged from the material. It is clear though, that the concerted use of alienation techniques does not merely intellectualise the film's satirical themes, but in itself becomes the subject of *Weekend*. The young Godard wrote about abolishing the distinction between conventional film-making techniques: 'montage is above all an integral part of *mise-en-scène*. Only at peril can one be separated from the other. One might just as well try to separate the rhythm from a melody' (Godard, 1972: 39). In *Weekend* Godard has gone further, the techniques of film-making no longer simply illustrate his themes, but have become the subject of his work: 'no film can accurately represent reality. It must therefore be presentational rather than representational' (Monaco, 1981: 336). It could be said that the presentational film-making that dominates Godard's work after *Weekend* is truer to his aesthetic, but it is certainly more stimulating as a spectator to witness Godard's labour pains, than be forced to see pictures of the baby.

The conclusion points out the limitations of the analysis. What might seem like a weakness is immediately and cleverly turned to an advantage: alienation leads nowhere (so the essay has, after all, said what must be said), because it is the real subject of the film. As with the previous essay, the final sentence finishes with a flourish, while at the same time making the case for a close analysis of this particular film.

FILMOGRAPHY

Weekend (1967) France, Jean-Luc Godard.

BIBLIOGRAPHY

Bordwell, David (1985a) *Narration in the Fiction Film* (London: Methuen & Co.).

Bordwell, David and Thompson, Kristin (1997) *Film Art: An Introduction* (New York: McGraw-Hill, 5th edn).

Bordwell, David *et al.* (1985b) *The Classical Hollywood Cinema: Film Style and Mode of Production to 1960* (London: Routledge).

Brecht, Bertolt (1978) *Brecht on Theatre: The Development of an Aesthetic* (London: Eyre Methuen).

Godard, Jean-Luc (1972a) *Godard on Godard* (New York: Da Capo Press).

Godard, Jean-Luc (1972b) *Weekend, and Wind from the East: Two Films* (New York: Simon and Schuster).

Henderson, Brian (1976) 'Towards a non-bourgeois camera-style', in *Films and Filming* **XXIV**(2), Winter, 1970–1971, 2–14. Reproduced in B. Nichols (ed.) *Movies and Methods: An Anthology* (University of California Press, Vol. 1).

MacBean, James Roy (1975) *Film and Revolution* (Bloomington: Indiana University Press).

Monaco, James (1981) *How to Read a Film: The Art, Technology, Language, History, and Theory of Film and Media* (New York: Oxford University Press, 2nd edn).

Spottiswoode, Raymond (1951) *Film and its Techniques* (Berkeley: University of California Press).

Stam, Robert *et al.* (1982) *New Vocabularies in Film Semiotics: Structuralism, Post-structuralism and Beyond* (London: Routledge).

Wollen, Peter (1982) *Readings and Writings: Semiotic Counter-Strategies* (London: Verso).

3. ON THE GAZE IN *MONSIEUR HIRE* (PATRICE LECONTE, 1989), BY ABIGAIL MURRAY*

This rather longer essay was originally a dissertation; it was eventually published in 1993 in the academic journal *Modern and Contemporary France* (**1**(3), 287–95), and was the only substantial academic article on the film until Duffy (2002). Leconte's film is one of the few films to deal directly with the act of viewing (the other major films are mentioned in the course of the essay). It is a remake of *Panique* (Duvivier, 1946), itself based on a novel by Simenon (*Les Fiançailles de Monsieur Hire*, 1933). All three tell the story of Monsieur Hire, a quiet, anti-social man, who spies on his neighbour Alice. He witnesses a murder, by Alice's boyfriend. Monsieur Hire becomes the prime suspect. A relationship develops between Alice and Hire when she realises that he has been watching her. He tries to persuade her to leave with him; when she refuses, he lets himself be chased and falls to his death, although he has left proof behind that it was not him but Alice's boyfriend who was the murderer.

The essay, like the two that precede it, is clearly argued and, like the first essay, has a simple ternary structure: theories of the gaze; the gaze is male; but the male is not always in the position of power. The argument is placed firmly within

*© Taylor and Francis Ltd (http://www.tandf.co.uk/journals)

Figure 4.3   Monsieur Hire

well-rehearsed debates concerning the gaze, showing how the gaze is not as monolithically 'male' as theorists had argued during the mid-1970s. It shows familiarity with those debates, and explains them coherently and clearly.

TEXT

Film-makers and critics alike have long been fascinated by the similarities between man's natural voyeuristic impulses and the viewing process in cinema. Conditions of screening (the darkened room) and narrative conventions in mainstream cinema (continuity editing as a means of effacing the methods of production, and the convention by which actors do not, generally speaking, directly address the camera), essentially make the film viewer a voyeur. Like the voyeur, we as viewers derive a certain sense of superiority that comes from experiencing events vicariously, hence without any real threat or danger to ourselves. Furthermore, when we are witness to things that are traditionally private, we feel we have a certain power over the object of our gaze; the look becomes a controlling one, a means of oppression.

This analogy has prompted critics to explore several related aspects of the way we view and experience films. For Christian Metz, voyeurism is a vital psychic mechanism associated with the cinema. In 'Story/Discourse: Notes on Two Kinds of Voyeurism' he states that the film, although it is exhibitionist, chooses to pretend that its audience does not exist, 'making it (at best) a beautiful closed object which must remain unaware of the pleasure it gives us'.[2] This situation invites a voyeuristic response, for by effacing its marks of *énonciation* and disguising itself as story (*histoire*) the film 'becomes an object presented by an agent who hides, rather than confronts our gaze.'[3] This interpretation offers a further

COMMENTARY

The introduction sets out a familiar argument, that the gaze in cinema is of paramount importance, and that it is usually defined as a male gaze. This context is given the right amount of theoretical support in the second and third paragraphs, which sketch out the positions taken by Metz and Mulvey in the 1970s. The theoretical framework is then supported by examples of films in which voyeurism plays a major part. The introduction ends by recalling the classic position, but indicating that the essay will question it on the basis of this film.

2 Metz, C. (1985) 'Story/Discourse: Notes on Two Kinds of Voyeurism', in B. Nichols (ed.) *Movies and Methods*, Vol. II (University of California Press), 546.
3 From the editor's Introduction to 'Story/Discourse: Notes on Two Kinds of Voyeurism', in NICHOLS, B. (ed.) op. cit., 543.

explanation of why the voyeuristic spectator feels so powerful – he or she now become the authoring agency having to make sense of the narrative events belonging to a story that no one seems to tell.[4]

This crucial positioning of the spectator as subject is also considered by Laura Mulvey, but from a feminist perspective. Taking as her basis the Freudian account of sexuality and the formation of the unconscious, according to which woman, within the patriarchal order, symbolise lack and the threat of castration, Mulvey examines how this patriarchal unconscious has managed to structure film form by reflecting and even playing on 'the straight, socially established inter-pretation of sexual difference which controls images, erotic ways of looking and spectacle'.[5] In a world struc-tured around sexual imbalance, pleasure in looking (scopophilia), Mulvey argues, 'has been split between active/male and passive/female'.[6] The controlling plea-sure in cinema is, therefore, male but this pleasure (contemplating woman as eroticised object), is not unproblematic owing to the castration threat that the female figure poses. Faced with this threat, however, two avenues of escape are open to the male spectator. He may build up the physical beauty of the object of his gaze, 'transforming it into something satisfying in itself'[7] (fetishism), or else he may derive sadistic plea-sure from 'ascertaining guilt . . . asserting control and subjecting the guilty person through punishment or forgiveness'[8] (voyeurism). It is with this second mani-festation of scopophilic pleasure, voyeurism, that this essay will principally concern itself.

The scenarios of the films which have, over the years, made voyeurism the subject of their narratives would

---

4 Metz, C., op. cit., 548.
5 Mulvey, L., 'Visual Pleasure and Narrative Cinema', in Nichols, B. (ed.) op. cit., 305.
6 Ibid., 309.
7 Ibid., 311.
8 Ibid., 311.

seem to bear out what Mulvey has to say about the active/male, passive/female dichotomy with regard to structures of looking, for the watcher is almost without exception male while his object (victim, in some cases) is almost exclusively female.[9] On a narrative level, this means that the former inevitably provides the main focus of the film, while the latter, already objectified by the controlling male gaze, tends to be marginalised and silenced. This manipulation of sympathies – that is, persuading the viewer to identify with the watcher and not the watched – is reinforced by the attempt, if not to justify, at least to account for the questionable activities of these men. 'Explanations' range from the absence or abuse of parental support and guidance (Tomek in *A Short Film About Love* (Kieślowski, 1989) is an orphan; Mark in *Peeping Tom* (Powell, 1960) was cruelly experimented on by his scientist father) to boredom resulting from physical confinement (Jeffries in *Rear Window* (Hitchcock, 1954) is wheelchair-bound).

A general pattern thus begins to emerge: the 'conventional' voyeur is insecure, sexually shy, emotionally or physically crippled – but there seems to be no matching consensus on the way in which the women, whose lives these men touch, should be portrayed:

> *Monsieur Hire* implies that Alice is flattered;
> in Powell's *Peeping Tom* ... the Anna
> Massey character feels afraid,
> compassionate, repulsed and morbidly
> fascinated; and in *Blue Velvet* Isabella
> Rossellini first offers violent aggression and
> then, masochistically, her love.[10]

Geoff Andrew concludes from this that 'men who make films are more confident about why members of

---

9 One could include among Monsieur Hire's cinematic predecessors: Jeffries in *Rear Window* (1954), Scottie in *Vertigo* (1958), Norman Bates in *Psycho* (1960) and Mark Lewis in *Peeping Tom* (1960) – and among his contemporaries, Tomek in *A Short Film About Love* (1989).
10 Andrew, G. (1990) 'On Voyeurism'. *Time Out* 1027 (25 April–2 May), 37.

their own sex become fully fledged voyeurs than about what may constitute a plausible, reasonable female reaction to being spied on'.[11]

In the light of these remarks I will begin by arguing that *Monsieur Hire* is, in many respects, conventional in its treatment of the theme of voyeurism. By setting up Monsieur Hire and Alice as male voyeur and female object of the gaze respectively, it will be shown how this film, superficially at least, perpetuates the myths of 'demarcated sex differences'.[12] At the same time, however, I believe that *Monsieur Hire*, as a product of a post-feminist context, offers a critique of the existing social structures based on these differences of gender, and I will therefore demonstrate how the apparent dominance of the male gaze in this film is, in fact, persistently challenged, questioned and undermined.

In *Women and Film: Both Sides of the Camera*, E. Ann Kaplan argues that 'our culture is deeply committed to myths of demarcated sex differences, called "masculine" and "feminine", which in turn revolve first on a complex gaze apparatus and second on dominance – submission patterns'.[13] In the light of this it would be pertinent to consider ways in which this gaze apparatus and these patterns, as they manifest themselves in *Monsieur Hire*, perpetuate the myths of gender differences by privileging the male gaze.

1a) The essay will be divided into two major parts, the first supporting the classic position, the second contrasting and modifying it. Here, the essay announces very clearly that it will explore the classic position of the powerful male gaze. This it does by careful analysis of *mise-en-scène*.

There can be no doubt that from his darkened room Monsieur Hire enjoys a privileged view of all that goes on in Alice's apartment – a privilege that has been enhanced by the film's use of *mise-en-scène*, which positions Hire's apartment one floor above Alice's so that, metaphorically as well as physically, he looks down

---

11 Ibid., 37.
12 Kaplan, E.A. (1990) *Women and Film: Both Sides of the Camera* (Routledge), 29. (First published by Methuen in 1983.)
13 Ibid., 37.

upon her (in the original Simenon novel the apartments were directly opposite each other).'[14] Leconte goes as far as to compare the power Hire exercises through his gaze to that of the director: 'On pourrait dire que Hire se fait son propre cinéma. Il est "voyeur" mais aussi "cadreur". [You might say that Hire is making his own film. He is a "voyeur" but also someone who puts things in a frame.]'[15]

In addition the camera relates to Hire and Alice in a way that further underlines their status as subject and object respectively. In the scenes in which we see him spying on Alice, Hire is filmed in profile and in extreme close-up, leaving just enough room in the frame to suggest the space his gaze has to travel. This has the effect of playing down the sense of a wider context and of directing us instead to the character's psychic state.[16] Repeatedly the camera tries to penetrate Hire's cold and expressionless exterior, to discover what lies behind the 'funereal visage'[17] as it prowls around behind him in the vast and lonely space of his room – sometimes sliding up to him by means of a slow-moving lateral tracking shot, at others descending upon him and finally 'peering' over his shoulder. Although what we and the camera come to discover in these scenes is that: 'What he has to convey (mainly in profile) is the quality of a loneliness so ingrained that it can communicate nothing, not even its own pain or the panic that Hire feels when the tables are turned . . .'[18]

This manifest interest of the camera in its masculine subject and his innermost thoughts stands in sharp contrast to its less involved relationship with Alice as passive object of the gaze. Framing her initially in

1b) In this section, the essay focuses on the way in which close-ups of Hire are contrasted with long shots of Alice, and thereby demonstrates Hire's dominance. This is made theoretically relevant by the introduction of a then recent analysis of male/female relationships by Ginette Vincendeau to show the dominance of the male and the submission of the female. The submission of the female will form the next major part of this section, as the other side of the coin to the male's dominance.

---

14 Simenon, G. (1990) *Les Fiançailles de Monsieur Hire* (Presses Pocket). (First published by Editions Fayard in 1933.)
15 From the director's notes in *L'Avant-Scène Cinéma* 390/391 (Mars/Avril 1990), 15.
16 Johnston, S. (1990) 'Tailor Plays the Dummy', *Independent* (26 April).
17 Younis, R. (1991) 'Monsieur Hire', *Cinema Papers* 83 (May), 56.
18 Buss, R. (1990) 'A Solitary Passion Shared', *Independent on Sunday* (29 April).

long-shot and then cutting to a medium-shot, the camera somehow never gives the impression in these scenes of wanting really to penetrate Alice's confident exterior, for to do so would alter completely the nature of the relationship between the two main characters as it is developed shot by shot. To have consistently shown Alice in close-up would have destroyed the inequality upon which the relationship between a voyeur and his unwitting object rests, as it would have destroyed the illusion of distance that separates Hire physically from the object of his desire and symbolically from a love that is freely given and not bought.

The same inequality that characterises this type of relationship also forms the basis of one of the 'master narratives' of French cinema of which *Monsieur Hire is* a variant – this is the father/daughter narrative as described by Ginette Vincendeau in a recent edition of *Sight and Sound*.[19] In her article Vincendeau demonstrates how, from the 1920s through to the 1940s, and with renewed vigour in the 1980s, French films have: 'explicitly (dramatised) the conflict of the aging man . . . torn between his erotic and his protective feelings towards a daughter, stepdaughter, adopted waif or very young wife.'[20]

Monsieur Hire is able to offer Alice protection because, like so many of the father figures in the films Vincendeau mentions, he is financially secure, but more importantly for the purposes of my argument, because he knows Alice's secret, he knows the truth about what happened the night Pierrette Bourgeois was murdered – and this privileged knowledge is due entirely to his voyeuristic activities. The gaze is powerful because it brings with it knowledge and, consequently, the ability to act.

---

19 Vincendeau, G. (1992) 'Family Plots. The Fathers and Daughters of French Cinema', *Sight and Sound* (March), 15.
20 Ibid., 16.

The marked difference in their positions – Alice the woman/child in need of protection and Hire the would-be controller of events – is clearly evident in the scene in the basement of the building where Alice and Emile have gone to watch a boxing match. A subjective shot from Hire's position in the doorway shows Alice huddled in the dark, her knees pulled up under her chin, a posture which suggests that of a small child. Most of the wide screen space is taken up by the basement wall, while Alice herself is pushed to the extreme right of the frame; her crouched position and the fact that she is filmed in long-shot clearly diminish her stature. It is the perfect opportunity for Hire to act out his fantasy of assuming control for his and Alice's future. Speaking with the disapproval of a real father, he tells Alice: 'Ce type ne vous mérite pas' [That guy doesn't deserve you]'. He then reveals his plans for their future, plans that, incidentally, fail to take any account of Alice's possible wishes and desires. Hire can only conceive of the future in terms of his actions and Alice's passive response. His attitude is a true reflection of the prevalent dominance/submission patterns that structure our culture and ideology, and within which woman occupies the latter position. Turning to Lacanian theory, Kaplan describes how this positioning evolves:

> The girl is forced to turn away from the illusory unity with the Mother in the prelinguistic realm and has to enter the symbolic world which involves subject and object. Assigned the place of object (lack), she is the recipient of male desire, passively appearing rather than acting. Her sexual pleasure in this position can thus be constructed only around her own objectification. [21]

1c) The essay illustrates the theoretical point made by using a concrete example taken from the film; this example will serve as the turning point between male dominance and female submission. In this section, the essay will, once again, refer to theoretical work so as to justify the general statements made about female submission, taking account towards the end of the final paragraph of the section of a possible objection, that Alice in fact controls Hire. That objection will be all the more readily dismissed by the following section on the Inspector.

---

21 Kaplan, E.A., op. cit., 26.

Referring to Nancy Friday's volumes, which collect together women's sexual fantasies, Kaplan shows how women construct for themselves a submissive, often masochistic role, and goes on to conclude that they have come to regard their position as 'to-be-looked-at' as sexually pleasurable. It is an issue that is brought sharply into focus by Alice herself when she tells Hire: 'C'est agréable d'être regardée. J'y prends du plaisir [It's nice to be looked at. I take pleasure in it.]' Whether a statement of fact, or a calculated ruse to force Hire to reveal what he knows about the crime, these words bring about a definite change in the way we are invited to consider Alice's character: initially the unwitting object of Hire's attentions, she is now aware of her position *vis-à-vis* the gaze and is willing to exploit her sexuality in response to it. Alice's visit to Hire's building, where she drops a bag of tomatoes down the stairs by his front door, is portrayed as a clear case of exhibitionism. As she proceeds to gather the tomatoes she leans forward provocatively, even brushing against the stupefied Hire as she reaches through his legs. In the scene that follows, Alice allows Emile to go on caressing and undressing her, even though she knows they are being watched, thus engineering the spectacle for Hire's benefit. However, Alice's ability to return the gaze in this way offers no positive alternative to the dominance/submission patterns outlined above for, as Kaplan argues with specific reference to Howard Hawks' *Gentlemen Prefer Blondes*, a woman's exploitation of her sexuality is *not* a sign of liberation.[22] Alice's control of narrative events is limited since Hire's final note to the Inspector foils her plans to frame him for the murder and her manipulations are geared towards her own submission to another man. For Alice's goal is to protect a relationship in which she clearly occupies a masochistic position, as she is well aware when she tells Emile: 'C'est pas grave si tu m'aimes qu'un peu, parce que

---

22 Ibid., 32–3.

moi, je t'aime pour deux [Don't worry if you only love me a bit, because I love you enough for both of us.]'

The notion of the male as dominant and the female as submissive is reinforced in a film in which the male figure as owner of the desire, a desire that is 'pinned to the actual process of investigation/scrutiny',[23] appears not once but twice, for Monsieur Hire and the Inspector are in fact two sides of the same coin.[24] Both are middle-aged unmarried men, one frustrated emotionally, the other professionally, and it is interesting to note how each is quick to perceive the other's weak point: 'A votre âge, ça doit pas être facile d'être un simple inspecteur [At your age it can't be easy to be no more than an inspector]' remarks Hire cynically on his first meeting with the Inspector, who in turn cannot resist goading Hire during one of their subsequent encounters: 'Dites-moi, Monsieur Hire, ça fait combien de temps que vous n'avez pas joui dans une femme? [Tell me, Monsieur Hire, how long is it since you last came inside a woman?]'

Each man's obsession with a younger woman (Hire with Alice and the Inspector with Pierrette) goes beyond the bounds of conventional romantic love and professional interest respectively, and is inextricably bound up with his strong voyeuristic tendencies. Hire, an amateur voyeur, literally cannot resist the urge to spy on Alice: 'Je vous ai d'abord regardée par hasard, et puis très vite, je n'ai pas pu détacher les yeux de votre fenêtre [I looked at you first of all by chance, and very quickly, I couldn't take my eyes off your window]', and this infatuation will ultimately lead to his destruction. The Inspector, on the other hand is, like Scottie in *Vertigo*, a voyeur by profession who, in

1d) In congruence with the major thrust of this first part of the essay, this section reinforces the notion of male domination by showing how Hire is doubled by the Inspector as a powerful 'gazer'. By the end of this section, then, the essay will have argued powerfully that Hire is a typically powerful voyeuristic male.

23 Kuhn, A. (1985) *The Power of the Image. Essays on Representation and Sexuality* (Routledge & Kegan Paul), 30.
24 '(L'Inspecteur) est aussi bizarre que Monsieur Hire et pourrait être en un sens, son double. Il est pareil, n'a pas de femme, vit seul . . . Lorsqu'il arrête Monsieur Hire, c'est en quelque sorte, par lassitude' [The Inspector is as weird as Monsieur Hire and could in a way be his double. He is the same, isn't married, lives alone. . . . When he arrests Monsieur Hire it's in a way through tiredness.] *L'Avant-Scène Cinéma* 390/391 (Mars/Avril 1990), 10.

his capacity as pursuer and investigator, is in a position to satisfy his scopic drives.[25] This is evident in the morgue scene in which the Inspector photographs Pierrette's corpse with a small pocket camera, presumably for his personal gratification – and also a little further on when, as part of his investigation, he seems to take pleasure in recreating, at least twice, an event of the night of the crime, staging it as spectacle with Monsieur Hire in the central role.[26]

This particular incident raises several important questions. How secure is Monsieur Hire's position of dominant specularity? And how far can the audience identify with him as spectator-within-the-text when, at key moments in the film (the display at the bowling alley, the reconstruction of the night of the crime, the fall at the ice rink and, most importantly, the final roof top scene), Hire is displaced as viewing subject and becomes instead the object of the gaze?

1e) The reader is thus all the more surprised by the calling into question of this classic position in the final paragraphs of the first part, and suggesting that Hire in fact occupies the position taken by the woman as object of the gaze. The essay recaps the classic argument before stating clearly that it will move on to question it in the second major part.

As I have argued above, textual operations such as extreme close-ups of Monsieur Hire, and the film's reproduction of dominance/submission patterns, tend to favour the male characters while relegating Alice to the margins of discourse by objectifying and infantilising her. I would now however like to consider ways in which this particular text manages, at the same time, to bring into question the superiority of the male position in relation to the gaze.

According to Mulvey: 'It is the place of the look that defines cinema, the possibility of varying it and exposing it. This is what makes cinema quite different in its voyeuristic potential from, say, strip-tease, theatre,

2a) The first part of the counterargument focuses on complicating the simplistic equation male

---

25 'Scottie's voyeurism is blatant: he falls in love with a woman he follows and spies on without speaking to. His sadistic side is equally blatant. He has chosen (and freely chosen for he had been a successful lawyer) to be a policeman, with all the attendant possibilities of pursuit and investigation.' Mulvey, L., op. cit., 313.
26 I make this claim based on the fact that the camera used seems to be the Inspector's own – it is certainly not a piece of professional equipment – and also because, as the audience knows, Pierrette's body has already been photographed for official purposes at the scene of the crime.

shows, etc.' [27] As a defining characteristic of cinema, this 'exposing' and more particularly this 'varying' of the look is crucial to the narrative of *Monsieur Hire* and its questioning of male visual pleasure. For what Leconte has in fact created is a complicated network of look and gazes, described by Claude Beylie as 'un univers de regards glacés' a universe of cold looks,[28] which establishes Hire's gaze, whatever narrative importance it may carry, as only one amongst many. Hire inhabits a world in which everyone, it seems, is trying to dominate or entrap somebody else, either through a voyeuristic process of investigation and scrutiny, or else by exhibitionistically playing to the look. His position as the most privileged spectator within the text is, therefore, more apparent than real.[29]

In at least one important respect Hire is less privileged than the Inspector, for it is the latter who effectively frames the whole film with his investigation of Pierrette's murder. It is the Inspector who, through the privileged discourse of a voice-over, tells us of the murder that has taken place prior to the film's opening and it is his act of reading Hire's note in the final scene that gives us access to the latter's commentary. However, my point is *not* that one privileged male discourse (Hire's) is simply usurped by another (the Inspector's), for ambiguities surrounding the presentation of the Inspector's character serve to undermine and question his own position as a figure of authority.

Hire's position of dominant specularity is further undermined by the fact that he is consistently set up as

= voyeur, female = object of voyeur, by reprising the points made at the end of the previous part: Hire is both subject and object, and is one gaze amongst many; amongst the many being the Inspector, which reprises the point about the doubling between Hire and the Inspector, suggesting that here too things are not so simple, since the Inspector is more powerful than Hire. By picking up points from the previous part of the essay and showing how they are more complex than initially presented helps to bind the essay's argument together more tightly.

2b) The major point of this second part of the

---

27 Mulvey, L., op. cit., 314.

28 Beylie, C. (1990) *L'Avant-Scène Cinéma* 390/391 (Mars/Avril), p. 4.

29 The notion of a power more apparent than real is captured by the film's much commented upon image of the voyeur at his window on the night of the storm. While the camera registers Alice's shock and fear in close-up, the cause of her alarm is portrayed as distant by cutting to an extreme long-shot of Monsieur Hire at his window. For the spectator at least, who is used to seeing Hire in extreme close-up, his status is somewhat diminished.

spectacle, not only in the literal sense as something to be 'looked at', but as spectacle in the additional sense of the word, i.e. as a distraction, entertainment or a digression from mundane, everyday reality. This point is underlined by the clearly artificial, almost theatrical lighting that dominates in certain key scenes. During the reconstruction of the night of the crime for example, the three key 'players' – Monsieur Hire, the Inspector and the taxi driver – as well as the small crowd that has gathered, are bathed in saturated reddish-orange tones and this reinforces the notion of an event that has been 'staged', doubly staged in fact: in the first place by the director Leconte, and within the confines of the text by the Inspector.

The lighting in this scene prefigures that of the bowling alley, where the same reddish hues dominate and where, since Hire is quite literally 'performing' for a crowd,[30] the link between performance and artificiality of lighting is no longer merely suggested but clearly underlined. Although in this particular instance Hire's objectification is a direct result of his willingness to exhibit himself, at other times it is indicative of a loss of control and of his inability to preserve his anonymity.

This loss of anonymity is important, for the sense of superiority that Hire derives from spying on his young neighbour rests precisely, and precariously, on the condition of his not being seen. As soon as Alice returns the gaze, the cloak of anonymity that shields Monsieur Hire vanishes, as does the illusion of power. Only when Alice is afraid, as she is on the night of the storm, does Hire have the courage to remain at his observation post, but as she becomes emboldened and

essay is that Hire is an object of the gaze too. This point is first made by exploring two key sequences in the film, before being underlined by the point that Alice returns Hire's gaze. This point, it will be remembered, was already made but dismissed in the first part; here it returns supported by different evidence (Hire as object of various spectacles) and thus finds its natural place in the argument.

---

30 Hire's blatant exhibitionism is not necessarily at odds with his voyeuristic tendencies. Freud clearly states in his *Three Essays On Sexuality* that: 'whenever we find in the unconscious an instinct of this sort which is capable of being paired off with an opposite one, this second instinct will regularly be found in operation as well. Every active perversion is thus accompanied by its passive counterpart: anyone who is an exhibitionist in his unconscious is at the same time a voyeur.', in Richards, A. (ed.) (1991) *On Sexuality* (Harmondsworth: Penguin), 81.

defiantly returns the gaze, Hire can only retreat behind the wall of his apartment, visibly threatened by this assault on a privilege he had doubtless come to regard as being exclusively his – exclusively male.

However, it is principally by portraying Monsieur Hire and the Inspector as highly ambiguous, even morally dubious, characters that this film undermines the dominant masculine position.

This questioning of male authority is especially apparent in the portrayal of the Inspector, for he is after all, supposed to represent the Law. Claude Baignères described him as 'un policier peu crédible' [a not very believable policeman][31] and few would disagree with this statement. His appearance alone actively works against our acceptance of him as a credible figure of responsibility and authority. His unkempt hair and 'unusual' dress sense (he sports the same duffel coat, yellow shirt and blue jumper throughout the film), make him the very antithesis of the suited, although equally dubious, Monsieur Hire. He is, like James Stewart's Scottie in *Vertigo,* a professional voyeur, a paid investigator, but even this official capacity fails to lend respectability to his strong scopic drives and he seems in many respects as suspicious as his chief suspect.

His behaviour in the morgue, for example, leaves the spectator with a very definite sense of unease. Even though we are not yet aware of his identity, there already seems to be something disturbing about André Wilms' playing of the scene 'comme s'il était le père de la jeune morte' [as if he were the father of the dead girl].[32] While wondering if the unidentified man is indeed the girl's father, one cannot help but be

2c) This section, like the previous one, picks up on a point made in part 1 of the essay – that the Inspector is a sort of double of Hire himself – and develops the point to show how this undermines the moral authority the powerful voyeuristic gaze might have had.

---

31 Baignères, C., 'L'homme de marbre', *Le Figaro* (22 Mai 1989), in *L'Avant-Scène Cinéma* 390/391 (Mars/Avril 1990), 76.
32 From the director's notes, *L'Avant-Scène Cinéma* 390/391, 11.

aware of the understated eroticism that pervades the whole scene. The Inspector clasps Pierrette's hands tightly, very slowly leans towards her as if about to kiss her, while all the time his intense gaze suggests a morbid fascination, if not attraction, towards the young girl. When he takes out a small pocket camera to photograph the corpse, his voyeurism becomes all the more alarming, suggestive even of a latent necrophilic tendency.

In the course of his investigation of Monsieur Hire, the Inspector continues to discredit himself, and his sadistic streak comes to the fore as he taunts the suspect about his sex life, reminds him of a murky past (six months in jail for indecent exposure), even becoming violently aggressive at one point as he presses Hire up against a wall after the boxing match. Ultimately, however, for all the power inherent in his male gaze and for all that he is given access to information and actual locations (such as the scene of the crime, the morgue, the homes of victims and suspects) closed off to the general public, the Inspector cannot solve the crime. Not only that, but he is also duped by Alice – he fails, that is, to 'see' the truth.

We come to see the Inspector as, literally, another face in the crowd, no longer a privileged and controlling spectator, but a passive, even impotent one. He can only watch on helplessly, along with those around him as Monsieur Hire falls to his death.

The film's central ambiguity, however, is that which surrounds the eponymous Monsieur Hire. He is an amalgam of disparate traits,[33] a fact reflected in the way the film is pieced together out of brief elliptical

2d) The issue of moral ambiguity developed for the Inspector returns in a different form for the

---

33 In an interview with *Independent*, Leconte described Hire as resembling 'Nosferatu, with a smattering of Peter Lorre' *(Independent* (6 April 1990); Peter Gutteridge finds Hire to be 'both repellent and sympathetic' *(The Times,* 26 April 1990); and Gérard Lenne compares him to folkloric monsters such as King Kong and the Phantom of the Opera, who are persecuted to such an extent that we sympathise with them *(Revue du Cinéma,* Juin 1989, 12).

scenes. For Julie Phillips,[34] Hire's eclectic nature undermines not only his subjective position within the text but the very integrity of the text itself. The aura of ambiguity that surrounds Monsieur Hire clearly sets him up as an enigmatic figure, whose demystification and final punishment, like that of the strong female protagonists in the Hollywood *film noir*, constitute the main narrative goal. By establishing Hire himself as the mystery to be solved and by frequently objectifying him, the film actually places him in the feminine position in relation to the male scrutinising gaze.

analysis of Hire. The essay cleverly suggests that Hire's enigmatic side makes him more like the *femme fatale* of film noir. This point might have seemed out of place earlier in the essay; the parallel with the Inspector has made this point a logical outcome of the argument, however provocative it might seem in itself.

Monsieur Hire initially sets up the gaze as male but only to bring into question the existing structures of looking in the cinema, which are based on the active/male, passive/female dichotomy. It plays with the 'socially established interpretation of sexual difference'[35] by positioning Hire as both active subject and passive object of the gaze, as both exploiter and victim.

Nevertheless it is questionable whether the film moves beyond a simple reversal of gender roles, which after all does not fundamentally alter the traditional patterns of dominance and submission. One of the film's final shots shows Alice standing at Monsieur Hire's window, in exactly the same spot from where he used to spy on her for hours on end. Only now, however, the tables are cruelly turned as Alice watches Hire fall to his death. The film closes as it opens – with a mystery to be solved. Could the female gaze replace the male gaze in cinema? And could this transformation bring about a qualitative change in the way we experience films and relate to representations of sexuality?

The conclusion briefly restates the main argument, that the traditional view of the male gaze has been questioned in this film. It finishes with a flourish, questioning whether strongly entrenched cultural and viewing habits could be changed; in other words, it evaluates the success of the argument.

---

34 Phillips, J. (1990) 'Monsieur Hire', *Village Voice* (24 April), 66.
35 Mulvey, L., op. cit., 305.

SEQUENCE ANALYSIS

We mean by sequence analysis the close and detailed analysis of a segment of film that functions as a distinct narrative unit. This could broadly be defined as the filmic equivalent of a chapter in a novel, or a scene in a play. Sequence analyses can frequently be found in articles or books on French cinema. A recent example is a university textbook by Francis Vanoye and Anne Goliot-Lété (1992), which takes the reader systematically through sequence analysis, as well as the analysis of a whole film; unfortunately, for our purposes, the films analysed are not French.[36] Calqued from the French literary tradition of the *explication de texte* (analysis of a literary passage), sequence analyses were developed mainly during the 1970s by film academics, as was explained in Chapter 2, and have remained a staple of Film Studies in the French arena.

AN APPROACH TO SEQUENCE ANALYSIS

In this brief introduction, we will cover the following questions.

- Why is a sequence analysis useful?
- How can a sequence analysis be selected?
- How long should a sequence be?
- What form should it take?

WHY IS A SEQUENCE ANALYSIS USEFUL?

During the 1990s, several publishers have brought out series on individual films. Whereas the British Film Institute (BFI) series 'Film Classics' and 'Modern Classics' both include French films,[37] neither has a standard format, reflecting the fact that both series are intended to address the film buff as well as the film student. In France, however, the Paris-based publisher Nathan, one of the several publishers working in the university market, brought out, as one of its film series, a series called 'Synopsis', intended specifically for film students. These are short 130–page handbooks,[38] with a standardised format:

- the life and films of the director
- the credits of the film to which the handbook is devoted

---

36 Alfred Hitchcock's *Rebecca* (1940) and Theo Angelopoulos's *Topio stin omichli/Landscape in the Mist* (1988).
37 At the time of writing (September 2001), these are *L'Argent* and *The Three Colours Trilogy* in the 'Modern Classics'; *Boudu Saved From Drowning, L'Age d'Or, L'Atalante, La Nuit américaine, Les Enfants du paradis, Napoléon* and *Pépé le Moko* in the 'Film Classics'.
38 The following handbooks have appeared since the late 1980s (French films only are listed): *À bout de souffle, A nos amours, Les Enfants du paradis, La Grande illusion, Hiroshima mon amour, Jules et Jim, Le Mépris, Mon Oncle, Les Parapluies de Cherbourg, Partie de campagne, Les 400 coups, La Règle du jeu, Un chien andalou/L'Âge d'or.*

- the historical and social context
- the credits
- the synopsis
- a detailed breakdown of the sequences in the film (what is known as a '*découpage*')
- the structure of the narrative
- the characters and the themes
- detailed analysis of two or more sequences
- critical views
- glossary
- bibliography

The sequence analyses therefore come at a point when the reader has considerable knowledge of the film; it is for this reason that we preface the analysis in each case with a brief synopsis and contextualisation. Sequence analysis is used as a kind of close-up on the way the film works at all levels. It is intrinsically a useful exercise, because it allows very detailed work to be done on the film, teasing out issues of *mise-en-scène*, cinematography and soundtrack, and thereby helping the film student to develop a deep, as opposed to superficial, visual and aural awareness. It is also often a useful way of illustrating some of the main points made in the course of an essay, helping the writer to pinpoint issues of style, characterisation, narrative and so on, which might have been discussed in more general terms as part of an essay's argument.

HOW CAN A SEQUENCE ANALYSIS BE SELECTED?

We will not discuss the issue of how one decides what forms a sequence. This was debated thoroughly during the 1960s by Christian Metz, as was explained in Chapter 2. In practice, the selection of a sequence of film for analysis can be determined, often intuitively, by specific cues such as an obvious lapse in time in the narrative, a substantive change of location or an aural cue such as a change in the non-diegetic music. None of these cues in themselves, or even taken together, necessarily signal what could be defined as a new sequence, which is why intuition is often the best guide, supported by the evidence provided by cues of this kind.

HOW LONG SHOULD A SEQUENCE BE?

Sequences, as Metz showed in the 1960s, can be of very different lengths and types. When choosing a sequence for analysis, it may be worth remembering that a very short sequence of, say, one or two minutes, may not yield enough material for a sustained argument. Conversely, a long sequence of, say, 15 minutes may well yield too much material. In practice our experience over the years has been that the optimal length for a sequence for detailed analysis is somewhere between 7 and 12 minutes.

WHAT FORM SHOULD IT TAKE?

We would recommend the practice, laborious though it may be, of detailed transcription of the image-track and soundtrack, what the French call *découpage*. One example of what this may look like can be found in the series published by *L'Avant-Scène du Cinéma*, an invaluable resource for students of French cinema (although the series has films other than French as well). These look like screenplays, with a detailed transcription of numbered shots, dialogue, camera and character movement (and, as an added benefit, usually contain substantial articles on the film and a review of reviews of the film). Another way of presenting a sequence analysis is in a tabular format, containing numbered shots, a description of their content, transcribed dialogue, and additional material when necessary, such as descriptions of the soundtrack, or cinematographic points of interest.

A second issue to do with the form of a sequence is that it may often be useful to compare material. In the sequences analyses that follow, we give two types of comparative sequence analysis. The first is to compare the film sequence with its equivalent in a source text, such as a novel; the second is to do the same with another film, particularly when the film chosen for analysis is a remake.

The key issue is that both of these formats encourage close viewing of and listening to the sequence, unlike the more general superficial awareness typical of a first-time viewing. It is often on the basis of such detailed empirical work that an analysis may be constructed, because it makes us more aware of patterns, repetitions and emphatic camerawork requiring comment.

LE JOUR SE LÈVE (MARCEL CARNÉ, 1939)

In *Le Jour se lève*, one of the great films from the French Poetic Realist tradition, Jean Gabin plays François, a worker in a sand-blasting factory, who has murdered Valentin (Jules Berry) because the latter had taunted him over François's girl-friend, Françoise (Jacqueline Laurent). He has holed up in his hotel bedroom, where he ruminates during the night on the events that led up to the murder. In this sequence (which is approximately six minutes long), the third hotel room sequence, the day has dawned and he addresses the crowd that has gathered below his hotel – Françoise, and his friends Gaston and Paulo arriving a little later with Clara (Arletty), also betrayed by Valentin, and in love with François.

In the column headed 'Camera' there are abbreviations for a variety of camera movements:

PR	pan right
PL	pan left
DF	dolly forwards
DB	dolly back
TU	tilt up
CU	crane up
CB	crane back

	Description of shot	Camera	Dialogue
1	Wardrobe (DISSOLVE)		
2	François in corner staring		
3	Brooch (close-up)		
4	François throws brooch out of window	PR/TU PL	
5	WIPE to building exterior		
6	François paces, lights cigarette, smashes mirror	PR PL DF/PR PL	
7	François walks to window	DB	
8	Sunrise		
9	Crowd/building (high angle)	TU	
10	François opens window (long shot; low angle)		
11	Crowd looks up (long shot; high angle)		
12	François at window (medium shot)		
13	Pair of individuals in crowd		
14	Different pair of individuals in crowd		
15	Different pair of individuals in crowd		
16	François (same as 12)		François: What are you looking at? What are you staring at, all of you? Eh?
17	Individuals of shot 13		Individuals: What's up with him? He's gone mad!
18	Individuals of shot 14		Individuals: Is he going to jump?

	Description of shot	Camera	Dialogue
19	Blind man in group		Blind man: What's going on? Individual: He's at his window. Blind man: But what's going on, eh?
20	François		François: I'm not a strange animal me. What are you waiting for? Ah, you're waiting for me to jump, ha! A murderer. Ah, now that's interesting isn't it, a murderer. I am a murderer. Yes, I'm a murderer. But murderers are everywhere! Everywhere! Everybody kills. Everybody kills a little bit, but they kill on the quiet, so you don't see it. It's like the sand, inside you, here inside you . . .
21	Crowd (long shot)		So just bugger off.
22	François		Bugger off. Go away. Go back home. You'll read about it in the papers, it'll be in print, everything will be in print . . .
23	Man in crowd (close-up)		. . . And you'll read it . . .
24	Woman in crowd (close-up)		. . . and you'll . . .
25	Youth in crowd (close-up)		. . . believe it . . .
26	François		Because you can find everything in the papers, they're jolly well informed. So bugger off, you're going to catch cold . . .
27	Couple at window (long shot)		. . . Go on, clear off . . .
28	Woman at window		
29	Different woman at window, F in background		. . . Leave me alone . . .
30	Building (extreme long shot)		. . . Alone you hear . . .
31	François		. . . I'm not asking anything from anyone, I just want to be left . . .

	Description of shot	Camera	Dialogue
32	Françoise arrives	CU/CB	. . . alone. Françoise: François. François.
33	François		François: Oh I'm tired, leave me alone . . .
34	Françoise, Gaston, Paulo (match on 32)		Group of friends: François. François.
35	François		François: I no longer trust anyone. It's over, over, you hear.
36	Françoise, Gaston, Paulo		Gaston: François, don't stay up there, there's no point.
37	Men in crowd		François: There are people who have killed other people. They haven't died as a result. Men: Come down, we can talk about it afterwards.
38	François		François: Hey, you lot, there's a job going, a good little job in my good little factory, with overtime. So go on, what are you waiting for? Happiness, a nice little lot of happiness.
39	Françoise, Gaston, Paulo		Paulo: François you ought to come down, we could sort something out.
40	François		François: What do you mean François? What François? There's no François any more. Don't know him, there's no François anywhere, anywhere, so leave me alone, bugger off, go away, leave me in peace.
41	Crowd		Voices: François, we know you, you're a good bloke . . . Don't dig your heels in . . . We'll speak up for you . . . Come on, come down, it's no good.
42	Crowd		(General hubbub)

	Description of shot	Camera	Dialogue
43	Three policemen		Policemen: So what do we do . . . We wait, that's orders.
44	Crowd		(General hubbub)
45	Arrival of riot police	PR PL	
46	Riot police get out of lorry (low angle)		
47	Riot police line up in front of crowd		
48	Ranks of riot police		
49	Riot police push crowd back		(General hubbub)
50	Crowd (high angle)		
51	François (long shot; low angle)		
52	Françoise, Gaston, Paulo pushed back	TU/PR	
53	Clara, Gaston, Paulo take Françoise to Clara's room	DB/PR PR	Paulo: She's fallen down, she probably knocked her head . . . We can't go leave her there . . . Clara: That's fine, take her up to my room. Hotel owner: Hey, where are you going, where are you going? Clara: She's hurt. Owner: Yes, but this isn't a hospital.
54	François on bed		
55	Wardrobe (DISSOLVE)	DF	

Amongst the important features of this sequence, two in particular stand out: first, the use of glass and the mirror; second, the three-pronged relationship between François, the crowd, and the authorities represented by the policemen and riot the police.

André Bazin wrote of the importance of glass in the film, pointing out how it could function as a metaphor for François' situation:

Glass is transparent but also reflects, both loyal, because you can see through it, and deceptive, because it separates you, and dramatic because if

> you forget about it it breaks and brings you bad luck; glass seems to
> comprise all the elements of François's drama. (Bazin, 1983: 62)

Small wonder, then, that both the glass of the window and the glass of the mirror are in this sequence shattered. François' face is framed in both. It is framed expressionistically with chiaroscuro lighting effects in the window (shot 7), suggesting a brooding caged beast, his world shattered as he remembers that Françoise, whom he believed to be pure and untainted by the mire of this world, has turned out to be Valentin's ex-lover; hence his fury as he throws the brooch out of the window (shots 3–4), since it represents Valentin and his lies to both Françoise and Clara, another ex-lover. The mirror functions as a device to tell François' 'story', with its photographs slipped into the frame, and the baubles propped against it on the mantelpiece. These were meaningless at the beginning of the film, but are invested with meaning by the time of this sequence, because we have seen where they came from. It is no surprise then that François should shatter the mirror (shot 6), caught in a moment of helpless anger in its frame as he destroys the 'old', gullible François who still believed in something. It is as if he were destroying his past in readiness for self-immolation, as Thiher points out:

> [The mirror] is quickly shattered by the gunfire and can then reflect only a
> distorted image corresponding to the shattered world that lies about
> François. In it François sees himself both as he is and, metaphorically, as a
> destroyed being. It is thus not surprising that he should finally smash the
> mirror in anger, which is on one level an attempt to abolish this image of
> himself and, on another level, an act that analogically foreshadows his
> suicide. The shattered mirror contains within itself the contradiction of the
> tragic circle that leads to self-destruction as the only release from tragic
> awareness. (Thiher, 1979: 124)

Bazin too speaks of this film as a tragedy, and points out how the crowd acts as a veritable Greek chorus, commenting on the action. The crowd has a more important role to play than mere comment, however. It frames François too, but very differently from the mirror and the window. This is not hard glass, but human beings, shown to have feelings by Carné, who carefully isolates individuals at key moments of François' oration. At first, the crowd is hostile; the gaze of individuals is silent, and the crowd is seen mostly in long shot, at a considerable distance from François. This is exacerbated by Alexandre Trauner's décor, comprising an excessively tall apartment block and a claustrophobic hotel bedroom. Bazin points out how the hotel is not realistic at all, set apart as it is from other buildings, and its excessive height emphasised by an unnaturally tall lamp-post; and Carné himself, in his autobiography, explains how the hotel bedroom was constructed as a kind of box; once the (real) bullets had destroyed the only exits (window and door), the only way in and out was by ladder.

The feeling of distance and claustrophobia thus generated is gradually dismantled by dialogue, cutting across François' oration. Dialogue between François and the crowd is introduced by an intermediary group, Françoise accompanied by François' friends, Gaston and Paulo, with a crane up signalling the breaking down of the hostility previously established. It is at this point that individuals, instead of commenting on his state of mind (as, for example, in shots 17–18), or just simply staring at him, begin to encourage him. The empathy generated between François and the crowd – after all, as the dialogue makes clear, they are like him, working people, who understand his resentment at working conditions and the fear of unemployment – carries a specific political purpose, as can be seen by the intro-duction of the riot police, who push back the murmuring crowd. They are clearly set up as repressive, partly by their contrast with the more individual and indecisive *gendarmes*, partly by the low camera angle that magnifies the threat they represent, the tramping of the feet in leather boots and the barked orders.

What seems to be gestured at here is a feeling of loss, almost of despair. All of the gains made by the left-wing coalition of the Popular Front government had been lost. The then innovative 40–hour working week had been suspended, there had been tax increases, a general strike had failed and, of course, war was approaching. Small wonder then that François, as his name suggests, the typical Frenchman, had revolted against his destiny, killing Valentin, the representative, as Jules Berry had also been in Renoir's *Le Crime de Monsieur Lange* (1936), of a dissolute and repres-sive bourgeoisie. Small wonder too that the narrative, brooding and inward-looking with its three increasingly urgent flashbacks (three months ago, one month ago, and the night before when François had killed Valentin), leads implacably to suicide as the only option.

37°2 LE MATIN (JEAN-JACQUES BEINEIX, 1986), AKA BETTY BLUE

This cult film from the 1980s is about a failed writer, Zorg, and his relationship with Betty, something of a rebel, who encourages him to write. She tries to have a baby and fails, eventually gouging her eye out and becoming catatonic, at which point Zorg kills her. The sequence is taken from early on in the film when Betty has moved into Zorg's beach house. Zorg, who works as an odd job man, has been asked by the owner of the beach houses to paint them all so as to earn his and

Betty's keep. Betty thinks painting is great fun, but revolts when she understands what the owner has asked Zorg to do.

Jean-Jacques Beineix came to prominence with his first film, *Diva* (1981), which has been called the first French postmodern film. Beineix's film style was much criticised, along with Besson's, during the 1980s, for its apparent superficiality and its tendency to prefer style over message.

	Description of shot	Camera	Dialogue
1	Zorg carries paint	DB	Zorg (voice-over): 500 bungalows, 500 façades, 1500 sides, thousands of shutters. Just a few odds and ends. Georges: Is it true that the two of you are going to paint all those houses by yourselves? You should paint the people too. Zorg: Listen, Georges, that's not what I'm going to do, but you just shut it, OK. Georges: Shit, are you mad at me? Zorg: How did you guess? I don't want you to speak about this in front of Betty, OK? Go on, go play your sax on the beach.
2	Zorg walks to house	DF	Betty: Hey, you could be a bit nicer. I was just explaining to these really nice people how we're going to paint their house.
3	Betty walks to Zorg	DF	Betty: What about me, what do I do? Zorg: You paint the shutters, and I'll paint around them. Here you are. Betty: Why are you sulking? Zorg: I'm not sulking at all. Betty: The first one to finish helps the other one?
4	Climb ladders		
5	Betty		Betty: Ready.
6	Old couple	Low angle	Woman: My God, I hope she doesn't fall. Man: Of course she won't, she's young.
7	Betty	Low angle	(Sax starts; to shot 21, except shot 14)
8	Betty and Zorg	Extreme low angle	

	Description of shot	Camera	Dialogue
9	Zorg	Extreme low angle	
10	Georges		
11	Betty and Zorg	Extreme low angle	Betty: Ready. Zorg: Bravo. Betty: I'll have a go at the wall. Zorg: OK, that's fine, have a go at the wall.
12	Old couple	Low angle	
13	Georges		
14	Betty and Zorg on ground	DF	Zorg: Shit, what a job. (Sax stops) Shit, shit, shit. Ah, that's no good. Betty: What's the problem? Zorg: No, it's my fault, I should have told you. Look, here, on the angle, you've gone over. Betty: Well, just look at the size of the brushes. Zorg: I know, but the other wall looks as though it's been started, you see. Betty: But why do we give a shit? Zorg: Why do we give a shit? Betty: But you're not going to paint only one part of their house are you? What's the point? Zorg: Hey, you're really nice, so you're going to paint their place so it looks like new. Betty: But of course I am. Zorg: But of course. You're a champion painter. Betty: But what did you think? Zorg: Good, well, go on then, I'll hold the bucket.
15	Georges		(Sax starts again)
16	Merry-go-round (from inside Zorg's house)		
17	Horizon (from inside Zorg's house)		

	Description of shot	Camera	Dialogue
18	Sun setting		
19	Georges		
20	Beach houses (merry-go-round in foreground)		
21	Sun setting		(Sax stops)
22	Zorg's house and merry-go-round against sky		
23	Zorg		Betty: You ready?
24	Betty sets camera		Betty: Now.
25	Betty joins Zorg	DB	Betty: Smile. Hold the roller higher.
26	Camera	DF	
27	Betty and Zorg	DB	
28	Camera clicks	DF	
29	They look at photos		Betty: So? But it's a really good one. Zorg: No it isn't, I'm frowning, look. Betty: But why are you frowning? Zorg: I'm not frowning, I'm smiling on both of them. Betty: The other one's better isn't it? Let's do another one, just one last one. Zorg: No, come on, stop. You've already done 50, Betty.
30	Owner arrives		
31	Betty and Zorg		Zorg: Come along, I'll buy you a beer. Owner: Well well. Betty: What does that fat pig want?
32	Owner	DL DF/PR DR	Owner: Looks like you've been hard at it, ho ho. Betty: Of course we have, what do you think? Owner: You're great. Well, we'll see if you can keep it up. Betty: He just said something I didn't understand. Zorg: What? What did he say? He didn't say anything. Betty: What do you mean, keep it up?

Description of shot	Camera	Dialogue
		Owner: Well, don't you worry, my darling, I'm not asking you to do all this without taking a break, I'm not a monster, ho ho. Just carry on doing that, fanning yourself, it suits you.
		Betty: But what do you mean, finish all this?
		Owner: But the other bungalows of course.
		Betty: He's joking?
		Owner: But do I look like I'm joking?
		Betty: I'll tell you in 5 seconds.
		Zorg: Betty (she pours paint over the car).
		Owner: Hey, hey, you're mad.
		Betty: I don't mind painting your old banger too much. So don't you go listening to your pals if they say they don't like it. But as for the houses there, I don't feel like it.
		Owner: Hey, is she mad or what?
33 Zorg wipes car		Zorg: Look, a quick wipe, and it's as good as new.
34 Zorg wipes windscreen	DF	Zorg: There you are. You'll have to forgive her, she's on her period. And then there's the sodding wind, it makes you mad. I'm sure she's sorry. There you are. I'll paint the dustbins and pylons as well if you like.
		Owner: I couldn't give a shit about the pylons, arsehole.

SEGMENTATION USING METZ'S GRANDE SYNTAGMATIQUE

- **1–6** look like a **scene**, because the event is continuous. There are two slight ellipses, however, at 3/4 (position on the ladders), and 7/8 (Betty has painted more of the shutter in 8 than 7). This sequence is therefore, strictly speaking, an **ordinary sequence**.
- **7–15**: 7 inaugurates a new syntagma, as is suggested by the combination of 'representative' shots of the two protagonists with the use of low angles and the introduction of the saxophone on the soundtrack. The alternation of

the two protagonists/old couple in one location and Georges in another location suggests an **alternating syntagma**, i.e. simultaneity of two parallel actions. The problem lies in deciding where this syntagma ends. The alternation principle covers shots 7–15, but 15 might well be interpreted as the first shot of a new syntagma.

- **15–22** are a sequence of discontinuous shots whose meaning lies in their juxtaposition, in this case, 'the end of the day'. This would suggest an **episodic sequence**. It might be possible to call this a **descriptive syntagma** in that the music suggests chronological continuity; on the other hand, the visual images are not chronologically continuous.

- **14**: if shot 15 is seen mainly as the first shot of a new syntagma, then the long shot 14 might well be seen as an **autonomous shot**.

- **23–34** look like a **scene**, but the slight ellipsis that occurs at 28/29 makes this sequence, strictly speaking, an **ordinary sequence**. An alternative reading could be to separate 23–29 as an **ordinary sequence**, and to propose 30–34 as a **scene**. The problem with this analysis is that 22–34 clearly suggest continuity. The alternative readings are as presented in the table below:

Alternative 1		Alternative 2	
1–6	ordinary/scene	1–6	ordinary/scene
7–15	alternating	7–13	alternating
		14	autonomous
15–22	episodic/descriptive	15–22	episodic/descriptive
23–34	ordinary/scene	22–29	ordinary/scene
		30–34	scene

ANALYSIS

There are two main issues of interest in this sequence. The first is the way in which the sequence constructs a relatively simplistic rebellious character for Betty. The second is the use of colour and camera, characteristic of the *cinéma du look*, and much criticised because it was felt to be technique for the sake of technique rather than technique in support of the narrative.

Betty

This sequence recounts the second event in the narrative to signal Betty's refusal to be exploited, after the first one which was quitting her job to go and live with Zorg. The sequence, which focuses principally on her splashing pink paint all over the owner's car (shot 33), suggests both her rebellion and also that her rebellion will eventually be contained. Narratively, it is Betty's refusal that seems the stronger element. She has violently rejected the owner's demeaning task by throwing its means of implementation, the paint, all over his car, by rejecting the task verbally, and by walking away with an obscene gesture of defiance. The *mise-en-scène* emphasises her refusal by having her centre frame, dressed in contrasting black, signalling rejection. Moreover, she is placed against the vivid green of a distant garage door, the only other major area of colour in the frame. The spectator's eye is therefore drawn to her all the more. She seems the strongest character, particularly in relation to Zorg, who feebly tries to make amends for her behaviour.

However, the *mise-en-scène* also suggests containment, on the following three counts.

- **Frames:** Betty is contained by a multiplicity of pink frames and a solid area of pink (the car) in what seems an excessive use of the motif of framing.
- **Betty's size:** Although she is centre-frame, she is a small figure in relation to the disembodied Zorg, whose conciliatory action dominates the foreground.
- **Use of the car:** The car is a symbol of power and mobility (Zorg and Betty do not have a car, and will hitch a lift from the beach later in the narrative). The black of the Citroën echoes the black worn by Betty, and it is significant in this respect that the car is covered by the same pink that surrounds her everywhere. Her action could have been an expression of power, but by throwing pink paint over the black car, Betty, the *mise-en-scène* is suggesting, is being recuperated; her gesture is a gesture of futile impotence.

Although narratively she may dominate the action, the film constantly works to reduce her dominance, in this case by emphasising male solidarity and its attributes.

Colour and camera

During the 1980s, many critics commented unfavourably on Beineix's use of images, suggesting that they pandered to the immediate gratification of the spectator, both by virtue of their resemblance to advertising images (isolation of the object by, for example, the use of odd camera angles, and by the systematic use of clear light), and by their excessive and excessively calculated nature. The then editor of the *Cahiers du cinéma*, Serge Toubiana, commented in his review of the film, for example, that 'the old man with the sax is beautiful once, but three times and it's no more than a picture postcard image' (Toubiana, 1986: 80). The same point concerning excess could be made in relation to the merry-go-round with which the saxophonist is associated, since the sequence of shots illustrating the setting of the sun (15–21) seems articulated around the focal point of the merry-go-round, which appears in shots 16 and 20, shot from different angles. The repeated images are redundant to the plot; they serve rather to evoke a particular type of atmosphere, one of nostalgia (end of day, out of season). This is emphasised by the visually striking image of Georges playing his saxophone as he leans on the miniature car of the merry-go-round, conjuring up an image of lost childhood. Aesthetic redundance, repetitive excess, strongly contrasted images, and nostalgic atmosphere are all hallmarks of the advertising clip and music clip style.

The use of odd camera angles (different levels of low angles) in the painting sequence are another instance of excess, since they distort the narrative action of painting. It is significant that the saxophonist occurs in the same sequence. Indeed, the saxophone music starts at the same time as the more excessive low angles, turning the action into an example of a typical, indeed stereotypical, action of painting, as is emphasised by the ellipses, accompanying soundtrack and use of colour. The extreme nature of the low angles could also be said to distort the actors, who are diminished by the objects of their action – the bungalows and the paint.

In Ostria's opinion, the painting sequence lacks verisimilitude (see Ostria, 1986: 60). The beach houses are not dilapidated enough to justify the need to have them repainted. Moreover, the result seems, as he puts it, to come straight out of a painter's manual; indeed, the paint used is Valentine, a pointed reference to television adverts made for Valentine paints by Beineix. The sequence fails, he contends, because the gesture of revolt (Betty throwing paint on the owner's car) is too obviously 'aesthetic'; it draws too much attention to itself, its aestheticism neutralising the force of the gesture. But it is also too obvious a gesture anyway, a simplistic expression of youth's revolt against the older, more materialistic generation. It could also be said that the juxtaposition of pastel paint colours (blue and pink), and the vivid primary colours of the oil drum and the merry-go-round, is yet another gesture towards simplistic but essentially redundant aesthetic contrasts.

Ostria's comments do not address the dynamics of the use of colour, however. Zorg tends to be associated with his environment in ways in which Betty does not, and this is articulated by the use of colour. Zorg is dressed in the same yellow-coloured vest as the sand of the beach and the beach houses prior to their being painted, and his skin colour matches the pink he is applying to them. Betty applies blue paint, on the other hand, suggesting a type of role reversal, blue usually being applied to boys and pink to girls. The role reversal is emphasised by other colour elements, such as her black dungarees, which establish a contrast with her environment. It is significant in this respect that Betty throws pink paint over the black car, helping to suggest the way in which she rebels against authority in a very active and graphic way.

Similarly, the red and green of the merry-go-round is echoed by the red and green of the oil drum on which Betty places the camera. The significance of the colours here is that both Georges and Zorg, seen together at the beginning of the sequence, are immobile when placed against these colours. Betty, on the other hand, is seen running away from the oil drum after setting the camera, and articulating a gesture of defiance in shot 33 as she is framed against the vivid green of the garage doors of a distant bungalow. Betty is therefore presented as the more proactive character by the use of colour, suggesting that Beineix's use of colour is not as redundant as might have been thought by prominent critics at the time.

COMPARATIVE SEQUENCE ANALYSIS: *37°2 LE MATIN* (NOVEL BY PHILIPPE DJIAN/FILM BY JEAN-JACQUES BEINEIX)

In this sequence Zorg has just learned that Betty is pregnant as he was about to deliver a piano to a client. He rushes off with his friend Bob in a borrowed lorry, and gets caught in a speed trap by the young policeman Richard, whom he had crossed before in town. In the table that follows overleaf, the dialogue in the film has the original passage from the novel next to it in the far right-hand column. The sequence analysis which follows the table takes account of the sequence mainly from the point of view of its adaptation from the novel, showing how humour is an essential part of the sequence, and its relationship to issues of the law.

	Description of shot	Dialogue	Text of novel
1	Bob	Bob: Look, what's the matter? You don't look at all right, you're all pale.	I hopped in the car and drove out of town. On the street I counted twenty-five women with strollers. My throat was dry. I had trouble getting my mind around what was happening — it was an eventuality I'd never seriously considered. Images raced through my mind like rockets. To calm myself down, I concentrated on the drive. It was beautiful. I passed the cop car, I was going eighty. A minute later he stopped me. Richard again. He had nice teeth and straight. He took out a pad and a pen.
2	Zorg (reverse shot)	Zorg: Oh la la, Bob, we're really . . .	
3	Foot on brake	(Brakes screech)	
4	Pram crosses	Bob: Shit. Zorg: Have you noticed the number of women walking around with prams, Bobbie? Bob: Ah no, that one almost copped it. Zorg: No she didn't.	
5	Piano on lorry	Bob: Oh la la, look here, we're going uphill, don't force the gears, this lorry is running in. Zorg: Look, I'm not forcing anything, it's a turbo after all, shit. Bob: Ah it's a turbo, it's a turbo, you tell that to Momo.	
6	Lorry	(Birdsong; lorry in distance)	
7	Zorg and Bob in cab	Zorg: Listen, shit, I'm only doing 40. Bob: You're doing 40, you're doing 40, you're not doing 40, you're doing 80.	
8	Lorry passes police	Zorg: Well all right I'm doing 80, it's not that serious.	
9	Richard stops them	Zorg: Oh shit.	
10	Bob	Bob: Oi, are you sure you've got your licence?	
11	Zorg (reverse shot)	Zorg: What? No, not really.	

12	Richard stops them	(Engine stops)	
13	Same as 11	(Birdsong and goat bells until 21)	
14	Richard and Zorg	Zorg: How are you doing? Do you remember me?	
15	Richard and Zorg (reverse shot)	Richard: You're doing 100 kh in a vehicle with a speed limit of 60 kh. On a section of a road classed as a local road, which has a limit of 50 kh. It's a good start, a good start. All right. Your papers, vehicle check, the whole thing. Zorg: Look, I'm sorry, I was dreaming. Richard: Don't you worry about it, if I find that you've got one or two grams of alcohol, I'll bring you down to earth. Zorg: If that was all, officer, but I've just learned that I am a father.	'Every time I see this car I know it means I have a job to do,' he whined. I had no idea what he wanted me for – no idea of what I was even doing on this road. I smiled at him dubiously. Perhaps he had been standing there in the sun all day, ever since dawn. 'Maybe you think that changing your tire gives you the right to drive like a maniac ... ?' I shoved my index finger and thumb into the corners of my eyes. I shook my head. 'Jesus, I was somewhere else,' I sighed. 'Don't worry. If I find two or three grams of alcohol in your blood, I'll bring you right back down to earth.' 'If it was only that,' I said. 'I just found out I'm going to be a daddy!'
16	Bob (reaction shot)	Richard: Sorry? Zorg: Yes ...	He seemed to hesitate for a moment, then he closed his pad, with his pen stuck inside, and put it back in his shirt pocket. He
17	Richard (reverse shot)	Zorg: A dad. Richard: You wouldn't have a cigarette would you? Zorg: Yes of course.	leaned over to me. 'You wouldn't have a cigarette, would you?' he asked.
18	Zorg and Bob in cab	Zorg: Here you are.	I gave him one. Then he leaned against my door, puffing
19	Same as 16 (camera further back)	Richard: Fathers are the last adventurers of modern times.	peacefully, and told me all about his eight-month-old son, who had just started crawling across the

20	Bob	
21	Same as 20	Richard: And so you'll see the joy, the sorrows too, the sorrows. (He sings Yves Duteuil song) *Take a child by the hand/To take him to tomorrow/To give him confidence in his steps/ Take a*
22	Bob (same as 21)	*child for a king/*
23	Same as 20	*Take a child in your arms/ For the first time* (Music starts)
24	Lorry leaves	
25	Lorry in sunset	

living room on all fours, and all the various brands of formula, and the thousand-and-one joys of fatherhood. I almost dozed off during his lecture on nipples. Finally he winked at me and said he'd look the other way this time, that I could go. I went.

(Djian, 1989: 225)

Vincendeau has defined the *cinéma du look* as 'youth-oriented films with high production values. ... The "look" of the *cinéma du look* refers to the films' high investment in non-naturalistic, self-conscious aesthetics, notably intense colours and lighting effects. Their spectacular (studio-based) and technically brilliant *mise-en-scène* is usually put to the service of romantic plots' (Vincendeau, 1996: 50). Her brief sketch does not mention key elements in the *cinéma du look*. The first is the recourse to comedy, which in Beineix's films is tinged with derision and irony. Excessive humour is one of the hallmarks of this film, and one of the major ways in which Beineix changes the novel is by pushing its irony into frankly absurdist humour. The visual effects, so criticised by reviewers during the 1980s, are a key component for an absurdist humour that repositions the spectator in a *Verfremdungseffekt* grounded in derision. This undermines the law, in its literal sense of the policeman as representative of the law, and in its film-theoretical sense of the law of the narrative. Both underminings generate a sense of marginality that is important for spectator positioning and for Beineix's self-positioning outside of the establishment.

A second issue unspoken by Vincendeau is the attraction to community as a concept, counterbalanced by a strong sense of independence, which manifests itself as marginality in Beineix's characters. That marginality is tinged with a rebellious Oedipal streak, which is no doubt one of the major reasons why youth audiences are attracted to the films of Beineix and Besson. Another major reason is the strong erotic charge of their work, one of the features most commented on, whether in relation to what the characters do (one thinks of the long opening sequence of *37°2 le matin* where Zorg and Betty make passionate love), or the way in which Beineix's images are frequently calculated to seduce the spectator, as Vincendeau points out.

The issue of the seductive surface forms part of the debate on postmodern cinema in the 1980s. Beineix's work was seen by many French establishment critics as typifying the worst excesses of this postmodern cinema. The critics of the *Cahiers du cinéma* in particular developed a sustained polemic centering on the changing nature of the film image during the 1980s. A typical response to Beineix's work is that of Toubiana, the editor of the *Cahiers* since the 1980s, who complained of excessively obvious stylistic features, focusing on cinematography:

> He always goes for what is easiest, for what will give the spectator pleasure. His strong point is technique; he loves constructing shots, or rather *images*, moving his camera. Going for a high angle is something he finds difficult to

resist, opening the spectator's visual field onto a sunset or a beautiful landscape. It's his thing, his visitor's card, his taste for the 'look'. I am thinking of the lorry travelling on a country road, with the nice policeman waving in the background (a sequence which makes you think of the good times), or the burning house, with Betty and Zorg leaving, the camera zooming upwards. . . . His shots bear his signature too overtly ['sur-signés': 'over-signed' as in 'over-determined'], their excess is in the end unsettling. . . . The house in moonlight, the sunset on this Eldorado for a washed out writer who receives the body of a sexy girl like manna from heaven, or the old saxophonist are beautiful once, but after three times, they are no more than picture postcards. (Toubiana, 1986: 80)

The 'picture postcard' effect, for such critics, tended to overwhelm the message, so that the message becomes the medium. This attachment to surface image, moreover, collapses the human into the material: objects in Beineix's films, several critics complained, become more important than characters. Indeed, they assume a life of their own, typical of what happens in advertising, which promotes consumer objects rather than people. When we consider the use made of *Betty Blue* in Dulux's advertising campaign, we can perhaps see that there might be a point.

What this analysis does not do is to make the link between seduction and derision, which a confrontation between the original novel and the film can help us to do. Both male and female spectators are positioned, by identification with Betty and Zorg, outside the law, just as the film positions itself outside the law of 'consistent' narrative by its sudden bursts of absurdist humour. The singing policeman sequence is not only a good example of such absurdist humour, but the one preferred by Beineix himself, for whom it is clearly an element not just of disruption, but of subversiveness:

The basis of laughter is the moment when things go wrong. Take power; when power becomes excessive, it becomes ridiculous. But it's also when one you place grand feeling, eternal truths next to the ephemeral. This gives rise to the comical. (Beineix, 1987: 42)

The sequence in the film compresses two consecutive sequences in the novel, a visit in the Mercedes to a prospective client, and the follow-up delivery in a lorry. Most of the material in the film is derived from the first visit in the Mercedes; indeed, a considerable section of the dialogue comes straight from the novel. Replacing the car with a lorry, however, allows a series of emphases.

- The first is the emphasis on speed, underlined by Bob's comment about the strain on the engine.
- The second is the emphasis on motherhood, underlined by quantity in the novel (25 prams), but by visual effect in the film, as an extreme low-angle shot shows the lorry braking abruptly in front of a single pram. Both of these emphases serve to underline Zorg's confusion at potentially being a father.
- A third emphasis is structured like the second: Richard is dominated by the lorry in a series of low-angle shots (Richard standing in front of the lorry as he calls for Zorg to stop; Richard looked down on by Zorg in the shot-reverse-shot conversation section), just as, interestingly, the mother was dominated by the lorry as she pushed the pram over the road.

The visual side of the sequence thus uses *mise-en-scène* literally to diminish the stature of the policeman, an effect that is emphasised even more by the dialogue. Whereas in the novel, Richard's talk of the joys of paternity is in reported speech, which conveys Zorg's feeling of not quite being able to focus on what Richard is saying, in the film Richard begins, absurdly, to sing a well-known sentimental song. The absurdity is underlined by Bob's reaction shot (a blankly uncomprehending face); and both the absurdity and the sentimentality are amplified in the various shots at the end of the sequence: a long-distance shot of Richard slowly and deliberately waving goodbye, framed by the lorry's ramps, followed by an extreme long shot of the lorry in the sunset, distorted by a wide lens, being waved at by people on the roadside. The singing avoids the need to replicate Richard's details about his son's feeding habits and other joys of paternity, thus serving a compressive function. That compressive function is largely outweighed, however, by the sequence's comic function, centring principally on the disruption of Richard's role as a policeman. What some saw as an advertising effect, excessive camera angles and framing at the service of the object, is in fact a key component of derision, which has little to do with objects, but a great deal to do with a critique of the law. There is a further point, however, and it has to do with the position of the spectator.

The immense leap from Richard as law dispenser to Richard as sentimental father is derisory in ways that the novel is not. It maintains the diffidence of the novel's narrator to the law, but introduces, as Beineix points out, caustic irony, a distancing for the spectator, which echoes the novel narrator's marginality from everything around him. Spectators laugh, but laugh *knowingly*; they watch themselves laughing. The spectator feels something like this: 'This is absurdly funny, so absurd that it does not square with what I was expecting, which only makes it funnier, but in so doing calls into question what I was really expecting, and thus calls my responses into question, which is absurd because this is a simple story, and the comedy that disrupts this simple story is itself simple, but that does not square with what I was expecting. . . .' and so on.

It is no coincidence that Beineix should emphasise the comical with sequences involving policemen. There is a 'doubling' effect. Spectators are implicated in the film's narrative through identification with Zorg, being made to feel his panic at the thought of being a father through the various techniques outlined above. But at the same time they are forced out of that identification by a complex derision, which works at the level of both character and narrative. There are two male characters, one a law enforcer, one a law breaker, both defined as fathers: the ultimate law. And yet neither is able to cohere with the stable role implied, the policeman because he switches to absurd sentimentality and therefore over-performs the law; the law breaker because he cannot comprehend his paternity, and therefore under-performs the law.

The instability of character is compounded by the instability of narrative tone. Beineix calls on spectators to stand back from the law of the narrative and, in a typically postmodern gesture, to put into question the notion of consistent tone upon which a simpler romantic narrative might have depended, to position themselves sideways in the elsewhere of mockery and, by implication, it could be suggested, self-mockery.

Beineix's project is as much to deflate pomposity, whether in terms of morals or in terms of film narrative, by derision. The excessive image criticised by Toubiana is not gratuitous at all, but an essential part of a system that calls upon spectators to marginalise themselves, not to take themselves or the narrative seriously. Like irony, derision functions as a kind of protection, both for the disempowered youth audiences of the 1980s, as well as, one may assume, for Beineix himself, in constant disagreement with the film 'establishment'.

PANIQUE (JULIEN DUVIVIER, 1946)/*MONSIEUR HIRE* (PATRICE LECONTE, 1989)

In this sequence analysis we will compare the opening sequences of two films adapted from the same novel, Georges Simenon's *Les Fiançailles de Monsieur Hire* (1933). Since these films and their directors are less well known than those used so far in this chapter, there follows rather more context than for previous sequence analyses.

Some 30 Simenon novels have been adapted for the screen. The most recent in relation to *Monsieur Hire* had been Tavernier's *L'Horloger de Saint-Paul* (1973). In the 1980s Tavernier was seen as a representative of the French quality tradition, a throwback to the films of the 1950s. Even more recently, Chabrol had adapted *Les Fantômes du chapelier* (1982), also dealing with lonely men. Patrice Leconte had made 14 films in the period 1969–1987 and, prior to this one, was known for light comedies, especially for the iconoclastic comic team of Le Splendid in the mid-1980s. The director of the earlier film, Julien Duvivier, made 51 films in the period 1922–1967. He is mostly remembered for the three great films made with Jean Gabin as star: *La Bandera* (1935); *La Belle Equipe* (1936), *Pépé le Moko* (1937). He had also already adapted a Simenon novel before this one, *La Tête d'un homme* (1932).

The opening sequences from the two films are very similar, but there are significant differences that the following sequence analysis will discuss. *Panique* opens with a tramp asleep on a bench in a city square being moved on. Monsieur Hire photographs the tramp before going into a butcher's shop to buy his slice of meat for the evening. While he is there, some circus men visiting the city discover a body on wasteland. Monsieur Hire goes to the cheesemonger's, where all the talk is of the discovery of a corpse; he is not interested in the talk. On his return home, he meets a little girl and talks to her, but her mother pulls her away from Hire angrily. Alice arrives in town; she and her boyfriend, Alfred, pretend that they do not know each other, and meet in the churchyard, where we learn that Alice has just come out of prison, having taken the rap for Alfred. In the second major opening sequence, we see Hire eating, and brushing his shoes. He sees Alice arrive in her hotel room opposite. She undresses, notices Hire and, sticking her tongue out at him, closes the window.

We have provided a shot-by-shot breakdown for the opening sequence of *Monsieur Hire* below, but the following outline will be useful for comparative purposes.

The Inspector deals with a body found on wasteland, and goes to the victim's bedroom to muse on the fragility of life. Monsieur Hire returns home and counts slowly with little Marie to get rid of her hiccups. The Inspector confronts Hire in his workshop, suggesting he might be the murderer. Hire eats in his darkened room; when the light streams in from a room opposite, he gets up and spies on Alice as she gets ready to leave her apartment. He listens to a piece of music as he watches her; we get the sense that this is a ritual.

SEGMENTATION USING METZ'S GRANDE SYNTAGMATIQUE

1	Corpse	**Ordinary**
2	Inspector	• 'Viewer skips the moments that have . . . no
3	Pierrette's room	direct bearing on the plot.'
4	Photos	**Episodic:**
5	Corpse at morgue	• 'The scenes are taken not as separate
6	Inspector photographs corpse	instances but only in their totality, which has
		the status of an ordinary sequence and which
		therefore constitutes an autonomous segment.
		In its extreme form (that is, when the
		successive episodes are separated by a long
		diegetic duration), this construction is used to
		condense gradual progressions.'
		• 'Symbolic summary of one stage in the fairly
		long evolution condensed by the total
		sequence.'
7	Marie and Hire's feet	**Scene:**
8	Hire	• 'Coincidence of screen time and diegetic
9	Hire's hand on Marie's head	time.'
10	Hire and Marie	• 'Continuity in the soundtrack.'
11	Marie watches Hire	
12	Hire sewing	**Scene:**
13	Hire sewing	• 'Coincidence of screen time and diegetic
14	Inspector at door	time', although there is a break between shots
15	Hire stops machine	14/15, so strictly it is an ordinary syntagma.
16	Hire's workshop	
17	Hire	
18	Inspector	
19	Hire	
20	Hire	
21	Photo of Pierrette	
22	Corpse being covered	**Autonomous insert:**
		• **Subjective:** 'Image conveying not the present
		instance, but an absent moment experienced
		by the hero of the film. Examples: images of
		memory, dream, fear, premonition.' Perhaps
		the Inspector's flashback?
		• **Displaced diegetic:** 'Image that, while
		remaining entirely "real", is displaced from
		its normal filmic position and is purposely

		intruded into a foreign syntagma. Example: Within a sequence showing the pursuers, a single shot of the pursued is inserted.' Taken from an earlier narrative event.
23	Hire	**Scene:**
24	Inspector	• 'Coincidence of screen time and diegetic
25	Inspector	time.'
26	Hire	
27	Inspector	
28	Hire	
29	Inspector	
30	Hire	
31	Inspector	
32	Hire eats	**Scene:**
33	Door	• 'Coincidence of screen time and diegetic
34	Egg	time.' Intuitively we read this as a single
35	Hire gets up	'theatrical' event. The soundtrack is diegetic
36	Hire at window	and continuous, as is clear from shot 41, even
37	Hire eats yoghurt	though there may be a break between shots
38	Alice dresses	35/36.
39	Hire puts yoghurt down	**Bracket:**
40	Object falls off table	• We might also read it as a 'typical event', a
41	Turntable	ritual, complete with the same music repeated
42	Hire at window	time after time. But note that the object
43	Alice	falling off (40) is unlikely to be a repeated
44	Hire moves at window	event, nor are the children banging at the
45	Hire and Alice in shot	door (33).

COMPARISON OF THE OPENING SEQUENCES OF *PANIQUE* AND *MONSIEUR HIRE*

There are significant differences in the way the two films open, even when on paper they appear to be similar; similarities would be, for example, the taking of the photograph, or the encounter with a little girl. The differences function to underline Hire's status. In *Panique* he is an individual who stands out from a community; in *Monsieur Hire*, he is an individual who is not merely an oddball, but disquietingly strange, a contrast emphasised by *mise-en-scène* and camerawork. The accosting of the little girl, to which we have just referred, indicates Hire's 'strangeness' in both films, but this is done explicitly in the 1946 film by having the girl's mother emerge from her apartment and pull her daughter away from Hire, suggesting that Hire is not a man to be trusted. In the modern film, Hire's strangeness is more implicit, conveyed by stark lighting (a cold blue), close-ups on the faces and a stylised shot of Marie's blank gaze at him, which is more difficult to interpret than the much more obvious reaction of the girl's mother in the earlier film. His strangeness is also conveyed implicitly, and most obviously, by the activity itself. In the earlier film Hire gives the girl an apple, whereas in the modern film the fact that he is helping the girl to overcome her hiccups is only made clear when he says that 'she no longer has them'; the spectator is left guessing as to what has been going on.

The sense of Hire's ambiguity and strangeness, more characteristic of the modern film, is also prevalent in the major differences between the two films. These are, first, that Hire and his reaction to the murder are introduced by contrasting him with a crowd in the 1946 film, but by contrasting him with an individual, the Inspector, in the 1989 film; second, that Alice and her boyfriend are introduced much earlier in the 1946 film; and, third, Hire's spying on Alice is presented as a habit in the 1989 film, whereas it is clearly the first occasion in the 1946 film.

In the 1946 film, Hire is seen shopping, along with many others. When news of the murder breaks, he is the only one not to manifest curiosity, his comments singling him out from the rest of the shoppers. This is emphasised by *mise-en-scène* and camerawork. Where the camera is concerned, for example, low-angle shots are associated with Hire (when he gets off the tram; when he goes up the stairs), whereas the square is associated with high-angle shots, establishing a spatial contrast between the community and Hire. Where *mise-en-scène* is concerned, Hire is consistently 'framed' in isolation (by dead meat in the butcher's, by the windows of the concierge's lodge, by his own window). Even the odd action of photographing the tramp (brought squarely to the spectator's attention by a rapid zoom combined with a tilt down) suggests that he has some kind of affinity with the tramp, underlining his own marginality and isolation, and the fact that people find him repellent, as the incident with the little girl's mother will go on to emphasise. The camera also, of course, associates him with voyeurism, the main theme of the film.

By contrast, in the modern film, it is the Inspector who takes a photograph, in this case of the corpse laid out in the morgue, turning the Inspector into as much of a disquieting figure as Hire himself. Indeed, even our sense of location is questioned in the modern film. Whereas in the earlier film, it is clear that the story is taking place in the city around a square, in the modern film, there are abrupt shifts of location (wasteland, bedroom, morgue, apartment block, workshop), which combine with the oddity of the characters to create considerable ambiguity for the spectator. Where are we exactly? Who exactly are these people? Patrice Leconte commented on the Inspector thus: 'I had asked Wilms to act the whole of this first part as if he were the father of the dead woman. It is only when he is with Monsieur Hire that we discover that he is a policeman' (*Monsieur Hire*, 1990:11).

The second major difference between the two films is that Alice and her boyfriend are introduced much earlier in the 1946 film. This, combined with the third major difference – that Hire's spying is a habit in the modern film – once more emphasises the fact that the modern film is about a set of lonely individuals, whereas the earlier film's concern is with the notion of community and the individual's place within it. To be more precise, the 1946 film, hardly surprisingly given its date, is concerned with how a community deals with individuals who do not quite fit (an allusion to those who collaborated in the Second World War), whereas the modern film is more concerned with the familiar notion of individuals alienated from each other by urban life. That contrast can be seen in the camerawork: *Panique* has a very mobile camera, with 22 shots out of 56 containing pans, tracking shots or crane shots; unusually, perhaps (because modern films tend to use more mobile cameras), *Monsieur Hire* only has 7 out of 44 shots with a similar mobile camera. The characters in the modern film are contained and framed as individuals isolated from each other much more than in the 1946 film.

A comparison of the two films, therefore, tells us much about choices made by scriptwriters and directors when adapting the original novel. It allows us to place those choices in relation to the society of the time, thus complementing the more psychoanalytical interpretation of the film proposed by Abigail Murray in her essay in the previous section of this chapter.

LA HAINE (MATTHIEU KASSOVITZ, 1995)

La Haine is one of the major films of the 1990s. It is characteristic of the *cinéma de banlieue*, films set in the outer suburbs of France's main cities, which focus on disaffected and usually jobless young men. It was the seventh most popular French film in 1995, and was shown to government ministers as an example of what would in the UK be called 'inner-city problems'. The film focuses on three friends, a black (Hubert), a white Jew (Vinz), and a *beur* (Saïd). There is tension on the housing estate because a young man has been beaten while in police custody. Vinz has managed to get hold of a policeman's gun, and speaks of exacting vengeance. The three friends go to Paris to clinch a drug-deal. Hubert and Saïd are picked up by the police, beaten, and released too late for them to get the last train back home. They wander around the city with Vinz, meeting, amongst others, a band of skinheads and an old man in a toilet, and they gatecrash the opening of an art exhibition. When they eventually return home, they meet an aggressive policeman who accidentally shoots Vinz dead. The film ends with Hubert holding the gun found by Vinz at the policeman's head, while the policeman holds his own gun to Hubert's head.

We have chosen two sequences for analysis. The first is the meeting with the old man in the public toilets; the second is the sequence where Vinz pretends that he is Robert de Niro in Scorsese's *Taxi Driver*. In this second sequence, we will be comparing and contrasting the US film with the French film.

GRUNWALSKI'S STORY

The three friends have been arguing in some public toilets about the value of violence when an old man emerges from a cubicle, and launches into a shaggy dog story. Surprisingly, they listen attentively, but at the end, it is made clear to us that they have no more idea why he told them the story than we might have. Here is a transcription of the sequence:

> **The old man:** It really does you good to have a decent shit. Do you believe in God? You shouldn't ask whether people believe in God, but whether God believes in us. I had a friend called Grunwalski. We were pals in Siberia. When you go to a camp in Siberia, they take you in cattle-wagons which cross the icy steppes for days without seeing a soul. You keep warm by huddling together. But the problem is that when you want to relieve yourself, you can't do it in the wagon. The only time you stopped was to put water into the locomotive. But Grunwalski was very prudish. He felt embarrassed at simply washing with other people. I often made fun of him because of that. Anyway, the train stopped and everybody makes the most of it to go and have a shit behind the wagon. I had gone on about it so much to Grunwalski that he preferred to go a bit further away. So the train sets off again, everybody jumps on. The problem is that Grunwalski has gone some way to hide behind a bush. He hadn't finished having a shit. He jumped up from behind his bush, holding his trousers in his hand so as not to trip over. He tried to catch up with the train. I held my hand out. But every time he stretched his out to me, he let go of his trousers, and they fell around his ankles. He picks up his trousers, starts running again, and every time his trousers fall down when he stretches out his hand to me.
> **Saïd:** So what happened?
> **The old man:** Well, nothing! Grunwalski died of cold. Bye-bye, bye-bye, bye-bye.
> **Saïd:** Why did he tell us that?

This sequence seems to have very little to do with the action. It seems rather to be a very conscious digression, a demonstration of wilful ambiguity, characteristic of the European art cinema, underlined by the heavy Polish accent of the old man. It is clearly intended to be funny:

- the form of the story — an extended joke without a punchline — is a familiar one
- the content of the story is lavatorial humour, corresponding to the location; indeed, the old man underlines the desperate need for a shit with a comical body gesture and an emphasis on the word '*chier*' (to shit)
- once the three friends have left, with Saïd repeating his final question, the camera remains fixed on the empty toilets for a few moments until an obviously frightened man peeks out of another cubicle to see if all is clear

The story clearly serves several functions, however. It is not just comical; the comedy is mixed with tragedy. At its most basic and functional level, the story interrupts the increasingly violent confrontation between the tearaway Vinz, who has been insisting that he will kill a cop, and the more reasonable Hubert, who points out that the violence will change nothing. The story also functions as a metaphor for issues of exclusion and solidarity. There are three overlapping issues here.

1   The fact that it interrupts a confrontation between Hubert and Vinz that centres on the moral and political value of violence suggests that the story can be seen as a comment on the need to stay together, otherwise tragedy will occur.
2   The story is about failing masculinity; it ridicules a man, suggesting very strongly the friends' disempowerment, and attempts at empowerment (by threatening to use the gun, for example).
3   The context of the story – deportation through the Siberian steppes – suggests the broader issue of the three friends' marginality both in relation to the urban centre (they live in a troubled estate), and in relation to French society in more general terms. Indeed, the story itself is one to which they do not have access: they do not understand why the old man has told them the story, and their incomprehension suggests their isolation from one of the principal ways in which a society constitutes itself, by remembering its history. For the three friends, marginalised from society, an absurd story about two men in the middle of the Siberian steppes means nothing, it is doubly absurd, because they have no notion of the events of the Second World War.

It might be argued that our attempt to 'make meaning' of what we first defined as a meaningless digression imposes interpretation, when the point of the story might well be that it is pointless. The kind of narrative coherence we are seeking here might, it could be argued, work against the incoherence which would help represent the aimlessness of the three friends. Nevertheless, film spectators, rightly or wrongly, attempt to make sense of the material presented to them, especially when that material is puzzling.

VINZ ACTS OUT TRAVIS BICKLE

If the previous sequence was 'European', this sequence is a much more obvious homage to US cinema. In it, Vinz acts out the famous sequence from Scorsese's *Taxi Driver* (1976) where Travis Bickle (Robert de Niro), who has become increasingly psychopathic, pretends that he is confronting nameless adversaries and draws his gun to frighten them. Here is a transcription of the dialogue from each film; for obvious reasons, in this case we have kept the French but given a translation of it for comparative purposes.

Vinz (French dialogue)	Vinz (English translation)	Travis Bickle
C'est à moi que tu parles?	You talkin' to me?	You talkin' to me?
C'est à *moi* que tu parles?	You talkin' to *me*?	You talkin' to *me*?
C'est à moi que tu parles enculé?	You talkin' to me, arsehole?	You talkin' to me?
C'est à moi que tu parles, hein?	You talkin' to me?	You talkin' to me?
Wo, wo, wo, wo.	Wo, wo, wo, wo.	Well, who the hell else are you talkin' to?
C'est à moi que tu parles enculé?	You talkin' to me, arsehole?	You talkin' to me?
C'est à moi que tu parles, putain?	Shit, you talkin' to me?	Well, I'm the only one here.
C'est à moi que tu parles comme ça, mec?	You talkin' to me, like that, man?	Who the fuck do you think you're talkin' to? Oh yeah? Oh yeah? OK.

The differences between the two sequences matter much more than the similarities. At their simplest, these differences signal Vinz's fragility compared with Travis Bickle; the first will be killed by the police, the second will be seen as a hero by police and public. This major difference is signalled in the detail of the sequences.

The dialogue may be much the same, but Bickle says something Vinz does not: 'Well, who the hell else are you talkin' to? . . . Well, I'm the only one here.' The statement recalls forcefully something that is relevant in both sequences: that the characters are talking to themselves. But the fact that this is drawn to our attention more in the Scorsese suggests by contrast that Vinz is considerably less alone than Bickle, forming part of a tight-knit male group, unlike Bickle's psychopathic loner. Arguably this should make Vinz stronger, but paradoxically he comes across as much weaker than Bickle, as the remaining details suggest.

It is not clear that Bickle is talking into a mirror, whereas this is made very clear at the beginning of the sequence in the French film, as the camera focuses on the back of Vinz's head before adopting the point of view of the mirror, i.e. Vinz's solipsistic micro-world (contrasted with Bickle's psychopathic world). Vinz's world is a micro-world in more sense than one, since there is an enormous difference in the décor: Bickle is in a large spacious apartment, whereas Vinz is compressed into a tiny bathroom. Bickle's apartment is a relatively neutral space; we are supposed to understand that this man does not really care much about his environment. Neither perhaps does Vinz, arguably, but the space in which he is forced to operate is not just small, it is also not his own, as is underlined by the painting in the background, which functions as a marker of lower-class taste and, with its tropical paradise full of palm trees, comments ironically on Vinz's situation, living with his parents in a run-down housing block. More obviously, though, Vinz is not just constrained in ways that Bickle is not, he is also more fragile: Bickle wears military-style fatigues, whereas Vinz in this sequence is undressed; and Bickle has a gun, whereas Vinz, who also has a gun, does not have it in this sequence. Finally, although the dialogue is very similar, the way in which the two actors deliver it is very different. They both have high-pitched voices, but de Niro speaks his lines deliberately, and comes across as 'friendly', emphasised by the smile. Cassel, on the other hand, is pure aggression, his dialogue delivered rapidly, in staccato style. Bickle suggests unpredictable malevolence, Vinz predictable aggression which, as the mirror suggests, will eventually turn against him.

We began by suggesting that the sequence is an unequivocal homage to Scorsese, which at one level it is. We have seen, however, that the differences in the sequences are what colour our perception of Vinz as a very specific example of a particular type of young Frenchman. In fact, the sequence is no more 'American' than 'French', since it also strongly recalls Jean-Paul Belmondo in Godard's *A bout de souffle* (1959) imitating Humphrey Bogart by running his fingers over the rim of his hat, and over his lips. As this interplay of references suggests (where does

'French' begin and 'American' stop?), the sequence underlines a point we have made elsewhere in this volume: that the French national cinema has a complex relationship with the American national cinema, and has had since the very beginning.

APPENDICES ☐

The majority of the statistics used in the following appendices are taken from Simsi (2000). The figures used are provided by the Centre National de la Cinématographie and represent the total number of spectators for the film in metropolitan France from its release to 1999.

TABLE 1: HISTORY OF THE FRENCH CINEMA (STARS, MOVEMENTS, DIRECTORS)

Major Stars	'Movements'		Other key directors
	1895–1920 Lumière, Méliès, Feuillade		
1920s Josephine Baker Max Linder Musidora	**1920s** **Impressionism** Dulac, Epstein, Gance, L'Herbier	**1925–30** **Surrealism** Buñuel	
1930s–1940s Arletty Martine Carol Jean Gabin Michèle Morgan Michel Simon	**1930s Poetic Realism** Renoir, Carné, Grémillon, Vigo		
	1940s–1950s Tradition **of quality** Autant-Lara, Becker, Christian-Jaque, Delannoy		

Table 1 – *contd*

Major Stars	'Movements'				Other key directors
1950s–1970s Brigitte Bardot Jean-Paul Belmondo Bourvil Alain Delon Catherine Deneuve Fernandel Louis de Funès Jean Marais Jeanne Moreau Gérard Philipe		1959–1964 New Wave Chabrol Demy Godard Malle Rivette Resnais Rohmer Varda Truffaut 1970s New quality Tavernier	1970s Realism Pialat	1970s Militant cinema Costa-Gavras, Godard	1950s–1960s Bresson Eustache Melville Tati 1970s–1980s Annaud Blier Leconte Lelouch Miller
1980s–1990s Isabelle Adjani Daniel Auteuil Emannuelle Béart Juliette Binoche Gérard Depardieu Isabelle Huppert Sophie Marceau	1980s Cinema of the look Beineix, Besson, Carax	1986 – Heritage Berri, Rappeneau, Wargnier	1980s Women's cinema Duras, Kurys, Varda 1990s New realism Kassovitz	1980s Beur cinema Charef, Chibane	

TABLE 2: FRENCH THEORISTS OF THE CINEMA

This table lists the key theorists and their texts in the history of French cinema; not all of these have been discussed in detail in Chapter 2 of this volume. The majority of these texts are also listed in the Bibliography, where the reader will find details of English translations where available.

1900–1945 Early Film Theory	Louis Delluc	*Photogénie* (1920)
1945–1960 André Bazin and the *politique des auteurs*	Alexandre Astruc André Bazin	'La Caméra-stylo' (1948) *Qu'est-ce que le cinema* (1958–1959)

1950–1970 Sociology and Structuralism	Gilbert Cohen-Séat	*Essai sur les principes d'une philosophie du cinema* (1946)
	Edgar Morin	*Le Cinéma, ou, l'homme imaginaire: essai d'anthropologie sociologique* (1956) *Les Stars* (1957)
	Jean Mitry	*Esthétique et psychologie du cinéma* (1963, 1965)
	Christian Metz	*Essais sur la signification au cinéma* (1968) *Langage et cinéma* (1971)
1968–1970 Ideology and Suture	Jean-Pierre Oudart	'La Suture' (1969)
	Jean-Louis Comolli and Jean Narboni	'*Young Mister Lincoln* de John Ford (1970)
1970–1980 Psychoanalysis and Postructuralism	Jean-Louis Baudry	'Cinéma: effets idéologiques produits pas l'appareil de base' (1971) 'Le Dispositif: approches métapsychologiques de l'effet de réalité' (1975) *L'Effet-Cinéma* (1978)
	Christian Metz	*Le Signifiant imaginaire* (1977)
The space(s) of cinema: Daney, Burch and Gardies	Noel Burch	*Une praxis du cinéma* (1967)
	Serge Daney	*La Rampe* (1983) *Le Salaire du zappeur* (1988) *Devant la recrudescence des vols de sacs à main* (1991) *L'Exercice a été profitable, Monsieur* (1993)
	André Gardies	*L'Espace au cinéma* (1993)
The movement(s) of cinema: Deleuze	Gilles Deleuze	*L'Image-mouvement* (1983) *L'Image-temps* (1983)
The sound(s) of cinema: Chion	Michel Chion	*La Voix au cinéma* (1982) *Le Son au cinéma* (1985) *La Toile trouée: la parole au cinéma* (1988) *L'Audio-vision: son et image au cinéma* (1990) *La Musique au cinéma* (1995)

TABLE 3 AND FIGURE 1: NUMBERS OF SPECTATORS 1945–1999

The figures presented here show that there has been a decline in spectator numbers since 1945. However, with the exception of the early 1950s, the decline in Paris has been slower and less dramatic than the decline over the whole of France. While Paris film theatres are sufficiently numerous and varied to continue attracting large numbers, elsewhere in France, particularly during the 1960s, spectators preferred to stay at home and watch television than go to their local cinema. The decline in the 1990s similarly reflects the advent of new cinema-oriented television channels such as Canal+ (in 1999, 1563 films were shown on French television, of which one nearly one-third (452) were on Canal+).

	Spectators in 000s			Spectators in 000s	
	France	Paris		France	Paris
1945	357 897	95 425	1973	175 961	42 158
1946	369 465	104 467	1974	179 437	43 814
1947	423 721	100 205	1975	181 670	45 168
1948	402 030	88 632	1976	177 290	45 026
1949	387 766	78 473	1977	170 256	44 478
1950	370 728	76 535	1978	178 540	45 129
1951	372 837	76 490	1979	178 100	44 271
1952	359 621	74 471	1980	175 430	44 565
1953	370 634	75 144	1981	189 230	45 450
1954	382 821	76 889	1982	201 930	45 150
1955	394 889	79 245	1983	198 870	43 010
1956	398 888	78 706	1984	190 870	41 880
1957	411 693	80 046	1985	175 080	38 412
1958	371 030	72 102	1986	168 130	34 953
1959	353 719	67 324	1987	136 940	30 890
1960	354 674	67 549	1988	124 750	29 200
1961	328 360	61 386	1989	120 910	28 320
1962	311 736	59 916	1990	121 920	27 260
1963	292 074	56 283	1991	117 490	27 310
1964	275 830	53 674	1992	116 050	27 260
1965	259 425	51 729	1993	132 720	28 080
1966	234 730	49 569	1994	124 420	26 010
1967	211 450	45 508	1995	130 240	24 730
1968	203 242	43 817	1996	136 740	26 260
1969	183 880	41 638	1997	149 410	26 520
1970	184 420	42 686	1998	170 100	27 130
1971	176 980	41 440	1999	155 630	26 920
1972	184 400	43 472			

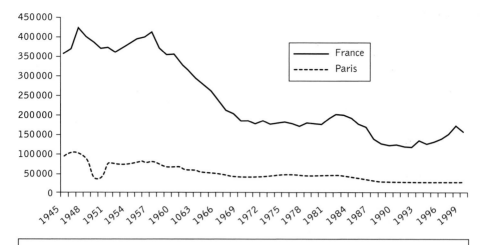

Figure 1 Numbers of spectators 1945–1999

TABLE 4 AND FIGURE 2: NUMBERS OF FILMS PRODUCED 1945–1999

Film production statistics are notoriously difficult to pin down, since they depend on the criteria used. The main problem is the status of co-productions. Is a film French if its director is French and its stars non-French, for example? The figures presented here should therefore be used with caution, and are intended as a guide rather than an accurate record. We have given statistics for a number of European countries, mainly so that the reader can place French film production in a context other than the US–French relationship. Where French statistics are concerned, we have given two different versions. The first, 'France (S)', is the version given by Simsi (2000); Simsi does not make his criteria clear, but is likely to have included some co-productions. 'France (V)', and the statistics for the other countries are those given by Ginette Vincendeau for the period 1945–1993 in the *Encyclopedia of European Cinema* (London: Cassell/British Film Institute, 1995); these have been supplemented for the period 1994–1998 by figures from the various BFI Film and Television Handbooks. Vincendeau's figures explicitly include co-productions, without making the proportions clear.

These difficulties aside, the figures show definable trends: French production has always been strong in European terms. It has taken over from Italy as the most prolific producer of films in Europe, Italy dominating the 1960s, and France dominating the 1980s and 1990s.

	Fr (S)	Fr (V)	UK	It	Ger	Sp
1945	50	72	51	–	–	33
1946	83	94	66	62	1	38
1947	88	72	73	60	9	49
1948	92	91	120	54	23	45
1949	100	108	125	76	62	36
1950	111	118	99	92	82	49
1951	113	112	102	104	60	42
1952	113	109	132	132	82	40
1953	106	111	142	146	114	44
1954	85	98	148	190	109	69
1955	82	110	115	126	128	56
1956	99	129	130	91	123	75
1957	114	142	164	137	107	72
1958	92	126	135	141	115	65
1959	105	133	140	164	106	67
1960	104	153	157	160	95	83
1961	109	167	151	205	80	91
1962	99	125	171	245	61	88
1963	104	141	150	230	66	114
1964	102	148	126	290	77	130
1965	86	142	97	203	72	151
1966	80	130	99	232	60	164
1967	96	120	140	247	96	125
1968	94	117	107	246	107	117
1969	97	154	112	249	121	125
1970	106	138	122	231	113	105
1971	103	127	67	216	99	91
1972	132	169	131	280	85	103

	Fr (S)	Fr (V)	UK	It	Ger	Sp
1973	170	200	98	252	98	118
1974	158	234	89	231	80	112
1975	175	222	91	230	73	110
1976	157	214	92	237	60	108
1977	149	222	73	165	52	102
1978	116	160	77	143	57	107
1979	151	174	77	144	65	89
1980	144	189	61	160	49	118
1981	131	231	66	103	76	137
1982	122	165	46	114	70	140
1983	107	131	56	110	77	99
1984	122	161	51	103	75	75
1985	130	151	53	89	64	77
1986	124	134	35	109	70	60
1987	126	133	48	116	65	69
1988	128	137	40	124	57	63
1989	128	136	27	117	68	48
1990	103	146	47	119	48	47
1991	123	156	46	129	72	64
1992	123	155	42	127	63	52
1993	124	152	60	106	67	56
1994	101	101	63	95	57	44
1995	122	122	76	75	70	59
1996	122	122	128	99	63	91
1997	165	165	116	110	61	80
1998	146	146	88	92	119	65
1999	164	164	–	–	–	–

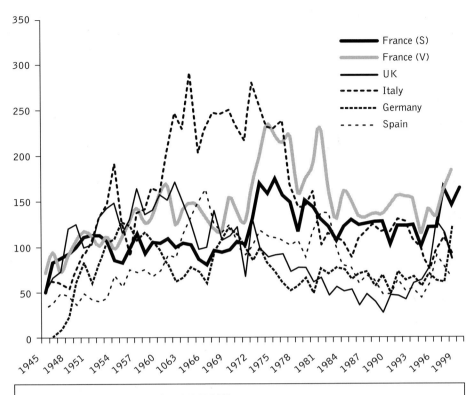

Figure 2   Numbers of films produced 1945–1999

TABLE 5 AND FIGURE 3: SHARE OF THE FRENCH MARKET 1945–1999

The figures show how British films have attracted more or less the same share of the French market for the last fifty years. US films, after a slow decline during the 1950s and 1960s, gradually came to dominate the French market after the mid-1980s, largely as a result of blockbuster and action films.

	France	USA	Great Britain			France	USA	Great Britain
1945	46.2	43.6	3.5		1973	58.5	19.8	4.1
1946	46.4	44.2	4.2		1974	53.9	21.3	4.1
1947	43.5	44.5	3.9		1975	50.7	27	4.1
1948	44.1	43.8	4		1976	52.1	27.7	5.3
1949	42.4	44.5	4.2		1977	46.5	30.5	6.3
1950	45.1	42.5	4.6		1978	46	32.6	4.2
1951	47.3	40	3.7		1979	50.1	29.3	5.1
1952	49.2	37.2	3.6		1980	47.1	35.9	4
1953	47.7	35.4	3.8		1981	49.7	30.8	6.3
1954	47.3	34.5	3.9		1982	53.4	30.1	4.6
1955	48.6	33.6	3.7		1983	46.8	35	6.3
1956	48.6	43.6	3.7		1984	49.3	36.9	4.8
1957	50	32.3	4.6		1985	44.6	39.3	8.1
1958	48.6	30.4	6.4		1986	43.7	43.3	8.1
1959	49.5	31.6	5.2		1987	36.2	45.7	6
1960	51.1	28.5	5.5		1988	39.1	45.7	3.9
1961	51.2	27.6	4.5		1989	34.3	55.5	4.4
1962	50.9	29.6	3.1		1990	37.6	55.9	1.5
1963	48.8	30.7	3.8		1991	30.6	58.2	7.2
1964	48.8	30.4	5.8		1992	34.9	58.2	1.6
1965	52.5	27	7.8		1993	35.1	57.1	2.7
1966	51	28	7.7		1994	28.3	60.9	7
1967	52.1	27.5	6.5		1995	35.2	53.9	6.5
1968	50	26.2	6.1		1996	37.5	54.3	5.1
1969	46.3	26.1	7.6		1997	34.5	53.8	7.3
1970	49	26	5.5		1998	34.5	53.8	7.3
1971	53	24.8	5.5		1999	29.7	53.9	8.7
1972	53.5	24.3	5					

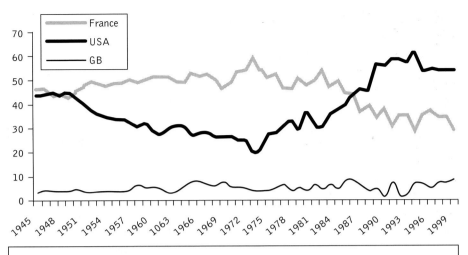

Figure 3   Share of the French market 1945–1999

TABLE 6: BEST-SELLERS 1945–1999

This list includes the first five French feature films, according to number of spectators, in each year since 1945, with their directors and main stars. The films include
co-productions where the main part is French.

Year	Director	No. spectators	Star(s)
1945			
La Cage aux rossignols	J. Dréville	5 085 489	M. Francey
Les Enfants du paradis	M. Carné	4 768 505	Arletty, J.-L. Barrault
Carmen	Christian-Jaque	4 277 813	V. Romance
Le Roi des resquillieurs	J. Devaivre	3 679 438	S. Dehelly, J. Batti
Le Cavalier noir	G. Grangier	3 672 572	M. Parély, G. Guétary
1946			
Mission spéciale	M. De Canonge	6 781 120	J. Holt, P. Renoir
La Symphonie pastorale	J. Delannoy	6 372 837	M. Morgan
Le Père tranquille	R. Clément	6 138 837	Noël-Noël
La Bataille du rail	R. Clément	5 727 203	J. Clarieux
Le Capitan	R. Vernay	5 098 185	P. Renoir

Year	Director	No. spectators	Star(s)
1947			
Le Bataillon du ciel	A. Esway	8 649 691	J. Crispin
Monsieur Vincent	M. Cloche	7 055 290	P. Fresnay
Pas si bête	A. Berthomieu	6 165 419	Bourvil
Quai des orfèvres	H.-G. Clouzot	5 526 341	B. Blier
Le Diable au corps	C. Autant-Lara	4 762 930	G. Philipe
1948			
La Chartreuse de Parme	Christian-Jaque	6 150 551	G. Philipe
La Bataille de l'eau lourde	T. Müller/ J. Dréville	5 373 377	
Clochemerle	P. Chenal	5 027 714	Maximilienne
Aux yeux du souvenir	J. Delannoy	4 559 689	M. Morgan
Les Casse-pieds	J. Dréville	4 328 290	M. Deval
1949			
Jour de fête	J. Tati	6 679 608	J. Tati
Barry	R. Pottier	4 086 921	P. Fresnay
L'Espagne sur la main	A. Berthomieu	3 657 951	Bourvil
Manon	H.-G. Clouzot	3 412 167	C. Aubry
L'Héroïque Monsieur Boniface	M. Labro	3 261 238	Fernandel
1950			
Nous irons à Paris	J. Boyer	6 658 693	R. Ventura
Uniformes et grandes manœuvres	R. Le Hénaff	4 588 407	Fernandel
Justice est faite	A. Cayatte	4 319 752	V. Tessier
Le Rosier de Madame Husson	J. Boyer	4 304 624	Bourvil
Meurtres	R. Pottier	4 013 769	Fernandel
1951			
Andalousie	R. Vernay	5 734 973	L. Mariano
Le Roi des camelots	A. Berthomieu	4 059 172	C. Ripert
Chacun son tour	A. Berthomieu	3 810 569	R. Lamoureux
Un grand patron	Y. Ciampi	3 737 966	P. Fresnay
Caroline chérie	R. Pottier	3 602 845	M. Carol

Year	Director	No. spectators	Star(s)
1952			
Le Petit monde de Don Camillo	J. Duvivier	12 790 676	Fernandel
Violettes impériales	R. Pottier	8 125 766	L. Mariano
Fanfan la tulipe	Christian-Jaque	6 712 512	G. Philipe
Jeux interdits	R. Clément	4 908 992	B. Fossey
Le Fruit défendu	H. Verneuil	4 002 100	Fernandel
1953			
Le Retour de Don Camillo	J. Duvivier	7 425 550	Fernandel
Le Salaire de la peur	H.-G. Clouzot	6 943 447	Y. Montand, C. Vanel
Les Trois mousquetaires	A. Hunebelle	5 354 739	G. Marchal
Les Vacances de Monsieur Hulot	J. Tati	4 945 053	J Tati
La Belle de Cadix	R. Bernard	4 328 273	L. Mariano
1954			
Si Versailles m'était conté	S. Guitry	6 986 788	S. Guitry
Papa, maman, la bonne et moi	J.-P. Le Chanois	5 374 131	R. Lamoureux
Touchez pas au grisbi	J. Becker	4 710 496	J. Gabin
Le Rouge et le noir	C. Autant-Lara	4 343 365	G. Philipe, D. Darrieux
Les Femmes s'en balancent	B. Borderie	4 314 139	E. Constantine
1955			
Le Comte de Monte Cristo	R. Vernay	7 780 642	P. Richard-Willm
Napoléon	S. Guitry	5 405 252	S. Guitry
Les Grandes manoeuvres	R. Clair	5 301 504	G. Philipe, M. Morgan
French-Cancan	J. Renoir	3 963 928	J. Gabin
Chiens perdus sans collier	J. Delannoy	3 905 504	J. Gabin
1956			
Michel Strogoff	C. Gallone	6 920 814	G. Page
Notre-Dame de Paris	J. Delannoy	5 693 719	A. Quinn
La Traversée de Paris	C. Autant-Lara	4 893 174	J. Gabin, Bourvil, L. de Funès
Le Chanteur de Mexico	R. Pottier	4 779 435	L. Mariano, Bourvil
Gervaise	R. Clément	4 108 173	M. Schell

Year	Director	No. spectators	Star(s)

1957

Le Triporteur	J. Pinoteau	4 888 151	D. Cowl
Le Chômeur de Clochemerle	J. Boyer	4 397 173	Fernandel
Porte des Lilas	R. Clair	3 946 553	P. Brasseur, G. Brassens
Honoré de Marseille	M. Regamey	3 755 963	Fernandel
Folies-Bergères	H. Decoin	3 513 397	E. Constantine, Z. Jeanmaire

1958

Les Misérables	J.-P. Le Chanois	9 966 274	J. Gabin, B. Blier, Bourvil
Les Tricheurs	M. Carné	4 953 600	P. Petit
Mon oncle	J. Tati	4 576 928	J. Tati
L'Eau vive	F. Villiers	4 083 521	P. Audret
Les Grandes familles	D. de la Patellière	4 042 041	J. Gabin

1959

La Vache et le prisonnier	Verneuil	8 849 752	Fernandel
La Jument verte	C. Autant-Lara	5 294 328	Bourvil
Babette s'en va en guerre	Christian-Jaque	4 657 610	B. Bardot
Les Liaisons dangereuses	R. Vadim	4 322 955	J. Moreau, G. Philipe
Archimède le clochard	G. Grangier	4 073 891	J. Gabin, D. Cowl

1960

Le Bossu	A. Hunebelle	5 845 980	J. Marais, Bourvil
La Vérité	H.-G. Clouzot	5 690 804	B. Bardot, S. Frey
Le Capitan	A. Hunebelle	5 177 612	J. Marais, Bourvil
Le Passage du Rhin	A. Cayatte	4 658 866	C. Aznavour
Normandie-Niemen	J. Dréville	3 485 432	P. Trabaud

1961

Un taxi pour Tobrouk	D. de la Patellière	4 945 868	L. Ventura, C. Aznavour
Le Comte de Monte-Cristo	C. Autant-Lara	4 448 776	P. Richard-Willm
Don Camillo Monseigneur	C. Gallone	4 280 338	Fernandel
La Belle Américaine	R. Dhéry	4 151 247	R. Dhéry
Le Miracle des loups	A. Hunebelle	3 784 157	J. Marais

Year	Director	No. spectators	Star(s)
1962			
La Guerre des boutons	Y. Robert	9 877 144	J. Dufilho
Lafayette	J. Dréville	3 747 642	M. Le Royer
Cartouche	P. de Broca	3 606 565	J.-P. Belmondo, C. Cardinale
Le Repos du guerrier	R. Vadim	2 872 723	B. Bardot
Les Mystéres de Paris	A. Hunebelle	2 736 818	J. Marais
1963			
La Cuisine au beurre	G. Grangier	6 396 439	Bourvil, Fernandel
Mélodie en sous-sol	H. Verneuil	3 518 083	J. Gabin, A. Delon, V. Romance
Les Tontons flingueurs	G. Lautner	3 321 121	L. Ventura
Bébert et l'omnibus	Y. Robert	3 012 415	P. Gibus, P. Richard
D'où viens-tu Johnny?	N. Howard	2 785 185	J. Hallyday, S. Vartan
1964			
Le Gendarme de Saint-Tropez	J. Girault	7 809 334	L. de Funès
L'Homme de Rio	P. de Broca	4 800 626	J.-P. Belmondo
Fantomas	A. Hunebelle	4 492 419	J. Marais, L. de Funès
Le Train	J. Frankenheimer	3 488 567	J. Moreau, M. Simon
Cent mille dollars au soleil	H. Verneuil	3 441 118	J.-P. Belmondo, L. Ventura
1965			
Le Corniaud	G. Oury	11 739 783	L. de Funès, Bourvil
Le Gendarme à New York	J. Girault	5 495 045	L. de Funès
Fantomas se déchaîne	A. Hunebelle	4 212 446	J. Marais, L. de Funès
Le Tonnerre de Dieu	D. de la Patellière	4 096 394	J. Gabin
Les Grandes gueules	R. Enrico	3 593 724	Bourvil, L. Ventura
1966			
La Grande vadrouille	G. Oury	17 267 607	L. de Funès, Bourvil
Paris brûle-t-il?	R. Clément	4 946 274	J.-P. Belmondo
Un homme et une femme	C. Lelouch	4 269 209	J.-L. Trintignant, A. Aimée
Le Grand restaurant	J. Besnard	3 878 520	L. de Funès
La Curée	R. Vadim	2 558 254	J. Fonda, M. Piccoli

Year	Director	No. spectators	Star(s)
1967			
Les Grandes vacances	J. Girault	6 986 777	L. de Funès
Oscar	E. Molinaro	6 120 862	L. de Funès
Fantomas contre Scotland Yard	A. Hunebelle	3 557 971	L. de Funès, J. Marais
Les Risques du métier	A. Cayatte	3 523 573	J. Brel, E. Riva
Vivre pour vivre	C. Lelouch	2 936 039	Y. Montand
1968			
Le Gendarme se marie	J. Girault	6 828 626	L. de Funès
Le Petit baigneur	R. Dhéry	5 542 755	R. Dhéry, L. de Funès
Le Tatoué	D. de la Patellière	3 211 778	J. Gabin, L. de Funès
Les Cracks	A. Joffé	2 946 373	Bourvil
Adieu l'ami	J. Herman	2 639 713	A. Delon
1969			
Le Cerveau	G. Oury	5 574 299	J.-P. Belmondo, Bourvil
Le Clan des Siciliens	H. Verneuil	4 821 585	J. Gabin, A. Delon, L. Ventura
Z	C. Costa-Gavras	3 952 913	Y. Montand, J.-L. Trintignant
Hibernatus	E. Molinaro	3 366 973	L. de Funés
Mon oncle Benjamin	E. Molinaro	2 722 179	J. Brel
1970			
Le Gendarme en balade	J. Girault	4 870 609	L. de Funès
Le Mur de l'Atlantique	M. Canus	4 770 962	Bourvil
Le Passager de la pluie	R. Clément	4 763 819	M. Jobert
Borsalino	J. Deray	4 710 381	J.-P. Belmondo, A. Delon
Le Cercle rouge	J.-P. Melville	4 339 821	Y. Montand, A. Delon, Bourvil
1971			
Les Bidasses en folie	C. Zidi	7 460 911	Les Charlots, J. Dufilho
Mourir d'aimer	A. Cayatte	5 912 404	A. Girardot
La Folie des grandeurs	G. Oury	5 562 576	Y. Montand, L. de Funès

Year	Director	No. spectators	Star(s)
Le Casse	H. Verneuil	4 410 120	J.-P. Belmondo
Les Mariés de l'an II	J.-P. Rappeneau	2 822 567	J.-P. Belmondo, M. Jobert

1972

Les Fous du stade	C. Zidi	5 744 270	Les Charlots
Les Charlots font l'Espagne	J. Girault	4 162 897	Les Charlots
Tout le monde il est beau, tout le monde il est gentil	J. Yanne	4 076 678	J. Yanne
L'Aventure c'est l'aventure	C. Lelouch	3 815 477	L. Ventura, J. Brel
Le Grand blonc avec une chaussure noire	Y. Robert	3 471 266	P. Richard, M. Darc, J. Rochefort

1973

Les Aventures de Rabbi Jacob	G. Oury	7 295 727	L. de Funès
Mais où est passé la 7e compagnie	R. Lamoureux	3 944 014	J. Lefebvre
Le Grand bazar	C. Zidi	3 913 477	Les Charlots, Coluche
L'Emmerdeur	E. Molinaro	3 354 756	J. Brel, L. Ventura
Le Magnifique	P. de Broca	2 803 412	J.-P. Belmondo

1974

Emmanuelle	J. Jaeckin	8 893 996	S. Kristel
Les Valseuses	B. Blier	5 726 031	G. Depardieu, P. Dewaere, Miou-Miou
Les Bidasses s'en vont en guerre	C. Zidi	4 154 509	Les Charlots
La Moutarde me monte au nez	C. Zidi	3 702 322	P. Richard
La Gifle	C. Pinoteau	3 385 541	L. Ventura, A. Girardot, I. Adjani

1975

Peur sur la ville	H. Verneuil	3 948 746	J.-P. Belmondo
On a retrouvé la 7e compagnie	R. Lamoureux	3 740 209	J. Lefebvre

Year	Director	No. spectators	Star(s)
Histoire d'O	J. Jaeckin	3 512 531	C. Cléry
Le Vieux fusil	R. Enrico	3 365 471	R. Schneider, P. Noiret
La Course à l'échalotte	C. Zidi	2 956 550	P. Richard

1976

L'Aile ou la cuisse	C. Zidi	5 841 956	L. de Funès, Coluche
A nous les petites anglaises	M. Lang	5 704 446	R Laurent
Un éléphant, ça trompe énormément	Y. Robert	2 925 868	J. Rochefort
Docter Françoise Gailland	J.-L. Bertuccelli	2 634 933	A. Girardot
Les Douze travaux d'Astérix	R. Goscinny/ A Uderzo	2 202 481	(animated film)

1977

L'Animal	C. Zidi	3 157 789	J.-P. Belmondo
Diabolo menthe	D. Kurys	3 013 638	E. Klarwein
Nous irons tous au paradis	Y. Robert	2 080 789	J. Rochefort
La Vie devant soi	M. Mizrahi	1 977 455	S. Signoret
Arrête ton char . . . bidasse!	M. Gérard	1 907 513	S. Hillel

1978

La Cage aux folles	E. Molinaro	5 406 614	M. Serrault
La Carapate	G. Oury	2 798 787	P. Richard
La Zizanie	C. Zidi	2 771 917	L. de Funès, A. Girardot
L'Hôtel de la plage	M. Lang	2 534 702	M. Boyer
Je suis timide mais je me soigne	P. Richard	2 308 644	P. Richard

1979

Le Gendarme et les extraterrestres	J. Girault	6 280 070	L. de Funès
Flic ou voyou	G. Lautner	3 950 691	J.-P. Belmondo
Et la tendresse? Bordel!	P. Schulman	3 359 170	J.-L. Bideau, B. Giraudeau
La Dérobade	D. Duval	2 764 084	Miou-Miou
Tess	R. Polanski	1 912 948	N. Kinski

Year	Director	No. spectators	Star(s)
1980			
La Boum	C. Pinoteau	4 378 430	B. Fossey, S. Marceau
Les Sous-doués	C. Zidi	3 985 214	M. Pacôme, M. Galabru
L'Inspecteur la bavure	C. Zidi	3 697 576	Coluche, G. Depardieu
Le Dernier métro	F. Truffaut	3 384 045	C. Deneuve, G. Depardieu
La Cage aux folles 2	E. Molinaro	3 015 152	M. Serrault
1981			
La Chèvre	F. Veber	7 079 674	P. Richard, G. Depardieu
Le Professionnel	G. Lautner	5 243 511	J.-P. Belmondo
La Guerre du feu	J.-J. Annaud	4 950 005	E. McGill
Les uns et les autres	C. Lelouch	3 234 549	R. Hossein
Le Maître d'école	C. Berri	3 105 596	Coluche, J. Balasko
1982			
L'As des as	G. Oury	5 452 593	J.-P. Belmondo
Deux heures moins le quart avant Jésus-Christ	J. Yanne	4 601 239	J. Yanne, M. Serrault, Coluche
Le Gendarme et les gendarmettes	J. Girault/ T. Aboyantz	4 209 139	M. Galabru
La Balance	B. Swaim	4 192 189	N. Baye, R. Berry, P. Léotard
La Boum 2	C. Pinoteau	4 071 585	S. Marceau, B. Fossey
1983			
L'Été meurtrier	J. Becker	5 137 040	I. Adjani, G. Souchon
Le Marginal	J. Deray	4 956 822	J.-P. Belmondo
Les Compères	F. Veber	4 847 229	P. Richard, G. Depardieu
Papy fait de la résistance	J.-M. Poiré	4 103 933	C. Clavier, M. Galabru
Tchao pantin	C. Berri	3 829 139	Coluche, P. Léotard
1984			
Marche à l'ombre	M. Blanc	6 168 425	M. Blanc, G. Lanvin
Les Ripoux	C. Zidi	5 882 397	P. Noiret, T. Lhermitte
Les Morfalous	H. Verneuil	3 621 540	J.-P. Belmondo

Year	Director	No. spectators	Star(s)
Joyeuses Pâques	G. Lautner	3 428 889	J.-P. Belmondo
La Vengeance du serpent à plumes	G. Oury	2 663 303	Coluche

1985

Trois hommes et un couffin	C. Serreau	10 251 465	A. Dussolier, M. Boujenah, R. Giraud
Les Spécialistes	P. Leconte	5 319 542	B. Giraudeau, G. Lanvin
Subway	L. Besson	2 920 588	C. Lambert, I. Adjani
P.R.O.F.S.	P. Schulman	2 845 580	F. Luchini, P. Bruel
L'Effrontée	C. Miller	2 761 141	C. Gainsbourg

1986

Jean de Florette	C. Berri	7 223 657	Y. Montand, G. Depardieu, D. Auteuil
Manon des sources	C. Berri	6 645 177	Y. Montand, D. Auteuil, E. Béart
Le Nom de la rose	J.-J. Annaud	4 955 664	S. Connery
Les Fugitifs	F. Veber	4 496 827	G. Depardieu, P. Richard
37°2 le matin	J.-J. Beineix	3 632 326	B. Dalle, J.-H. Anglade

1987

Au revoir les enfants	L. Malle	3 488 460	G. Manesse
Le Grand chemin	J.-L. Hubert	3 175 537	Anémone, R. Bohringer
Lévy et Goliath	G. Oury	2 166 907	R. Anconina
Association de malfaiteurs	C. Zidi	1 194 563	F. Cluzet
Les Keufs	J. Balasko	1 071 467	J. Balasko, J.-P. Léaud, I. de Bankolé

1988

Le Grand bleu	L. Besson	9 192 732	J.-M. Barr, J. Reno
L'Ours	J.-J. Annaud	9 136 266	T. Karyo
La Vie est un long fleuve tranquille	E. Chatiliez	4 088 009	H. Vincent, D. Gelin
Itinéraire d'un enfant gâté	C. Lelouch	3 254 397	J.-P. Belmondo
Camille Claudel	B. Nuytten	2 717 136	I. Adjani, G. Depardieu

Year	Director	No. spectators	Star(s)
1989			
Trop belle pour toi	B. Blier	2 031 131	G. Depardieu, C. Bouquet, J. Balasko
Noce blanche	J.-C. Brisseau	1 819 295	B. Cremer, V. Paradis
Hiver 54, l'Abbé Pierre	D. Amar	1 645 755	L. Wilson, C. Cardinale
La Petite voleuse	C. Miller	1 834 940	C. Gainsbourg
Noce blance	J.-C. Brisseau	1 819 295	V. Paradis
1990			
La Gloire de mon père	Y. Robert	6 286 547	P. Caubère
Cyrano de Bergerac	J.-P. Rappeneau	4 732 136	G. Depardieu
Le Château de ma mère	Y. Robert	4 269 318	P. Caubère
Nikita	L. Besson	3 787 845	A. Parillaud, T. Karyo, J.-H. Anglade
Ripoux contre ripoux	C. Zidi	2 910 070	P. Noiret, T. Lhermitte
1991			
Tous les matins du monde	A. Corneau	2 152 966	G. Depardieu, J.-P. Marielle
Une époque formidable	G. Jugnot	1 672 754	R. Bohringer, G. Jugnot
La Totale	C. Zidi	1 639 813	Miou-Miou, T. Lhermitte
Opération corned beef	J.-M. Poiré	1 475 580	J. Reno, C. Clavier
Mon père, ce héros	G. Lauzier	1 428 871	G. Depardieu
1992			
Indochine	R. Wargnier	3 198 663	C. Deneuve, V. Perez, J. Yanne
L'Amant	J.-J. Annaud	3 156 124	J. March
Christophe Colomb 1492	R. Scott	3 082 110	G. Depardieu
Les Nuits fauves	C. Collard	2 811 124	C. Collard, R. Bohringer
La Crise	C. Serreau	2 350 189	V. Lindon
1993			
Les Visiteurs	J.-M. Poiré	13 728 242	C. Clavier, J. Reno
Germinal	C. Berri	6 139 961	G. Depardieu, Miou-Miou

Year	Director	No. spectators	Star(s)
Tout ça pour ça	C. Lelouch	1 847 381	V. Lindon
La Soif de l'or	G. Oury	1 517 890	C. Clavier, C. Jacob
L'Enfant lion	P. Grandperret	1 255 917	W. Liking, S. Koli

1994

Un indien dans la ville	P. Hervé	7 870 802	T. Lhermitte
Léon	L. Besson	3 546 077	J. Reno
La Cité de la peur	A. Berbérian	2 216 436	A. Chabat
La Vengeance d'une blonde	J. Szwarc	2 039 370	C. Clavier, M.-A. Chazel, T Lhermitte
Grosse fatigue	M. Blanc	2 015 230	M. Blanc, C. Bouquet, J. Balasko

1995

Les Trois frères	D. Bourbon/ B. Campan	6 667 549	D. Bourbon, B. Campan
Les Anges gardiens	J.-M. Poiré	5 734 059	G. Depardieu, C. Clavier
Le Bonheur est dans le pré	E. Chatiliez	4 929 723	M. Serrault, E. Mitchell, S Azéma
Gazon maudit	J. Balasko	3 990 094	V. Abril, A. Chabat, J. Balasko
Élisa	J. Becker	2 473 193	V. Paradis, G. Depardieu

1996

Pédale douce	G. Aghion	4 158 212	P. Timsit
Le Huitième jour	J. van Dormael	3 597 960	D. Auteuil
Un air de famille	C. Klapisch	2 411 224	J.-P. Bacri, A. Jaoui
Le Jaguar	F. Veber	2 390 580	J. Reno, P. Bruel
Le Plus beau métier du monde	G. Lauzier	2 269 925	G. Depardieu

1997

Le Cinquième élément	L. Besson	7 696 667	B. Willis
La Vérité si je mens!	T. Gilou	4 879 200	R. Anconina
Le Pari	D. Bourdon/ B. Campan	3 825 825	D. Bourdon, B. Campan

Year	Director	No. spectators	Star(s)
Didier	A. Chabat	2 881 278	A. Chabat, J.-P. Bacri
Marius et Jeannette	R. Guédiguian	2 653 960	A. Ascaride

1998

Year	Director	No. spectators	Star(s)
Le Dîner de cons	F. Veber	9 231 507	J. Villeret, .T Lhermitte
Les Couloirs du temps	J.-M. Poiré	8 035 342	C. Clavier, J. Reno
Taxi	G. Pirès	6 464 411	S. Naceri
La Vie rêvée des anges	E. Zonca	1 445 312	E. Bouchez, N. Régnier
1 chance sur 2	P. Leconte	1 055 037	J.-P. Belmondo, A. Delon, V. Paradis

1999

Year	Director	No. spectators	Star(s)
Astérix et Obélix contre César	C. Zidi	8 944 457	C. Clavier, G. Depardieu
Jeanne d'Arc	L. Besson	2 984 144	M. Jovovich
Himalaya	E. Valli	2 355 765	T. Lhondup
Les Enfants du marais	J. Becker	2 119 186	J. Villeret, A. Dussolier
Quasimodo d'el Paris	P. Timsit	1 706 110	P. Timsit

TABLE 7: THE TOP 50 FRENCH FILMS 1945–1999 (BY NUMBER OF SPECTATORS)

	Title	Year	Director	No. Spectators	Stars
1	*La Grande vadrouille*	1966	G. Oury	17 267 607	L. de Funès, Bourvil
2	*Les Visiteurs*	1993	J.-M. Poiré	13 728 242	C. Clavier, J. Reno
3	*Le Petit monde de Don Camillo*	1952	J. Duvivier	12 790 676	Fernandel
4	*Le Corniaud*	1965	G. Oury	11 739 783	L. de Funès, Bourvil
5	*Trois hommes et un couffin*	1985	C. Serreau	10 251 465	A. Dussolier, M. Boujenah, R. Giraud
6	*Les Misérables*	1958	J.-P. Le Chanois	9 966 274	J. Gabin, B. Blier, Bourvil
7	*La Guerre des boutons*	1962	Y. Robert	9 877 144	J. Dufilho
8	*Le Dîner de cons*	1998	F. Veber	9 231 507	J. Villeret, T. Lhermitte
9	*Le Grand bleu*	1988	L. Besson	9 192 732	J.-M. Barr, J. Reno
10	*L'Ours*	1988	J.-J. Annaud	9 136 266	T. Karyo
11	*Astérix et Obélix contre César*	1999	C. Zidi	8 944 457	C. Clavier, G. Depardieu
12	*Emmanuelle*	1974	J. Jaeckin	8 893 996	S. Kristel
13	*La Vache et le prisonnier*	1959	Verneuil	8 849 752	Fernandel
14	*Le Bataillon du ciel*	1947	A. Esway	8 649 691	J. Crispin
15	*Violettes impériales*	1952	R. Pottier	8 125 766	L. Mariano

Title	Year	Director	No. Spectators	Stars
16 *Les Couloirs du temps*	1998	J.-M. Poiré	8 035 342	C. Clavier, J. Reno
17 *Un Indien dans la ville*	1994	P. Hervé	7 870 802	T. Lhermitte
18 *Le Gendarme de Saint-Tropez*	1964	J. Girault	7 809 334	L. de Funès
19 *Le Comte de Monte Cristo*	1955	R. Vernay	7 780 642	P. Richard-Willm
20 *Le Cinquième élément*	1997	L. Besson	7 696 667	B. Willis
21 *Les Bidasses en folie*	1971	C. Zidi	7 460 911	Les Charlots, J. Difilho
22 *Le Retour de Don Camillo*	1953	J. Duvivier	7 425 550	Fernandel
23 *Les Aventures de Rabbi Jacob*	1973	G. Oury	7 295 727	L. de Funès
24 *Jean de Florette*	1986	C. Berri	7 223 657	Y. Montand, G. Depardieu, D. Auteuil
25 *La Chèvre*	1981	F. Veber	7 079 674	P. Richard, G. Depardieu
26 *Monsieur Vincent*	1947	M. Cloche	7 055 290	P. Fresnay
27 *Si Versailles m'était conté*	1954	S. Guitry	6 986 788	S. Guitry
28 *Les Grandes vacances*	1966	J. Girault	6 986 777	L. de Funès
29 *Le Salaire de la peur*	1953	H.-G. Clouzot	6 943 447	Y. Montand, C. Vanel
30 *Michel Strogoff*	1956	C. Gallone	6 920 814	G. Page
31 *Le Gendarme se marie*	1968	J. Girault	6 828 626	L. de Funès
32 *Mission spéciale*	1946	M. De Canonge	6 781 120	J. Holt, P. Renoir
33 *Fanfan la tulipe*	1952	Christian-Jaque	6 712 512	G. Philipe
34 *Jour de fête*	1949	J. Tati	6 679 608	J. Tati
35 *Les Trois frères*	1995	D. Bourbon/ B. Campan	6 667 549	D. Bourbon, B. Campan
36 *Nous irons à Paris*	1950	J. Boyer	6 658 693	R. Ventura
37 *Manon des sources*	1986	C. Berri	6 645 177	Y. Montand, D. Auteuil, E. Béart
38 *Taxi*	1998	G. Pirès	6 464 411	S. Naceri
39 *La Cuisine au beurre*	1963	G. Grangier	6 396 439	Bourvil, Fernandel
40 *La Symphonie pastorale*	1946	J. Delannoy	6 372 837	M. Morgan
41 *La Gloire de mon père*	1990	Y. Robert	6 286 547	P. Caubère
42 *Le Gendarme et les extraterrestres*	1979	J. Girault	6 280 070	L. de Funès
43 *Marche à l'ombre*	1984	M. Blanc	6 168 425	M. Blanc, G. Lanvin
44 *Pas si bête*	1947	A. Berthomieu	6 165 419	Bourvil
45 *La Chartreuse de Parme*	1948	Christian-Jaque	6 150 551	G. Philipe
46 *Germinal*	1993	C. Berri	6 139 961	G. Depardieu, Miou-Miou
47 *Le Père tranquille*	1946	R. Clément	6 138 837	Noël-Noël
48 *Oscar*	1967	E. Molinaro	6 120 862	L. de Funès
49 *Mourir d'aimer*	1971	A. Cayatte	5 912 404	A. Girardot
50 *Le Bossu*	1960	A. Hunebelle	5 845 980	J. Marais, Bourvil

TABLE 8: FRENCH PRIZES 1945–1999

Only major prizes have been listed (Best Film, Palme d'Or, International and Special Jury Prizes, Best Director, Best Actor and Best Actress). The year given is the year of release of the film.

	Cannes	Louis Delluc
1945		L'Espoir, A. Malraux
1946	La Bataille du rail, R. Clément: Best Director; International Jury Prize La Symphonie pastorale, J. Delannoy: Best Film; Best Actress (Michèle Morgan)	La Belle et la bête, J. Cocteau
1947		Paris 1900, N. Védrès
1948		Les Casse-pieds, J. Dréville
1949	Au-delà des grilles, R. Clément: Best Director; Best Actress (Isa Miranda)	Les Rendez-vous de juillet, J. Becker
1950		Journal d'un curé de campagne, R. Bresson
1951		
1952	Nous sommes tous des assassins, A. Cayatte: Special Jury Prize Fanfan la tulipe, Christian-Jaque: Best Director	Le Rideau cramoisi, A. Astruc
1953	Le Salaire de la peur, H.-G. Clouzot: Best Film; Best Actor (C. Vanel)	Les Vacances de Monsieur Hulot, J. Tati
1954	Monsieur Ripois, R. Clément: International Jury Prize	Les Diaboliques, H.-G. Clouzot
1955	Du rififi chez les hommes, J. Dassin: Best Director	Les Grandes manœuvres, R. Clair
1956	Le Monde du silence, J.-Y. Cousteau/L. Malle: Palme d'Or Le Mystère Picasso, H.-G. Clouzot: Special Jury Prize Un condamné à mort s'est échappé, R. Bresson: Best Director	
1957		Ascenseur pour l'échafaud, L. Malle
1958	Mon oncle, J. Tati: Special Jury Prize	

	Cannes	Louis Delluc
1959	Les 400 coups, F. Truffaut: Best Director / Orfeu Negro, M. Camus: Palme d'Or	On n'enterre pas le dimanche, M. Drach
1960	Moderato Cantabile, P. Brook: Best Actress (Jeanne Moreau)	Une aussi longue absence, H. Colpi
1961	Une aussi longue absence, H. Colpi: Palme d'Or	Un Cœur gros comme ça, F. Reichenbach
1962		L'Immortelle, A. Robbe-Grillet / Le Soupirant, P. Étaix
1963	Procès de Jeanne d'Arc, R. Bresson: Special Jury Prize	Les Parapluies de Cherbourg, J. Demy
1964	Les Parapluies de Cherbourg, J. Demy: Grand prix du Festival international du film	Le Bonheur, A. Varda
1965		La Vie de château, J.-P. Rappeneau
1966	Un homme et une femme, C. Lelouch: Grand prix du Festival international du film	La Guerre est finie, A. Resnais
1967		Benjamin ou les mémoires d'un puceau, M. Deville
1968		Baisers volés, F. Truffaut
1969	Z, C. Costa-Gavras: Jury Prize; Best Actor (J.-L. Trintignant)	Les Choses de la vie, C. Sautet
1970		Le Genou de Claire, E. Rohmer
1971		Rendez-vous à Bray, A. Delvaux
1972	Nous ne vieillirons pas ensemble, M. Pialat: Best Actor (Jean Yanne)	État de siège, C. Costa-Gavras
1973	La Maman et la putain, J. Eustache: Grand Prix Spécial / La Planète sauvage, R. Laloux: Special Prize	L'Horloger de Saint-Paul, B. Tavernier
1974	Violons du bal, M. Drach: Best Actress (Marie-José Nat)	La Gifle, C. Pinoteau

Year	Cannes	Louis Delluc	Césars (began 1976)			
			Best Film	Best Director	Best Actor	Best Actress
1975	Les Ordres, M. Brault: Best Director Section spéciale, C. Costa-Gavras: Best Director	Cousin, cousine, J.-C. Tachella	Le Vieux fusil, R. Enrico	Que la fête commence, B. Tavernier	Le Vieux fusil, R. Enrico (P. Noiret)	L'Important c'est d'aimer, A. Zulawski (R. Schneider)
1976		Le Juge Fayard, dit 'Le Shériff', Y. Boisset	Monsieur Klein, J. Losey	Monsieur Klein, J. Losey	Le Juge et l'assassin, B. Tavernier (M. Galabru)	Docteur Françoise Gailland, J.-L. Bertucelli (A. Girardot)
1977		Diabolo menthe, D. Kurys	Providence, A. Resnais	Providence, A. Resnais	Le Crabe-tambour, P. Schoendoerffer (J. Rochefort)	La Vie devant soi, M. Mizrahi (S. Signoret)
1978	Violette Nozière, C. Chabrol: Best Actress (Isabelle Huppert)	L'Argent des autres, C. de Chalonge	L'Argent des autres, C. de Chalonge	L'Argent des autres, C. de Chalonge	La Cage aux folles, E. Molinaro (M. Serrault)	Une histoire simple, C. Sautet (R. Schneider)
1979	Mon oncle d'Amérique, A. Resnais: Special Jury Prize	Le Roi et l'oiseau, P. Grimault	Tess, R. Polanski	Tess, R. Polanski	La Guerre des polices, R. Davis (C. Brasseur)	La Dérobade, D. Duval (Miou-Miou)
1980		Un étrange voyage, A. Cavalier	Le Dernier métro, F. Truffaut	Le Dernier métro, F. Truffaut	Le Dernier métro, F. Truffaut (G. Depardieu)	Le Dernier métro, F. Truffaut (C. Deneuve)

	Cannes	Louis Delluc	Césars (began 1976)			
			Best Film	Best Director	Best Actor	Best Actress
1981	Best Actress (Isabelle Adjani for Quartet, J. Ivory and Possession, A. Zulawski)	Une étrange affaire, P. Granier-Deferre	La Guerre du feu, J.-J. Annaud	La Guerre du feu, J.-J. Annaud	Garde à vue, C. Miller (M. Serrault)	Possession, A. Zulawski (I. Adjani)
1982	La Balance, B. Swaim: Best Film	Danton, A. Wajda	La Balance, B. Swaim	Danton, A. Wajda	La Balance, B. Swaim (P. Léotard)	La Balance, B. Swaim (N. Baye)
1983	L'Argent, R. Bresson: Best Director	À nos amours, M. Pialat	À nos amours, M. Pialat Le bal, Ettore Scola	Le Bal, Ettore Scola	Tchao pantin, C. Berri (Coluche)	L'Été meurtrier, J. Becker (I. Adjani)
1984	Un dimanche à la campagne, B. Tavernier: Best Director	La Diagonale du fou, R. Dembo	Les Ripoux, C. Zidi	Les Ripoux, C. Zidi	Notre histoire, B. Blier (A. Delon)	Un dimanche à la campagne, B. Tavernier (S. Azéma)
1985	Rendez-vous, A. Téchiné: Best Director	L'Effrontée, C. Miller	Trois hommes et un couffin, C. Serreau	Péril en la demeure, M. Deville	Subway, L. Besson (C. Lambert)	Sans toit ni loi, A. Varda (S. Bonnaire)
1986	Tenue de soirée, B. Blier: Best Actor (Michel Blanc) Thérèse, A. Cavalier: Jury Prize	Mauvais sang, L. Carax	Thérèse, A. Cavalier	Thérèse, A. Cavalier	Manon des sources, C. Berri (D. Auteuil)	Mélo, A. Resnais (S. Azéma)

1987	Sous le soleil de Satan, M. Pialat: Palme d'Or	Au revoir les enfants, L. Malle Soigne ta droite, J.-L. Godard	Au revoir les enfants, L. Malle	Au revoir les enfants, L. Malle	Le Grand chemin, J.-L. Hubert (R. Bohringer)	Le Grand chemin, J.-L. Hubert (Anémone)
1988		La Lectrice, M. Deville	Camille Claudel, B. Nuttyens	L'Ours, J.-J. Annaud	Itinéraire d'un enfant gâté, C. Lelouch (J.-P. Belmondo)	Camille Claudel, B. Nuttyens (I. Adjani)
1989	Trop belle pour toi, B. Blier : Special Jury Prize	Un monde sans pitié, E. Rochant Le Petit criminel, J. Doillon	Trop belle pour toi, B. Blier	Trop belle pour toi, B. Blier	La Vie et rien d'autre, B. Tavernier (P. Noiret)	Trop belle pour toi, B. Blier (C. Bouquet)
1990	Cyrano de Bergerac, J.-P. Rappeneau: Best Actor (G Depardieu)	Le Mari de la coiffeuse, P. Leconte	Cyrano de Bergerac, J.-P. Rappeneau	Cyrano de Bergerac, J.-P. Rappeneau	Cyrano de Bergerac, J.-P. Rappeneau (G. Depardieu)	Nikita, L. Besson (A. Parillaud)
1991	La Belle noiseuse, J. Rivette: Grand Prix	Tous les matins du monde, A. Corneau	Tous les matins du monde, A. Corneau	Tous les matins du monde, A. Corneau	Van Gogh, M. Pialat (J. Dutronc)	La Vieille qui marchait dans la mer, L. Heynemann (J. Moreau)
1992		Le Petit prince a dit, C. Pascal Smoking/No Smoking, A. Resnais	Les Nuits fauves, C. Collard Smoking/No Smoking, A. Resnais	Un coeur en hiver, C. Sautet Smoking/No Smoking, A. Resnais	Le Souper, E. Molinaro (C. Rich) Smoking/No Smoking, A. Resnais (Pierre Arditi)	Indochine, R. Wargnier (C. Deneuve)
1993						Trois Couleurs: Bleu, K. Kieślowski (J. Binoche)

	Cannes	Louis Delluc	Césars (began 1976)			
			Best Film	Best Director	Best Actor	Best Actress
1994	*La Reine Margot*, P. Chéreau: Jury Prize; Best Actress (Virna Lisi)	*Les Roseaux sauvages*, A. Téchiné	*Les Roseaux sauvages*, A. Téchiné	*Les Roseaux sauvages*, A. Téchiné	*Le Fils préféré*, N. Garcia (G. Lanvin)	*La Reine Margot*, P. Chéreau (I. Adjani)
1995	*La Haine*, M. Kassovitz: Best Director *N'oublie pas que tu vas mourir*, X. Beauvois: Jury Prize		*La Haine*, M. Kassovitz	*Nelly et Monsieur Arnaud*, C. Sautet	*Nelly et Monsieur Arnaud*, C. Sautet (Michel Serrault)	*La Cérémonie*, C. Chabrol (I. Huppert)
1996	*Ridicule*, P. Leconte: Best Film *Le Huitième jour*, J. van Dormael: Best actors (D. Auteuil, P. Duquenne)	*Y aura-t-il de la neige à Noël?*, S. Veysset	*Ridicule*, P. Leconte	*Ridicule*, P. Leconte *Capitaine Conan*, B. Tavernier	*Capitaine Conan*, B. Tavernier (P. Torreton)	*Pédale douce*, G. Aghion (F. Ardant)
1997	*Western*, M. Poirier: Jury Prize *La Vie de Jésus*, B. Dumont: Special Mention	*Marius et Jeannette*, R. Guédiguian *On connaît la chanson*, A. Resnais	*On connaît la chanson*, A. Resnais	*Le Cinquième élément*, L. Besson	*On connaît la chanson*, A. Resnais (André Dussolier)	*Marius et Jeannette*, R. Guédiguian (A. Ascaride)

		L'Ennui, C. Kahn	La Vie rêvée des anges, E. Zonca	Ceux qui m'aiment prendront le train, P. Chéreau	Le Dîner de cons, F. Veber (J. Villeret)	La Vie rêvée des anges, E. Zonca (Elodie Bouchez)
1998	La Vie rêvée des anges, E. Zonca: Best Actresses (Elodie Bouchez and Natacha Régnier) / La Classe de neige, C. Miller: Jury Prize					
1999	L'Humanité, B. Dumont: Grand Prix; Best Actor (E Schotte); Best Actress (S Caneele) / Rosetta, L. and J.-P. Dardenne: Palme d'Or; Best Actress (E. Duquenne)	Adieu plancher des vaches, O. Iosselani / Voyages, E. Finkiel	Vénus beauté, (Institut) T. Marshall	Vénus beauté, (Institut) T. Marshall	La Fille sur le pont, P. Leconte (D. Auteuil)	Haut les coeurs!, S. Anspach (K. Viard)

TABLE 9: OSCAR FOR BEST FOREIGN FILM WON BY FRENCH FILMS

The year given in the table below is the year of the Oscar; the film was generally released the previous year. Numbers of spectators are for France.

1958	*Mon oncle*	J Tati	4 576 928
1960	*Orfeu Negro*	M Camus	3 690 517
1970	*Un homme et une femme*	C Lelouch	4 269 209
1973	*Le Charme discret de la bourgeoisie*	L Buñuel	1 490 924
1974	*La Nuit américaine*	F Truffaut	827 665
1977	*La Victoire en chantant*	J-J Annaud	173 150
1979	*Préparez vos mouchoirs*	B Blier	1 321 087
1985	*La Diagonale du fou*	R Dembo	337 105
1992	*Indochine*	R Wargnier	3 198 663

TABLE 10: KEY TECHNICAL TERMS IN ENGLISH AND FRENCH

Camera distance (using the human figure as measure)		
extreme long shot	*plan général, plan de grand ensemble*	far distance
long shot	*plan d'ensemble*	full figure
medium long shot	*plan moyen, plan demi-ensemble*	knees up
medium	*plan américain*	thighs up
medium close	*plan rapproché*	waist or shoulders up
close-up	*gros plan*	face
extreme close-up	*très gros plan*	part of face
background	*arrière-plan*	
foreground	*premier plan*	

Camera movement		
crane up	*plan grue (haut)*	camera mounted on crane
crane down	*plan grue (bas)*	
dolly forwards	*travelling avant*	camera mounted on trolly;
dolly back	*travelling arrière*	often on a rail-track so also
dolly right	*travelling latéral (droite)*	known as *tracking shot*
dolly left	*travelling latéral (gauche)*	
pan right	*panoramique (droite)*	camera swivels on horizontal

pan left	*panoramique (gauche)*	or vertical axis; 'pan' is short for 'panorama'
tilt down	*panoramique vertical (haut)*	
tilt up	*panoramique vertical (bas)*	
high angle	*en plongée*	camera from high to low
low angle	*en contre-plongée*	camera from low to high

Other Terms Associated with the camera

image track	*bande-image*	
reel	*bobine*	
lens	*objectif*	
intertitles	*intertitres*	
deep focus	*profondeur de champ*	background and foreground are equally clear
fade in	*fondu au noir*	
fade out	*ouverture au noir*	
superimposition	*fondu enchaîné*	
framing	*cadrage*	
fast motion	*accéléré*	
slow motion	*ralenti*	
blurred	*flou*	
wipe	*volet*	a sweeping effect across the screen to close a shot
zoom	*zoom*	lens with variable focus allowing travelling effects without moving the camera
off screen	*hors cadre* ('hors champ' is more specifically used for visuals, 'off' for sound)	

Lighting/*Lumière*

key light	*lumière principale*
filler light	*lumière d'ambiance, lumière de face*
back light	*lumière de derrière*
filter	*filtre*

Soundtrack/*Bande-Son*

| sound effects | *bruitage* |

fully/simple diegetic (la diégèse/diégétique)	*diégétique*	soundtrack coincides with what the spectator sees on screen (the story space, or diegesis)
external diegetic	*diégétique externe*	sound in the story space, but unseen, although the spectator assumes that characters are aware of it
displaced diegetic	*diégétique déplacée*	ditto, but sound is anterior or posterior to image
semi-diegetic	*demi-diégétique*	voice-over by character
internal diegetic	*diégétique interne*	dialogue assumed to be in the mind of character
non-diegetic	*non-diégetique*	not part of story space, e.g. commentary 'off' ('*voix off*')
voice-over	*voix off*	a character speaks from 'outside' the story space (or diegesis)
dubbing	*doublage, dubbing*	
subtitled	*sous-titré*	

Music

redundant; empathetic	*musique empathique*	conveys the emotions of characters
contrapuntal; a-empathetic	*musique anempathique*	music indifferent to the drama, distances the spectator
contrapuntal; didactic	*musique didactique*	music asks the spectator to adopt a distanced, even ironic position

Editing

credits	*générique*	
establishing shot	*plan général*	a shot, usually a long shot, that shows the spectator the general location of the scene that follows; it often provides essential information and orientates the spectator

shot	*plan*	
link shot	*raccord*	the linking of two shots through movement, sound, etc.
shot – reverse shot	*champ/contrechamp*	conventional organisation of shots in a sequence, as in a conversation where the camera switches from one interlocutor to the other as each speaks
false continuity	*faux raccord*	
insert	*insert*	an inserted shot, e.g. a close-up (see the section on Metz in Chapter 2 of this volume for other examples)
flashback	*flashback*	
flash forward	*flash forward*	

Mise-En-Scène

A commonly used term in both English and French, meaning literally 'what is put into the scene'. It covers everything the spectator sees that is not camera-specific: lighting and colour; costume, hair and make-up; settings and props; facial expressions and body language; positioning of characters and objects within the frame.

FURTHER READING

Writing on the French cinema is extensive. We confine ourselves here to major works published in the last 20 years or so, which students may find helpful in thinking about French cinema. We have not listed encyclopaedias or dictionaries (of which there are many published in French and, increasingly, in English); nor have we listed volumes on individual directors, since these are too numerous; many of them are referred to in Chapter 3 of this volume. It is also worth signalling Manchester University Press's recent French Directors series which, at the time of writing, has volumes on Besson, Beineix, Blier, Bresson, Chabrol, Kurys, Méliès, Renoir, Serreau, Truffaut and Varda, with volumes on Carax, Cocteau, Duras, Godard, Leconte, Resnais, Tavernier, Téchiné and Vigo to appear. These volumes give critical bibliographies for the directors.

The following reading list is split into two sections: the first for books in English, the second for books in French.

BOOKS IN ENGLISH

Abel, Richard (1984) *French Cinema: The First Wave, 1915–1929* (Princeton, NJ: Princeton University Press). Abel's work is essential reading if you are interested in early French cinema.

Abel, Richard (1994) *The Cine Goes to Town: French Cinema, 1896–1914* (Berkeley: University of California Press).

Austin, Guy (1996) *Contemporary French Cinema: An Introduction* (Manchester University Press). Very good on the cinema of the 1980s and 1990s.

Crisp, Colin (1993) *The Classic French Cinema: 1930–1960* (Bloomington: Indiana University Press). An essential study, with excellent background on the industry for this period.

Forbes, Jill (1992) *The Cinema in France after the New Wave* (Basingstoke, Hampshire: Macmillan). An essential volume by the writer to whom this book is dedicated.

Greene, Naomi (1999) *Landscapes of Loss: The National Past in Postwar French Cinema* (Princeton, N.J.: Princeton University Press). Explores the way in which the past resurfaces in film; see the appraisal in Chapter 3 of this volume.

Hayward, Susan (1993) *French National Cinema* (London and New York: Routledge). A key volume that attempts to redefine the history of French cinema.

Kline, T. Jefferson (1992) *Screening the Text: Intertextuality in New Wave French Cinema* (Baltimore and London: Johns Hopkins University Press). An innovative study of a key period of French cinema.

Mazdon, Lucy (2000) *Encore Hollywood: Remaking French Cinema* (London: BFI). A clear introduction to one of the more interesting features of 1980s film production; see the appraisal in Chapter 3 of this volume.

Mazdon, Lucy (ed.) (2001) *France on Film: Reflections on Popular French Cinema* (London: Wallflower). A collection of essays on recent cinema. Films covered include *Jean de Florette*, *Les Visiteurs*, *Gazon Maudit*, *Romance*.

Powrie, Phil (1997) *French Cinema in the 1980s: Nostalgia and the Crisis of Masculinity* (Oxford: Clarendon Press). A set of essays on individual films covering three major genres: heritage, police thriller and comedy.

Powrie, Phil (ed.) (1999) *French Cinema in the 1990s: Continuity and Difference* (Oxford: Oxford University Press). Essays, mainly on individual films from the 1990s, preceded by a long introduction.

Tarr, Carrie with Brigitte Rollet (2001) *Cinema and the Second Sex: Women's Filmmaking in France in the 1980s and 1990s* (New York and London: Continuum). An essential history that complements Powrie (1997; 1999).

Vincendeau, Ginette (2000) *Stars and Stardom in French Cinema* (London, New York: Continuum). An essential volume by one of the leading academics in French Film Studies; see the appraisal in Chapter 3 of this volume.

Williams, Alan Larson (1992) *Republic of Images: A History of French Filmmaking* (Cambridge, Ma: Harvard University Press). Good on the early periods, skimpy on the1980s.

Wilson, Emma (1999) *French Cinema since 1950: Personal Histories* (London: Duckworth). A useful complement to Forbes (1992) and Greene (1999), particularly in its focus on trauma.

BOOKS IN FRENCH
General histories

Billard, Pierre (1995) *L'Age classique du cinéma français: du cinéma parlant à la Nouvelle Vague* (Paris: Flammarion). Well-known film reviewer; large, detailed and very accessible volume produced for the centenary of the cinema.

Frodon, Jean-Michel (1995) *L'Age moderne du cinéma français: de la Nouvelle Vague* à nos jours (Paris: Flammarion). *Le Monde*'s film reviewer; large, detailed and very accessible volume produced for the centenary of the cinema.

Jeancolas, Jean-Pierre (1995) *Histoire du cinéma français* (Paris: Nathan). Perhaps the best short introduction by a respected historian and regular contributor to the journal *Positif*.

Prédal, René and Michel Marie (1991) *Le Cinéma français depuis 1945* (Paris: Nathan). A useful complement to Frodon (1995) by two academics.

Siclier, Jacques (1990) *Le Cinéma français* (Paris: Editions Ramsay). Vol.1: *De La Bataille du rail à la Chinoise, 1945–1968*; Vol.2: *De Baisers volés à Cyrano de Bergerac, 1968–1990*.

Specific periods

Buache, Freddy (1987) *Le Cinéma français des années 60* (Renens: 5 Continents/Paris: Hatier).

Buache, Freddy (1990) *Le cinéma français des années 70* (Renens: 5 Continents/Paris: Hatier).

Chirat, Raymond and Micheline Presle (1985) *La IVe République et ses films* (Renens: 5 Continents/Paris: Hatier).

Guillaume-Grimaud, Geneviève (1986) *Le Cinéma du Front Populaire* (Paris: Lherminier).

Jeancolas, Jean-Pierre (1983) *15 ans d'années trente: le cinéma des Français, 1929–1944* (Paris: Stock).

Marie, Michel (2000) *La Nouvelle Vague: une école artistique* (Paris: Nathan).

Predal, Rene (2002) *Le jeune cinéma français* (Paris: Nathan). More academic than Trémois.

Trémois, Claude (1997) *Les Enfants de la liberté: le jeune cinéma français des années 90* (Paris: Seuil). A useful introduction by the film critic of *Télérama*.

Theoretical and practical issues

Aumont, Jacques and Michel Marie (1988) *L'Analyse des films* (Paris: Nathan). Although a university textbook, this is sometimes heavy going in its outline of the various film theories.

Aumont, Jacques, Alain Bergala and Michel Marie (1983) *L'Esthétique du film* (Paris: Nathan). A standard textbook in France and a very thorough introduction to film analysis.

BIBLIOGRAPHY

Abel, Richard (1984) *French cinéma: The First Wave, 1915–1929* (Princeton, NJ: Princeton University Press).

Abel, Richard (1988) *French Film Theory and Criticism: A History/Anthology, 1907–1929* (Princeton, NJ: Princeton University Press).

Abel, Richard (1994) *The Cine Goes to Town: French Cinema, 1896–1914* (Berkeley: University of California Press).

Aitken, Ian (2001) *European Film Theory and Cinema: A Critical Introduction* (Edinburgh: Edinburgh University Press).

Andrew, Dudley (1984) *Concepts in Film Theory* (Oxford, New York: Oxford University Press).

Andrew, Dudley (1995) *Mists of Regret: Culture and Sensibility in Classic French Film* (Princeton, NJ: Princeton University Press).

Astruc, Alexandre (1948) 'La caméra-stylo', *Écran français* **144**.

Atack, Margaret (1999) *May 68 in French Fiction and Film: Rethinking Society, Rethinking Representation* (Oxford: Oxford University Press).

Aumont, Jacques (1989) *L'Œil interminable: cinéma et peinture* (Paris: Librairie Séguier).

Aumont, Jacques (1990) *L'Image* (Paris: Nathan).

Aumont, Jacques (1997) *The Image* (London: British Film Institute).

Aumont, Jacques (1999) *Amnésies: fictions du cinéma d'après Jean-Luc Godard* (Paris: POL).

Austin, Guy (1996) *Contemporary French Cinema: An Introduction* (Manchester: Manchester University Press).

Austin, Guy (1999) *Claude Chabrol* (Manchester: Manchester University Press).

Azzopardi, Michel (1997) *Le Temps des vamps 1915–1965 (Cinquante ans de sex-appeal)* (Paris: L'Harmattan).

Baudry, Jean-Louis (1971) 'Cinéma: effets idéologiques produits pas l'appareil de base', *Cinéthique* **7/8**. Translated as 'Ideological effects of the basic cinematographic apparatus' in the following: *Film Quarterly* (1974/75) **28**(2), 39–47; *Movies and Methods: An Anthology*, Vol.2, ed. B. Nichols (Berkeley and Los Angeles: University of California Press, 1985), 531–42; *Narrative, Ideology, Apparatus: A Film Theory Reader*, ed. P. Rosen (New York: Columbia University Press, 1986), 286–98; *Film Theory and Criticism*, ed. G. Mast and M. Cohen (New York and London, Oxford University Press, 1992), 302–12.

Baudry, Jean-Louis (1975) 'Le dispositif: approches métapsychologiques de l'effet de réalité', *Communications* **23**, 56–72. Translated as 'The Apparatus: metapsychological approaches to the impression of reality in the cinema' in the following: *Camera Obscura* (1975) **23**, 104–28; *Narrative, Ideology, Apparatus: A Film Theory Reader*, ed. P. Rosen (New York: Columbia University Press, 1986), 299–318; *Film Theory and Criticism*, ed. G. Mast and M. Cohen (New York and London, Oxford University Press, 1992), 690–707.

Baudry, Jean-Louis (1978) *L'Effet-Cinéma* (Paris: Albatros).

Bazin, Andre (1958) *Qu'est-ce que le cinema? 1: Ontologie et langage* (Paris: Éditions du Cerf).

Bazin, Andre (1959) *Qu'est-ce que le cinema? 2: Le cinéma et les autres arts* (Paris: Éditions du Cerf).

Bazin, Andre (1974a) *What is Cinema?* Vol. 1 (Berkeley: University of California Press).

Bazin, Andre (1974b) *What is Cinema?* Vol. 2 (Berkeley: University of California Press).

Bazin, Andre (1983) *Le Cinéma français de la libération à la Nouvelle Vague (1945–1958)* (Paris: Editions de L'Etoile), 50–69.

Beineix, Jean-Jacques (1987) 'Interview', *Séquences* **129**, 40–47.

Bellour, Raymond (1975) 'Le blocage symbolique', *Communications* **23**, 235–350.

Bergala, Alain (1999) *Nul mieux que Godard* (Paris: Cahiers du cinéma).

Bertin, Célia (1994) *Jean Renoir cineaste* (Paris: Gallimard).

Bessy, Maurice (1989) *Jean Renoir* (Paris: Pygmalion/G. Watelet).

Billard, Pierre (1995) *L'Âge classique du cinema francais: du cinema parlant à la Nouvelle Vague* (Paris: Flammarion).

Blanchet, Christian (1989) *Claude Chabrol* (Paris: Rivages).

Bonitzer, Pascal (1985) *Peinture et cinéma: décadrages* (Paris: Éditions de L'Étoile).

Bonitzer, Pascal (1991) *Eric Rohmer* (Paris: Cahiers du cinéma).

Bordwell, David (1997) *On the History of Film Style* (Cambridge, MA: Harvard University Press).

Braudy, Leo (1989) *Jean Renoir: The World of his Films* (New York: Columbia University Press).

Brewster, Ben (1973) 'Notes on the text, *Young Mr Lincoln*, by the Editors of *Cahiers du cinéma*', *Screen* **14**(3), 29–43; *Screen Reader 1* (London: Society for Education in Film and Television, 1977), 156–70.

Burch, Noël (1967) *Praxis du cinéma* (Paris: Gallimard).

Burch, Noël (1973) *Theory of Film Practice* (London: Secker & Warburg).

Burch, Noël (1986) *Une praxis du cinéma* (Paris: Galllimard).

Cahiers du cinéma (1970) 'Young Mister Lincoln de John Ford', *Cahiers du cinéma* **223**. Translated as 'John Ford's *Young Mister Lincoln*' in the following: *Screen* **13**(3) (1972), 5–34; *Screen Reader 1* (London: Society for Education in Film and Television, 1977), 113–51; *Movies and Methods: An Anthology*, Vol. 1, ed. B. Nichols (Berkeley and Los Angeles: University of California Press, 1976), 493–528; *Narrative, Ideology, Apparatus: A Film Theory Reader*, ed. P. Rosen (New York: Columbia University Press, 1986), 444–82.

Chapuy, Arnaud (2001) *Martine Carol filmée par Christian-Jaque: un phénomène du cinéma populaire* (Paris: L'Harmattan).

Chateau, René (1996) *Le Cinéma français sous l'Occupation 1940–1944* (Paris: René Chateau).

Chion, Michel (1988) *La Toile trouée: la parole au cinéma* (Paris: Cahiers du cinéma).

Chion, Michel (1990) *L'Audio-vision: son et image au cinéma* (Paris: Nathan).

Chion, Michel (1993) *La Voix au cinéma* (Paris: Cahiers du cinéma). First published 1982.

Chion, Michel (1994) *Le Son au cinéma* (Paris: Cahiers du cinéma). First published 1985.

Chion, Michel (1994) *Audio-vision: Sound on Screen* (New York and Chichester: Columbia University Press).

Chion, Michel (1995) *La Musique au cinéma* (Paris: Fayard, 'Les chemins de la musique').

Chion, Michel (1999) *The Voice in Cinema* (New York: Columbia University Press).

Cohen-Séat, Gilbert (1946) *Essai sur les principes d'une philosophie du cinéma* (Paris: Presses Universitaires de France).

Colombat, Andre Pierre (1993) *The Holocaust in French Film* (Metuchen, NJ and London: Scarecrow Press).

Comolli, Jean-Louis and Jean Narboni (1970) '*Cinéma/idéologie/critique*', *Cahiers du cinéma* **216**. Translated as 'Cinema/ideology/criticism' in the following: *Movies and Methods: An Anthology*, Vol. 1, ed. B. Nichols (Berkeley, Los Angeles: University of California Press, 1976), 22–30; *Screen Reader 1* (London: Society for Education in Film and Television, 1977), 2–11; *Cahiers du cinéma 1969–1972: The Politics of Representation* (Cambridge, MA: Harvard University Press, 1990), 58–67; *Film Theory and Criticism*, ed. G. Mast and M. Cohen (New York and London, Oxford University Press, 1992), 682–9.

Crisp, Colin (1988) *Eric Rohmer: Realist and Moralist* (Bloomington: Indiana University Press).

Crisp, Colin (1993) *The Classic French Cinema: 1930–1960* (Bloomington: Indiana University Press).

Daney, Serge (1983) *La Rampe: cahier critique 1970–1982* (Paris: Gallimard).

Daney, Serge (1988) *Le Salaire du zappeur* (Paris: Ramsay).

Daney, Serge (1991) '*Devant la recrudescence des vols de sacs à main*': *cinéma, télévision, information 1988–1991* (Lyon: Aléas).

Daney, Serge (1993) *L'Exercice a été profitable, Monsieur* (Paris: POL).

Darke, Chris (1993) 'Rupture, continuity and diversification: *Cahiers du Cinéma* in the 1980s', *Screen* **34**(4), 362–79.

Deleuze, Gilles (1983) *Cinéma 1: L'image-mouvement* (Paris: Minuit).

Deleuze, Gilles (1985) *Cinéma 2: L'Image-temps* (Paris: Minuit).

Deleuze, Gilles (1989) *Cinema 2: The Time Image* (London: Athlone).

Deleuze, Gilles (1992) *Cinema 1: The Movement-Image* (London: Athlone).

Deleuze, Gilles and Felix Guattari (1972) *L'Anti-Oedipe: Capitalisme et Schizophrenie* (Paris: Éditions de Minuit).

Delluc, Louis (1920) *Photogénie* (Paris: M. de Brunoff).

Desbarats, Carole (1989) *L'Effet Godard* (Toulouse: Milan).

Deschamps, Hélène (2001) *Jacques Rivette: théâtre, amour, cinéma* (Paris, L'Harmattan).

Dine, Philip D. (1994) *Images of the Algerian War: French Fiction and Film, 1954–1992* (Oxford: Clarendon Press).

Dixon, Wheeler W. (1997) *The Films of Jean-Luc Godard* (Albany: State University of New York Press).

Djian, Philippe (1986) *37°2 le matin* (Paris, J'ai Lu, No.1951. First published Paris: Bernard Barrault, 1985).

Djian, Philippe (1989) *Betty Blue: The Story of a Passion*. Translated by Howard Buten (London: Abacus); translation first published in Great Britain by London, Weidenfeld and Nicolson, 1988.

Douin, Jean-Luc (1989) *Jean-Luc Godard* (Paris: Rivages). Revised edition 1994.

Duffy, Jean (2002) 'Message versus mystery and *film noir* borrowings in Patrice Leconte's *Monsieur Hire*', *French Cultural Studies* **XII**, 209–24.

Durham, Carolyn A. (1998) *Double Takes: Culture and Gender in French Films and their American Remakes* (Hanover and London: University Press of New England).

Eagleton, Terry (1983*) Literary Theory: An Introduction* (Oxford: Basil Blackwell).

Ezra, Elizabeth (2000a) *The Colonial Unconscious: Race and Culture in Interwar France* (Ithaca, NY and London: Cornell University Press).

Ezra, Elizabeth (2000b) *Georges Méliès* (Manchester: Manchester University Press).

Faulkner, Christopher (1986) *The Social Cinema of Jean Renoir* (Princeton and Guildford: Princeton University Press).

Flitterman-Lewis, Sandy (1990) *To Desire Differently: Feminism and the French Cinema* (Urbana: University of Illinois Press).

Forbes, Jill (1992), *The Cinema in France after the New Wave* (Basingstoke, Hampshire: Macmillan).

Forbes, Jill and Sarah Street (ed.) (2000) *European Cinema: An Introduction.* (Basingstoke: Palgrave).

Frappat, Hélène (2001) *Jacques Rivette: secret compris* (Paris: Cahiers du cinéma).

Frodon, Jean-Michel (1995) *L'Age moderne du cinema francais: de la Nouvelle Vague à nos jours* (Paris: Flammarion).

Gardies, André (1993) *L'Espace au cinéma* (Paris: Méridiens Klincksieck).

Gillain, Anne (1991) *François Truffaut: le secret perdu* (Paris: Hatier).

Greene, Naomi (1999) *Landscapes of Loss: The National Past in Postwar French Cinema* (Princeton, NJ: Princeton University Press).

Haffner, Pierre (1988) *Jean Renoir* (Presses Universitaires Nancy).

Harris, Sue (2001) *Bertrand Blier* (Manchester: Manchester University Press).

Hayes, Graeme (2001) '*T'es beau, tu sais*: Alain Delon and the Spectacle of

Masculinity', paper given at the 'Exploring Masculinities and Film' conference, Newcastle upon Tyne.

Hayward, Susan (1993) *French National Cinema* (London and New York: Routledge).

Hayward, Susan (1998) *Luc Besson* (Manchester: Manchester University Press).

Hayward, Susan and Ginette Vincendeau (1990) *French Film: Texts and Contexts* (London and New York: Routledge); 2nd edn, 2000.

Henderson, Brian (1973) 'Critique of cine-structuralism (Part 1)', *Film Quarterly* **27**(1), 25–34.

Henderson, Brian (1973/74) 'Critique of cine-structuralism (Part 2)', *Film Quarterly* **27**(2), 37–46.

Higgins, Lynn A. (1996) *New Novel, New Wave, New Politics: Fiction and the Representation of History in Postwar France* (Lincoln: University of Nebraska Press).

Holmes, Diane and Robert Ingram (1998) *François Truffaut* (Manchester: Manchester University Press).

Hughes, Alex and Keith Reader (eds) (1998) *Encyclopedia of Contemporary French Culture* (London: Routledge).

King, Norman (1984) *Abel Gance: A Politics of Spectacle* (London: BFI).

Kline, T. Jefferson (1992) *Screening the Text: Intertextuality in New Wave French Cinema* (Baltimore and London: Johns Hopkins University Press).

Kuntzel, Thierry (1975) 'Le travail du film, 2', *Communications* **23**, 136–89.

Lapsley, Robert and Michael Westlake (1988) *Film Theory: An Introduction* (Manchester: Manchester University Press).

Le Berre, Carole (1993) *François Truffaut* (Paris: Editions de l'Étoile/Cahiers du cinéma).

Leperchey, Sarah (2000) *Alain Resnais: une lecture topologique* (Paris: L'Harmattan).

McMahan, A. (2002) *Alice Guy Blaché: Lost Visionary of the Cinema* (New York: Continuum)

Magny, Joël (1986) *Eric Rohmer* (Paris: Rivages). New edition, 1995.

Magny, Joël (1987) *Claude Chabrol* (Paris: Cahiers du cinéma).

Magny, Joël (1995) *Maurice Pialat* (Paris: Éditions de L'Etoile/Cahiers du cinéma).

Mazdon, Lucy (2000) *Encore Hollywood: Remaking French Cinema* (London: BFI).

Mazdon, Lucy (ed.) (2001) *France on Film: Reflections on Popular French Cinema* (London: Wallflower Press).

Metz, Christian (1968) *Essais sur la signification au cinéma* (Paris: Klincksieck).

Metz, Christian (1971) *Langage et cinéma* (Paris: Larousse).

Metz, Christian (1975a) 'Le Signifiant imaginaire', *Communications* **25**, 3–55.

Metz, Christian (1975b) 'Le film de fiction et son spectateur', *Communications* **23**, 108–35.

Metz, Christian (1977) *Le Signifiant imaginaire: psychanalyse et cinéma* (Paris: Union générale d'éditions).

Metz, Christian (1982) *Psychoanalysis and Cinema: The Imaginary Signifier* (London: Macmillan).

Mitry, Jean (1963) *Esthétique et psychologie du cinéma: les structures* (Paris: Éditions universitaires).

Mitry, Jean (1963) (1965) *Esthétique et psychologie du cinéma: les formes* (Paris: Éditions universitaires).

Monaco, James (1976) *The New Wave: Truffaut, Godard, Chabrol, Rohmer, Rivette* (New York: Oxford University Press).

Monaco, James (1978) *Alain Resnais: The Role of Imagination* (London and New York: Secker & Warburg/Oxford University Press).

Mondragon (1949) 'Comment j'ai compris *Un chien andalou*', *Revue du Ciné-Club* **8/9** (May–June).

Monsieur Hire (1990) *Monsieur Hire*, suivi de Julien Duvi ior, *Panique*, *L'Avant-Scène Cinéma*, 390–91.

Morin, Edgar (1956) *Le Cinéma, ou, l'homme imaginaire: essai d'anthropologie sociologique* (Paris: Éditions de Minuit).

Morin, Edgar (1957) *Les Stars* (Paris: Seuil).

Morin, Edgar (1961) *The Stars* (New York: Grove Press).

Mulvey, Laura (1975) 'Visual pleasure and narrative cinema', *Screen* **16**(3), 6–18.

Nichols, Bill (1975) 'Style, Grammar, and the Movies', *Film Quarterly* **28**(3), 33–48.

Nora, Pierre (1986–1992) *Les Lieux de mémoire*, 3 vols (Paris: Gallimard).

Norindr, Panivong (1996) *Phantasmatic Indochina: French Colonial Ideology in Architecture, Film, and Literature* (Durham and London: Duke University Press).

O'Shaughnessy, Martin (2000) *Jean Renoir* (Manchester: Manchester University Press).

Ostria, Vincent (1986) '*37°2 le matin*', *Cinématographe* **118**, 60.

Oudart, Jean-Pierre (1969) 'La suture', *Cahiers du cinéma* **211**, 36–9 and **212**, 50–5. Translated as 'Cinema and Suture, *Screen* (1977–1978) **18**(4), 35–47.

Passek, Jean-Loup (1987) *Dictionnaire du cinéma français* (Paris: Larousse).

Pérez, Michel (1994) *Les Films de Carné* (Paris: Ramsay).

Powrie, Phil (1997) *French Cinema in the 1980s: Nostalgia and the Crisis of Masculinity* (Oxford: Clarendon Press).

Powrie, Phil (ed.) (1999) *French Cinema in the 1990s: Continuity and Difference* (Oxford: Oxford University Press).

Powrie, Phil (2001a) '(De)constructing the male body in 1920s French cinema', paper given at the 'Men's Bodies' conference, University of Nottingham.

Powrie, Phil (2001b) *Jean-Jacques Beineix* (Manchester: Manchester University Press).

Powrie, Phil (2002) 'Out of this (world) cinema: French cinema studies now', *Journal of Romance Studies* **1**(3), 81–91.

Prédal, René (1996) *L'Itinéraire d'Alain Resnais* (Paris: Lettres Modernes).

Rabourdin, Dominique (1995) *Truffaut: le cinéma et la vie* (Paris: Mille et Une Nuits).

Reader, Keith (1987) 'The scene of the action is different', *Screen* **23**(3), 99.

Reader, Keith (2000) *Robert Bresson* (Manchester: Manchester University Press).

Richards, I.A. (1948) *Principles of Literary Criticism* (London: Routledge).

Rollet, Brigitte (1998) *Coline Serreau* (Manchester: Manchester University Press).

Rodowick, David N. (1997) *Gilles Deleuze's Time Machine* (Durham, NC: Duke University Press).

Ross, Kristin (1995) *Fast Cars, Clean Bodies: Decolonization and the Reordering of French Culture* (Cambridge, MA, and London: MIT Press).

Rousso, Henri (1991) *The Vichy Syndrome: History and Memory in France since 1944* (Boston: Harvard University Press).

Schrader, Paul (1972) *Transcendental Style in Film: Ozu, Bresson, Dreyer* (Berkeley: University of California Press).

Sellier, Geneviève and Noel Burch (1996), *La Drôle de guerre des sexes du cinéma français* (Paris: Nathan).

Serceau, Daniel (1985) *Jean Renoir: la sagesse du plaisir* (Paris: Cerf).

Serceau, Michel (2000) *Eric Rohmer: les jeux de l'amour du hasard et du discours* (Paris: Cerf).

Sesonske, Alexander (1980) *Jean Renoir, the French Films, 1924–1939* (Cambridge, MA: Harvard University Press).

Sherzer, Dina (1996) *Cinema, Colonialism, Postcolonialism: Perspectives from the French and Francophone Worlds* (Austin: University of Texas Press).

Silverman, Kaja and Harun Farocki (1998) *Speaking about Godard* (New York and London: New York University Press).

Simsi, Simon (2000) *Ciné-Passions: 7ᵉ art et industrie de 1945–2000* (Paris: Editions Dixit).

Smith, Alison (1998) *Agnès Varda* (Manchester: Manchester University Press).

Souriau, Etienne (1947) *La Correspondance des arts*: *éléments d'esthétique comparée* (Paris: Flammarion).

Stacey, Jackie (1994) *Star-gazing: Hollywood Cinema and Female Spectatorship* (London: Routledge).

Stam, Robert (1999) *Film Theory: An Introduction* (Malden, MA: Blackwell).

Sterritt, David (1999) *The Films of Jean-Luc Godard: Seeing the Invisible* (Cambridge: Cambridge University Press).

Sutton, Paul (2001) '*Nachträglichkeit* in Psychoanalysis and Film: A Paradigm for Spectatorship'. PhD Thesis, University of Bradford.

Tarr, Carrie (1999) *Diane Kurys* (Manchester: Manchester University Press).

Temple, Michael and James S. Williams (2000) *The Cinema Alone: Essays on the Work of Jean-Luc Godard 1985–2000* (Amsterdam: Amsterdam University Press).

Thiher, Allen (1979) 'Prévert and Carné's *Le Jour se lève*: Proletarian Tragedy', in Allen Thiher, *The Cinematic Muse: Critical Studies in the History of the French Cinema* (Columbia and London: University of Missouri Press), 113–28.

Tortajada, Maria (1999) *Le Spectateur séduit: le libertinage dans le cinéma d'Eric Rohmer et sa fonction dans une théorie de la représentation filmique* (Paris: Kimé).

Toubiana, Serge (1986), 'Les oripeaux du look', *Cahiers du cinéma* **383**(4), 79–80.

Truffaut, François (1976) 'A Certain Tendency of the French Cinema', in *Movies and Methods: An Anthology*, Vol. 1, ed. by B. Nichols (Berkeley and Los Angeles: University of California Press), 224–36. Originally published in *Cahiers du cinéma* **31** (1954).

Tudor, Andrew (1974) *Image and Influence: Studies in the Sociology of Film* (London: Allen & Unwin).

Turk, Edward Baron (1989) *Child of Paradise: Marcel Carné and the Golden Age of French Cinema* (Cambridge, MA: Harvard University Press).

Vanoye, Francis and Anne Goliot-Lété (1992) *Précis d'analyse filmique* (Paris: Nathan).

Vincendeau, Ginette and Claude Gauteur (1993) *Jean Gabin: anatomie d'un mythe* (Paris: Nathan).

Vincendeau, Ginette (1996) *The Companion to French Cinema* (London: Cassell and BFI).

Vincendeau, Ginette (2000) *Stars and Stardom in French Cinema* (London and New York: Continuum).

Vincendeau, Ginette (2001) *Film/Literature/Heritage: A Sight and Sound Reader* (London: BFI).

Viry-Babel, Roger (1994) *Jean Renoir: le jeu et la règle* (Paris: Ramsay).

Williams, Alan Larson (1992) *Republic of Images: A History of French Filmmaking* (Cambridge, MA: Harvard University Press).

Waldron, Darren (2001) 'Incorporating Qualitative Audience Research into French Film studies: The Case of *Gazon Maudit*', paper given at the 'Studies in French Cinema' annual conference.

Wilson, Emma (1999) *French Cinema since 1950: Personal Histories* (London: Duckworth).

Wilson, Emma (2000) *Memory and Survival: The French Cinema of Krzysztof Kieslowski* (Oxford: Legenda).

Wollen, Peter (1969) *Signs and Meaning in the Cinema* (London: Secker & Warburg). Revised eds 1972, 1998.

Wollen, Peter (1972) 'Afterword', *Screen* **13**(3), 44–50; *Screen Reader 1* (London: Society for Education in Film and Television, 1977), 152–5.

INDEX

For the purposes of indexing the initial definite/indefinite article is ignored.
Titles starting with numbers are indexed as spelled in the language of the title.
Page numbers in italics refer to illustrations.